Studies in Rhetorics and Feminisms

Series Editors, Cheryl Glenn and Shirley Wilson Logan

Other Books in the Studies in Rhetorics and Feminisms Series

Regendering Delivery
The Fifth Canon and Antebellum Women Rhetors
Lindal Buchanan

Feminism Beyond Modernism
Elizabeth A. Flynn

Liberating Voices
Writing at the Bryn Mawr Summer School for Women Workers
Karyn L. Hollis

Gender and Rhetorical Space in American Life, 1866–1910
Nan Johnson

Appropriate[ing] Dress
Women's Rhetorical Style in Nineteenth-Century America
Carol Mattingly

The Gendered Pulpit
Preaching in American Protestant Spaces
Roxanne Mountford

Rhetorical Listening
Identification, Gender, Whiteness
Krista Ratcliffe

Vote and Voice
Women's Organizations and Political Literacy, 1915–1930
Wendy B. Sharer

A Feminist Legacy

A Feminist Legacy

THE RHETORIC AND PEDAGOGY OF GERTRUDE BUCK

Suzanne Bordelon

Southern Illinois University Press
Carbondale

Library of Congress Cataloging-in-Publication Data
Bordelon, Suzanne, 1962–
   A feminist legacy : the rhetoric and pedagogy
of Gertrude Buck / Suzanne Bordelon.
       p. cm. — (Studies in rhetorics and feminisms)
   Includes bibliographical references and index.
   ISBN-13: 978-0-8093-2748-5 (cloth : alk. paper)
   ISBN-10: 0-8093-2748-1 (cloth : alk. paper)
   1. Buck, Gertrude, 1871–1922. 2. Feminists—United
States—Biography. 3. Women college teachers—
United States—Biography. 4. Vassar College—
Officials and employees—Biography. 5. Feminist
theory. 6. Feminist literary criticism. I. Title.

HQ1413.B83B67 2007
305.42092—dc22
[B]   2006102588

Printed on recycled paper. ♻
The paper used in this publication meets the minimum
requirements of American National Standard for Information Sciences—Permanence of Paper for Printed
Library Materials, ANSI Z39.48-1992. ∞

For my grandmothers, Helen and Mary,
my husband, Bob,
and my son, Nicholas

CONTENTS

ILLUSTRATIONS

ACKNOWLEDGMENTS

*M*any people have helped make this book a published, hard-copy reality. I am fortunate to have wonderful colleagues and friends in San Diego. Glen McClish and Jacqueline Bacon have been extremely generous in reading various versions, providing advice, and encouraging my efforts. Ellen Quandahl also has provided support and perceptive feedback. My friends outside of San Diego have been equally helpful. I am particularly grateful to Lisa Mastrangelo for her knowledge of the Seven Sisters colleges, for sharing relevant sources, and for her willingness to read and comment on numerous versions of this project. Alexis Easley has also provided invaluable assistance, with her constant encouragement and helpful comments on many earlier versions of this manuscript. Thanks also to Rich Carr, Lillian Corti, Julia Garbus, and Susan North for their willingness to read and comment on earlier versions of this manuscript. I also am indebted to Barbara McManus for her thoughtful suggestions and for providing me with a copy of her typed summary of letters from the Helen Drusilla Lockwood collection. The summary was a tremendous help. Vassar College historian Betty Daniels also shared stories about the college's English Department and generously assisted me in negotiating Vassar's archives. In addition, I'm deeply grateful to John Gage, my doctoral advisor, for introducing me to Gertrude Buck's work in his course on nineteenth-century rhetoric and for his continued support of my professional endeavors. I would also like to thank Lisa Ede, Suzanne Clark, Jim Crosswhite, and Barbara Welke for their valuable feedback while I worked on a very early version of this project at the University of Oregon.

Studies in Rhetorics and Feminisms series editors Cheryl Glenn and Shirley Wilson have been extremely supportive, generous, and knowledgeable throughout this process. I feel very fortunate that they were the editors. I would also like to thank outside reviewer Katherine H. Adams for her insightful revision suggestions and overall support of the project. In addition, I would like to thank Karl Kageff, editor-in-chief at Southern Illinois University Press, and Bridget Brown, acquisitions assistant, for answering my many questions and for allowing more pictures in the final project.

I would like to express my gratitude to previous scholars who have examined Buck's work. In particular, I would like to thank Barbara L'Eplattenier, JoAnn Campbell, Vickie Ricks, Kevin James Koch, and Dana Hood Morgan for their dissertations and master's projects. Their work was extremely helpful to me in completing my own project. I am grateful to Barbara L'Eplattenier for her willingness to read earlier versions; for her depth of knowledge about Buck, Wylie, and the English Department; and for her generous advice. In addition, I thank Vickie Ricks and Dana Hood Morgan for reading and commenting on an early version of this project when I was in Oregon.

Special appreciation also goes to those librarians who helped me access archival materials that were integral to this project. I am particularly grateful to Dean Rogers at Vassar, who provided beyond-the-call-of-duty assistance in locating a number of sources. I am equally indebted to Nancy S. MacKechnie, former curator of rare books and manuscripts at Vassar, who located Buck's Vassar Workshop notebook. Thanks also to Karen L. Jania at the Bentley Historical Library, Patricia Albright at the Mount Holyoke Archives and Special Collections, Virginia Dent at the Harvard Theatre Collection, Megan Sniffin-Marinoff at Harvard University Archives, and Margaret J. Kimball at Stanford University Archives. In addition, I would like to thank William P. Sosnowsky for his kind help with the photograph of Harriet M. Scott, as well as Mary J. Wallace of the Walter P. Reuther Library at Wayne State University. I also am especially indebted to James A. McDonald Jr. of Kindred Roots Genealogical Society for his invaluable assistance in allowing me to use the photographs of Buck and her mother and father.

The completion of this project wouldn't have been possible without the support and funding I received from several organizations. I am indebted to San Diego State University for providing a teaching release that allowed me to finish revising the manuscript and to the Department of Rhetoric and Writing Studies for helping to offset the cost of indexing. I also am grateful to the University of Alaska Fairbanks for supporting one of my trips to Vassar. In addition, I would like to thank the Center for the Study of Women in Society at the University of Oregon for providing a travel grant that allowed me to make my initial visit to Vassar's archives.

I also would never have finished this book without the support and encouragement of my family. I would like to thank my parents, Ian and Eileen Mackie, and my in-laws, Jim and Anne Bordelon. In addition, I would like to extend a heart-felt thanks to my husband, Bob, and my son, Nicholas, for their encouragement, humor, and patience throughout the researching, writing, and revising process.

Portions of this book were published previously in the following academic journals and anthologies:

My thanks to Parlor Press for permission to reprint a revised version of "The 'Advance' Toward Democratic Administration: Laura Johnson Wylie and Gertrude Buck of Vassar College," *Historical Studies of Writing Program Administration: Individuals, Communities, and the Formation of a Discipline,* ed. Barbara L'Eplattenier and Lisa Mastrangelo (West Lafayette, IN: Parlor Press, 2004) 91–115. This segment constitutes part of chapter 3.

I would also like to thank Barry Tharaud, editor of *Nineteenth-Century Prose,* for permission to reprint a revised version of "Gertrude Buck: Revisioning Argumentation and the Role of Women in a Participatory Democracy," ed. William W. Wright, *Nineteenth-Century Prose* 27 special issue (2000): 138–58, which makes up part of chapter 4. In addition, I thank Kim Lovejoy, editor of the *Journal of Teaching Writing,* for permission to reprint a revised version of "Gertrude Buck's Approach to Argumentation: Preparing Women for a More Active and Vocal Role in a Democracy," ed. Gail Stygall, *Journal of Teaching Writing* 16 special issue (2000): 233–62, which makes up part of chapter 4.

Finally, I thank Gregory Clark, former editor of *Rhetoric Society Quarterly,* for permission to reprint a revised version of "Contradicting and Complicating Feminization of Rhetoric Narratives: Mary Yost and Argument from a Sociological Perspective," which appeared in *Rhetoric Society Quarterly* 35 (2005): 101–24, and which makes up part of chapter 6.

A Feminist Legacy

INTRODUCTION

I was first drawn to the writing of Gertrude Buck (1871–1922) while studying nineteenth-century rhetoric in graduate school during the mid-1990s.[1] In this course, we had the opportunity to examine nineteenth-century rhetoric textbooks from the library's abundant collection. I was attracted to the work of Buck, a teacher and textbook writer at Vassar College during the early decades of the twentieth century, because I was impressed by her emphasis on inclusiveness and the need for equality in the communicative process. After reviewing her dissertation and various writing textbooks, I read Albert R. Kitzhaber's 1953 dissertation. Kitzhaber was the first scholar to rediscover her ideas, and although he praises Buck for her originality, his work is also an example of how traditional scholarship contains conflicting assessments of women's contributions. For instance, in discussing the work of Fred Newton Scott, Kitzhaber asserts that Scott "stood alone" (*Rhetoric* 94). He continues, "For nearly all other men of the time, rhetoric was a much narrower and more pedestrian subject that was wholly identified with teaching young people how to write in such a manner as to avoid social censure" (94). Kitzhaber's contention that Scott "stood alone" reveals how women's work and achievements have been set apart from and viewed as insignificant compared to men's. His statement is particularly telling given that Buck had a broad, interdisciplinary view of rhetoric. Later, when he discusses her approach to the metaphor, Kitzhaber asserts she was "undoubtedly ahead of her time" (185). His words provided me with a rationale for writing about her work.

This book focuses on Buck's writing and life, with references also to the work of Laura Johnson Wylie, her longtime professional associate, friend, and housemate. The first book-length analysis of Buck's contribution to the field of rhetoric and composition, this study places her ideas within the context of Progressive America and white, middle-class women's activism.[2] A common thread woven throughout Buck's life and work was an ethical perspective aimed at eliminating hierarchies and power imbalances. Since she viewed society as a dynamic, interactive social organism, Buck's ethics underscored participation, relationships, and interdependence. This perspective was central to her feminism and her rhetoric, which challenged male/female hierarchies, revised traditional approaches to rhetoric, and sought social transformation. As will become evident in the first chapter, Buck's social philosophy and teaching practices represent important antecedents to modern feminist approaches to ethics and pedagogy.

Buck formulated her ethics in response to the social reform activities in which she participated, including progressive education, women's suffrage, and the Little Theater movement. By analyzing Buck's work against the backdrop of the Progressive Era (1890–1920), I show how she conceptualized these different activities as important sites for rhetorical theory and action.[3] In so doing, this study pushes beyond Buck's better known academic achievements to consider her broader political and social involvements and the dialectic between these activities and her approach to argumentation and pedagogy. Like Katherine H. Adams's examination of the first generations of women who used their collaborative training in college to develop as writers, this study contributes to the understanding of how these influential women were educated. Drawing on a variety of archival sources, including textbooks, department reports, student information, and previously unexamined materials, the study details the impact Buck's writing and work with Wylie had on the English Department curriculum and on the lives of their students. It demonstrates how, at Vassar, it was assumed that these women would be active, thoughtful, and vocal leaders in their communities.

A significant and ironic aspect of Buck's context to consider is the gendered historical nature of this period. Like that of her colleague Lucy Maynard Salmon, Buck's vision was deeply influenced "by her status as a woman in a time when few women were educated and most were disenfranchised" (Bohan, "Lucy Maynard" 48). Buck developed an approach to rhetoric that stressed full participation, challenged unequal power relations, and sought to heal divisions and promote cooperation when she and other women were denied the right to vote and socially oppressed. She crafted a method particularly suited to a democracy and was committed to these ideals, despite or perhaps because her status as a citizen was limited and ambiguous (Crocco 10). Thus, Buck encouraged her female students to debate issues of social concern, helping them to develop the skills they would need once the vote was a reality. Her efforts to break down barriers between the college and the community were also aimed at promoting women's intervention in the public realm.

As is apparent from Kitzhaber's words, one significant reason the contributions of women like Buck have been marginalized is because of the gendered nature of the traditional histories of rhetoric and education. Although Margaret Smith Crocco discusses the construction of social studies as an academic discipline, her argument shares significant parallels with the establishment of Composition and Rhetoric as a discipline. Crocco asserts that from the beginning, "securing a place for the social sciences in universities and professional organizations has involved contests over power" (6). One consequence of these contests is that gendered and racialized perspectives have molded the field. Thus, in social sciences and history, Crocco argues that "[w]here women appear in the history of the disciplines at all, they typically are featured as followers rather than leaders; their work is associated with practice rather than theory; their ideas are devalued simply because they are propounded by women. Rarely are women portrayed as original thinkers" (8).

This pattern of marginalization is also evident in Composition and Rhetoric because, like social studies, the field has stressed "monocultural and masculinist modes masquerading as universal ways of thinking, being, and acting" (Crocco 8). This marginalization is particularly apparent among groups that have been regularly suppressed by sociopolitical power formations. For example, in her study of literacy and social change among nineteenth-century African American women, Jacqueline Jones Royster emphasizes how pervasive this marginalization has been. As Royster asserts, "The presence of African American women as writers of worth has typically been neutralized and their achievements devalued" (4). By demonstrating the contributions of these women, Royster's scholarship on African American women's literate practices responds to the erasure that has occurred in traditional accounts of nineteenth-century history.

Gendered perspectives have also significantly patterned the field's landscape. Joan Wallach Scott provides a helpful two-part definition of gender, which I will draw upon: "[G]ender is a constitutive element of social relationships based on perceived differences between the sexes, and gender is a primary way of signifying relationships of power" (42). Thus, as Scott notes, "[c]hanges in the organization of social relationships always correspond to changes in representations of power . . ." (42–43). A benefit of viewing gender difference as historically constructed and contested is that it allows me "to forge a double-edged analytic tool that offers a way to generate new knowledge about women and sexual difference *and* to inspire critical challenges to the politics of history . . ." (9–10, emphasis in original). As Scott explains, feminist history becomes not only an effort to enhance or correct previous histories but also a way to discern how history functions as a location in producing knowledge about gender (10). Such an analytic tool reveals the power politics behind traditional histories.

The gendered nature of Composition and Rhetoric is evident in the positioning of Buck's work within the field. For instance, although her work is often mentioned in histories of nineteenth-century North American rhetoric and composition, scholars (Kitzhaber, Berlin, Crowley) have focused on well-known male rhetoricians at all-male colleges. These histories often neglect women's contributions. One reason Buck's work has been neglected is that her achievements typically have been viewed only in relation to those of Fred Newton Scott, her teacher at the University of Michigan. Although Buck was influenced by Scott's democratic rhetoric, she extended his theories to her situation, a context shaped by the women with whom she worked and taught at Vassar and the activism that was integral to her life.

More frequently, scholars (Kitzhaber, Berlin, Burke, Mulderig, Allen, Koch, and Vivian) have unintentionally isolated Buck from her Progressive-Era context, often analyzing her work in relation to contemporary composition practices instead of viewing it as interconnected with her other ethical, pedagogical, and social interests. While I, too, consider Buck's work in relation to current practices, a major focus of my analysis is to investigate her ideas within their specific historical setting. By contextualizing her ideas within this larger frame, I will add to the understanding of Buck by showing her participation in broader reform efforts emphasizing social justice. In this way, scholars may gain deeper insight into how Buck was not necessarily ahead of her time but very much a product of her own period.

By situating Buck's work historically, I also complicate claims that composition was feminized and personalized by the loss of argumentation and debate during the latter part of the nineteenth century.[4] Extending the feminist critique of this perspective, the project underscores the social and political nature of Buck's work by showing how the "feminized" has been misclassified as "personal."[5] More significantly, instead of viewing this transformation as the loss of argumentation and debate, I demonstrate how it represents the rise of a more ethical approach to argumentation. Buck's rhetorical theory, with its stress on ethical behavior, directly responds to the more agonistic, persuasion-oriented rhetoric that scholars have emphasized. In reflecting male cultural practices, this agonistic approach ignored women's experiences and was antithetical to the democratic values that Buck and several other Progressive-Era rhetoricians supported.

To forward such arguments, scholars have tended to depict argument as male and narrative as female, reinscribing binary and essentialist conceptions of gender. As Joy S. Ritchie and Kate Ronald argue, defining certain genres in terms of gender "not only may be inaccurate but also may limit women's rhetorical options and ignore the rhetorical power of much of women's writing throughout history" ("Riding" 234–35). A significant aspect of women's rhetorical history has included women's argumentation, such as women arguing for their right to vote and defending their right to education (Ritchie and Ronald, "Riding" 232). At certain points in my analysis, I also generalize, universalize, and essentialize; however, I try to do so self-consciously, employing Gayatri Chakravorty Spivak's concept of "strategic essentialism"—the judicious use of such discourse to gain power to dismantle systems of oppression (11–12). I realize, though, the provisionality of my position and try to limit my claims to specific historical situations, considering "an inquiry into feminism and composition as a situated knowledge . . ." (Clark, "Argument" 97).

My research demonstrates that Vassar College, specifically through the work of Buck, Wylie, and their students, represents an undervalued yet important site in the history of women's argumentation and pedagogy. It also underscores the need to continue searching for women's traditions, while at the same time complicating scholars' understanding of these practices. Doing so will allow scholars to see beyond black-and-white conceptions of gender to understand the shades of gray, the ways women worked against and within patriarchal modes while at the same time establishing their own traditions. As Ritchie emphasizes, feminism's strength is "its ability to hold in tension an array of theoretical and practical perspectives and, thus, to arrive at a clearer understanding of the varied nature of women's positions" (85). This tension is evident in Buck's life and work.

In a broader sense, this study illuminates historians' understanding of the rhetorical activities of women during this period, adding to feminist scholarship detailing the contributions of women to rhetorical history and theory. Although not the first, a prominent early example of this scholarship is Karlyn Kohrs Campbell's two-volume *Man Cannot Speak for Her: A Critical Study of Early Feminist Rhetoric* (1989), which recovers and examines the rhetorical activities of women reformists during the women's rights/suffrage movement. As Campbell explains, a goal of such scholarship is to "make some of the voices of these once silenced women heard again" ("Biesecker Cannot Speak" 158). In recovering the contributions of Buck and Wylie to rhetorical history, I hope to advance these efforts to redress the marginalization and erasure of women in the history of rhetoric and composition.

As noted, a goal of this study is to gain recognition for Vassar College as an important site in the history of women's argumentation and teaching. In so doing, this research builds on Cheryl Glenn's efforts to *remap* the traditional rhetorical landscape to include women.[6] In *Rhetoric Retold: Regendering the Tradition from Antiquity through the Renaissance,* Glenn regenders rhetoric from the classical period through the Renaissance by recovering women's contributions. According to Glenn, "Such a methodology implies not only a new history of women but also a new rhetorical history, in short, an entirely new map of rhetoric" (3). Thus, such efforts involve a complete rethinking of rhetoric, history, and methodology.

This remapping is well underway and is evident in a number of revisionist anthologies and book-length studies, which have broadened understanding of women's contributions to the history of rhetoric.[7] Like these anthologies and studies, my work contributes to efforts to regender the history of rhetoric. More specifically, this analysis builds on recent work exploring formal writing instruction at alternate educational levels and settings.[8] Traditionally, nineteenth-century rhetoric and composition scholars have focused on first-year writing instruction within U.S.

(primarily male) colleges. Recently, scholars have shifted their focus to different sites of instruction. Although not all of these texts are specifically about women rhetoricians, Adams's examination of advanced writing instruction during the Progressive Era, Lucille M. Schultz's work on nineteenth-century children's composition texts, Susan Kates's study of students often excluded from traditional higher-education instruction, and Karyn L. Hollis's treatment of the Bryn Mawr Summer School for Women Workers expand understanding of how writing was taught during the nineteenth and early part of the twentieth centuries. My study builds upon Schultz's work, exploring democratic writing practices in American schools by examining how Buck and Wylie introduced similar practices at the college level. It also applies Kates's concept of "activist education" to the work of Buck and Wylie, demonstrating how these women were part of this activist legacy in rhetorical education. In addition, it underscores connections between the Bryn Mawr Summer School for Women Workers and Vassar's English Department faculty, and it explores drama as a significant site of rhetorical activity.

Another way this study broadens efforts to write women into the history of rhetoric is by asking questions that have only recently been raised by feminist historians. In *Gender and Rhetorical Space in American Life, 1866–1910,* Nan Johnson adds another layer of complexity to the remapping project by asking not only who has been "silenced or overlooked" but also "why women were silenced and how programs of rhetorical silencing were deployed" (12).[9] I agree with Johnson that both questions need to be asked. In analyzing the work of Buck and Wylie, I draw upon primary materials to recover the rhetorical activities of these two women. Since this is the first book-length investigation of both women, a major focus is the recovery of their words and achievements. However, I also explore why their accomplishments are missing from the traditional map of rhetoric. In other words, I examine "the complicated relationship between rhetorical practices and the inscription of cultural power . . ." (Johnson 1). As Johnson points out, this relationship emphasizes contradictions because "pedagogies and histories of rhetoric are always simultaneously empowering and disenfranchising" (18). These contradictions can be seen, for example, in the fact that Buck and Wylie were preparing women to be vocal and active participants in a society that, at the time, had no place for them.

My approach resembles the "Theory from Practice" methodology outlined by Campbell.[10] In other words, it is inductive, developing its theory based on an analysis of specific practices rather than beginning with preselected theoretical frameworks. As Christine Mason Sutherland suggests, it can be "potentially dangerous" when scholars, who reject any attempts at objectivity, search for affirmations of their current selves in the texts of the past (14). Such an approach can lead to "the danger of anachronism" and ultimately amount to "cultural appropriation" (Sutherland 14). Instead, Sutherland urges "a sympathetic listening to the voices of the past—a listening which may involve reading across the grain of our own preferences and political agendas" (14). Although some might view this study's feminist lens as "preselected," I contextualize Buck's work in relation to the Progressive Era and white, middle-class women's reform efforts in an attempt to listen with a sympathetic ear and to guard against the danger of cultural appropriation and a forced theoretical fit. In so doing, I hope to add to the scholarship developing feminist methodologies of historiography and to revisionary efforts to explore women's contributions to rhetorical theory and history.

In addition, I hope to contribute to scholarly efforts aimed at revising current approaches to archival methodology. I agree with Barbara E. L'Eplattenier's contention that archival researchers need to be more open in discussing how they gather and present their material.[11] In qualitative studies, for example, L'Eplattenier emphasizes that researchers typically disclose the specifics of how the information was gathered. She also points out that the current citation system, the Modern Language Association method, does not require researchers to include important details about where the materials came from, such as box and file numbers. I would like to respond to this call for more explicitness in terms of what researchers *do* in the archives by noting that I have been completing research on Buck off and on for the past ten years. During those years, I have visited the Vassar archives three times for a week each time. After visits, I have also made many requests for further material, based on what I have found during previous trips. Although I physically have not visited these libraries, I have also requested material from the Bentley Historical Library at the University of Michigan, the Harvard Theatre Collection, Harvard University Archives, the Kalamazoo Public Library, Mount Holyoke Archives and Special Collections, Stanford University Archives, and the

Walter P. Reuther Library at Wayne State University. In presenting my materials, I separate primary from secondary sources for ease of future researchers. In addition, I try to indicate box and file numbers so that other researchers may find and examine specific documents that I discuss. By including these details, I hope to contribute to the process of rethinking archival methodology.

Like other researchers, I also try to resist descriptions of Buck as "the great woman" and to simply valorize her efforts.[12] As noted, to guard against such characterizations, I consider Buck's work within the broader context of Progressive America and early-twentieth-century middle-class women's reform efforts. In addition, I feel it's important to examine some of the limitations and contradictions apparent in the Progressive Era, Vassar College, and Buck. Although the Progressive Era is known for its reforms and women figured prominently in progressivism, historians also have stressed the complexity of this period and the term *progressives*. As Daniel T. Rodgers asserts, "Progressives could be found who admired the efficiency of the big corporation and who detested the trusts, who lauded the 'people' and who yearned for an electorate confined to white and educated voters, who spoke the language of social engineering and the language of moralistic uplift, or (to make matters worse) did all these things at once" (122). Rodgers questions the notion that a coherent ideology framed the era and instead emphasizes a more dynamic and fragmentary perspective. His words highlight the complex nature of the period.

Turn-of-the-twentieth-century Vassar also wasn't without its contradictions and limitations. For instance, while Vassar and the other Seven Sisters colleges have been recognized for their academic achievements and notable alumnae, during this period the Seven Sisters colleges were "identified with the daughters of the White Anglo-Saxon Protestants of the middle and upper classes" (Perkins 104). The discriminatory nature of Vassar is evident in the fact that it was the last of the Seven Sisters colleges to formally admit African American students (Perkins 106). Anita Florence Hemmings, who graduated from Vassar in 1897, is the college's first known African American student. However, according to Linda M. Perkins, a "scandal" emerged in the northeast when authorities learned that the light-skinned Hemmings was African American (107). Perkins adds that college officials "clearly felt that the presence of African-American women, even those with a slight tinge of black blood, would detract from the image it sought to project as an institution for the aristocratic and genteel woman" (107). It wasn't until 1940 that Vassar changed its policy to formally admit students of color.

Like the period and Vassar College, Buck, Wylie, and their students were also multifaceted and contradictory. Although Buck challenged hierarchies and class distinctions, she still favored her own class- and culture-based values, a contradiction she seemed unaware of given her background and life at a prestigious college. These oppositions meant that Buck was committed to the democratic values of equality while, at the same time, she assumed a hierarchy of cultural advancement and intellect that upheld her own values and assumptions. It's important to note, though, that while most of Buck and Wylie's efforts focused on educating their highly privileged Vassar students, they were involved in projects that extended beyond the elite society of Vassar. Buck helped to develop the Poughkeepsie Community Theatre, which sought to involve diverse members of the town in dramatic productions. After retiring from Vassar, Wylie also taught at the Bryn Mawr School for Women Workers, a pioneer effort in extending higher education opportunities to working-class women. In addition, their student, Helen Lockwood, was involved in worker education for more than forty years; and after retiring, she made significant donations to Vassar's Center for Black Studies (Gleason, Mace, and Turner 1).

These efforts also weren't free of contradictions. According to Rita Rubinstein Heller, the Bryn Mawr Summer School for Women Workers "defies easy summaries. It was simultaneously elitist and egalitarian, conservative and radical, exclusive but also heterogeneous and inclusive" ("The Women of Summer" 1).[13] The same could be said of Buck's and Wylie's efforts both in and outside of Vassar. As Linda J. Rynbrandt notes, contemporary critiques of progressive women reformers for their racism and elitism may be well grounded, but the relationships may be more involved than these critiques suggest (203). While it is difficult to discern the rationales behind their efforts, the work of Buck, Wylie, and Lockwood also suggests the complexity of these attempts to move across race and class lines. And although there are these multiple layers of contradictions, what emerges in investigating these Vassar teachers is a pattern, an approach to rhetoric and pedagogy that was imbued with a democratic spirit that sharply contrasted with dominant rhetorical theories in the late-nineteenth and early-twentieth centuries.

In the chapters that follow, I examine Buck's social theory of rhetoric and pedagogy in relation to different reform movements in order to show how her ideas were connected to a new democratic ethics emerging during this period. Emphasizing freedom, equality, and cooperation, this ethics was central to Buck's feminism, which, through her pedagogy, empowered her female students at Vassar. She wanted her students to be active, critical citizens who would recognize and work against systems of dominance and oppression, beginning at the level of the communicative process.

Chapter 1 details Buck's life and achievements, and it investigates her "social" perspective, examining how it shaped her approach to ethics and rhetoric, and her classroom practices. The chapter argues that Buck developed women-centered alternatives to Kantian ethics and traditional approaches to rhetoric. Buck's early ideas and her efforts to democratize pedagogy are explored in chapter 2. More specifically, I examine Buck's participation in progressive education and her work with Harriet M. Scott, Fred Newton Scott's older sister, who was the principal of the Detroit Normal Training School. In so doing, the chapter reveals the gendered nature of traditional histories of rhetoric, which have ignored women's efforts in the normal and common schools. The chapter also demonstrates how Buck and Scott's pedagogy anticipates contemporary discussions of the significance of care ethics to moral education. In addition, it shows how this ethics was integral to Buck's approach to the metaphor and rhetoric.

Chapter 3 focuses on the way Buck's experience at Vassar shaped her ideas by exploring her work in the English Department and her professional relationship with Laura Johnson Wylie. After examining Wylie's background and her ideas about writing, I investigate the feminist administrative approach of the English Department, which was headed by Wylie and Buck. For twenty-four years, both women worked together and developed a collaborative model of administration that encouraged members of the English Department to take an active role in running the department. Chapter 4 contextualizes Buck's approach to argumentation and debate within the women's suffrage movement at Vassar and her involvement in such activities. I show how Buck's textbooks and debating activities at the college encouraged Vassar women to think about women's issues and demonstrate the feminist effects of her approach to argumentation, with its emphasis on action, communal interests, free inquiry, and equality. I reveal how Buck's approach to argumentation anticipates efforts by contemporary feminists to develop alternate approaches to argument.

I investigate Buck's participation in the Little Theater movement in chapter 5. Not only was Buck a leader in introducing the new drama curriculum in women's colleges, but she also helped to organize the Poughkeepsie Community Theatre, which created a vital, democratic connection between the people of Poughkeepsie and Vassar College. I argue that Buck's involvement in this movement represented her response to the context of the time—an attempt to break down the barriers between the neighboring community and the college. In addition, I show how the Little Theater movement, in significant ways, was an offshoot of the middle-class women's reform movement and how it expressed Buck's feminism. In a broader sense, I agree with Adams's assertion that in the first half of the twentieth century, collaborative workshop formats like Buck's contributed to the transformation of writing itself by "making a Male/Writer definition no longer really possible and the male grip on cultural formation harder to maintain" (*Group* xviii). The sixth and concluding chapter surveys the achievements of students of Buck and Wylie, Mary Yost and Helen Lockwood. More significantly, the chapter shows how these women carried on Buck and Wylie's feminist tradition of encouraging democratic communication, activism, and broader intellectual and social responsibility for women.

Buck forged a distinct theory of rhetoric and pedagogy that was inseparable from her feminism, middle-class women's activism, and linked to Progressive-Era reform. Her approach provided an alternative set of assumptions from those offered by mainstream educators and rhetoricians. Buck's goal was to empower Vassar women to become engaged and thoughtful citizens capable of intervening in their communities and resisting systems of dominance. Central to her approach was her belief in the importance of human relationships, specifically the need to foster equality in relationships in order to transform society. By examining Buck's work within the classroom, department, and broader community, it is possible to gain an understanding of the depth of her work and the lasting impact she had on the lives of others: her feminist legacy.

I

BUCK'S "SOCIAL" VIEW OF
ETHICS AND RHETORIC

But one short life! Thou niggard God, for shame!
Canst give no more? A thousand doors stand wide.
Wilt close them all save one thou bidst me name?
I will not choose. I claim those lives denied!
　　　　　　　—Gertrude Buck, "The Complaint of
　　　　　　　Youth," from *Poems and Plays*

*A*lthough Gertrude Buck drafted these lines for her poem "The Complaint of Youth," her words also capture her life. Buck lived only fifty years, but she did, indeed, seem to enter through as many of life's doors as she could. A talented English professor and theorist at Vassar College during the Progressive Era, Buck has left a significant feminist legacy as a woman, teacher, rhetorician, administrator, and community leader. In her brief life, Buck distinguished herself as an advocate for suffrage and democratic reform, a pioneer in progressive education, and an educator and mentor of women during the early development of women's higher education. In addition, she was a rhetorician who challenged traditional approaches to argument, an administrator who fostered a collaboratively run department, and the founder of the Vassar Workshop and the Poughkeepsie Community Theatre. Like an ever-broadening circle rippling in a pool, Buck's feminism permeated all aspects of her life.

While Buck identified with women's causes and feminism was an inextricable aspect of her life, she did not specifically call herself a *feminist,* a term that wasn't widely used until the 1920s (Crocco, Munro, and Weiler 5). Nevertheless, her feminism was implied in her approach to pedagogy, rhetoric, administration, and drama. At the center of Buck's feminism was her focus on the "social," which is particularly evident in her ethics and approach to rhetoric. As mentioned, Buck privileged her own class and values; however, she still viewed "social" as meaning that all would participate and benefit, a commitment that "include[d] all people, particularly women and the underprivileged" (Ricks 7). Buck connected her social perspective with democracy because it meant that communal interests, equality, and freedom of thought would be stressed. As Vickie Ricks points out, Buck was "more a progressive educator for the masses than a radical feminist" (6). Her feminism resembled what scholars have called "social feminism," which emphasized broader social reform rather than women's rights alone (Lemons viii). However, because Buck's ideas underscored a "social" perspective at a time when women were socially oppressed and disenfranchised, they had feminist implications, particularly in terms of her female students. Buck and the English Department faculty empowered their students to become active participants in the creation of a more democratic society.

Buck's social perspective was integral to her ethics and approach to rhetoric. Her ethics provided an inclusive method of dealing with conflict and stressed the importance of democratic relationships. It also reduced the traditional duality between feelings and reason because both were necessary for moral action. Value judgments were based on the interplay between an individual's own desires and a broad critical analysis of the consequences in terms of their social outcomes. In rhetoric, Buck's social perspective meant that all would participate and that discourse had the potential to promote cooperation and equality. Like other progressive educators of her period, she stressed democratic forms of education and communication. One major consequence of this progressive influence in rhetoric was a shift in the early decades of the twentieth century from sophistic to neo-Platonic approaches to discourse. A leader in the development, Buck developed a feminist theory of argument quite separate from the agonistic, patriarchal approach that Robert Connors contends was displaced after women entered higher education but also different from the "irenic rhetoric" that he claims took its place (*Composition-Rhetoric* 24). Buck's approach challenged the traditional persuasion-oriented focus and instead emphasized the social significance of argument in terms of communication and community building.

Buck's social perspective was particularly evident in her work at Vassar. She blended her teaching with a commitment to suffrage and reform through her efforts in progressive education, which applied democratic principles to the teaching of writing; her teaching of argumentation, which encouraged Vassar women to take a more active and public role in society; her work in criticism, which helped students to see the social implications of literature; and her efforts in the community theater, which brought together the college and the community. In every aspect of her work, Buck urged her students to think critically about broader social issues. This emphasis was also evident in the work of students who were influenced by Buck and Laura Johnson Wylie, Chair of the English Department and Buck's colleague, friend, and housemate.[1] Joan Shelley Rubin, for example, specifically discusses Buck and Wylie's social views of literature "as the source of [Constance] Rourke's progressive social attitude and methods for studying American culture. . . . Through her studies and attendance at Vassar, Rourke began to feel herself part of a nationwide movement of women in social reform" (Gordon 130).[2] A 1907 graduate of Vassar who served as an instructor in the English Department from 1910 to 1915, Rourke was an originator of American Studies.

Buck and Wylie participated in this nationwide movement and in related reform efforts highlighting an egalitarian politics. In significant ways, Buck's ethics can be seen as her response to the different reform movements in which she participated during the Progressive Era, including efforts associated with women's suffrage, education, and the Little Theater movement. By exploring Buck's work in relation to these movements, her ideas can be viewed as part of a broader social consciousness emerging in a variety of middle-class women's reform efforts during this period. Jane Addams, who was dedicated to social reform during the Progressive Era, aptly summarized key aspects of this new ethics. Addams wrote that reformers like herself were motivated "by a desire to get back to the people, to be identified with the common lot; each of them magnified the obligation inherent in human relationships as such" (55).[3]

In a 1929 address, Vassar economics professor Herbert E. Mills described this time of awakened social consciousness during the last decade of the nineteenth century and the first decade of the twentieth century:

[T]hose who could leave their own homes were plunging into the woman's suffrage movement, into social settlement life, into assistance in shirt waist and other strikes, into work for family relief, for child welfare, for child labor legislation, for improved recreational opportunities for the masses, for the advancement of the cause of socialism. Willingly they accepted small incomes, sacrificed careers the world would have applauded, proudly they marched in militant processions, joyfully they accepted arrest and imprisonment for the sake of "votes for women," for free speech and to help a strike. (*College Women* 4–5)

This new sense of social consciousness for women was especially evident during the fiftieth-anniversary celebration of the opening of Vassar College in 1915, which featured speakers such as Lillian Wald, Julia Lathrop, and Emily James Putnam, an associate in History at Barnard College, whose topic was "Women and Democracy."[4] In her presentation, "New Aspects of Old Social Responsibilities," Wald, of the Henry Street Settlement in New York City, emphasized the important role women now were playing in fulfilling social responsibilities:

Women have been experiencing the growth of a new consciousness, an integral element in the evolution of self-government; and as a result many more women than ever believe that *they* can best represent human interests in government. . . . They are more earnestly aware of the social responsibility that rests upon them. . . . She is a freer being, capable of doing more and being more. (107–8, emphasis in original)

This social consciousness, felt by many middle-class white women during the Progressive Era, also influenced Buck. These ideas were reinforced by "[t]he atmosphere of social action" that pervaded Vassar during this period (Rubin 10). In her life and work, Buck emphasized accepting broader social obligations and breaking down the barriers that separate people.

An Overview of Gertrude Buck

To better understand Buck's feminist legacy, it is necessary to know something about her life. In reviewing her achievements, it is easy to understand why several scholars have viewed her as a person who was "ahead of her time." Throughout her life, she frequently was ahead of her colleagues, both male and female. For instance, she was the first person in the United States to receive a Ph.D. in composition-rhetoric, the first Ph.D. student in rhetoric to graduate from Fred Newton Scott's program at the University of Michigan,[5] among the first teachers to pioneer the "Dewey school of thought," among the first women to attend George Pierce Baker's playwriting and stage production course, and among the first teachers to implement the new playwriting curriculum in women's colleges (Connors, "Teaching and Learning" 137; Campbell, "Gertrude Buck" 1; Snyder 118; Flanagan 16). The creator of the "47 Workshop" at Harvard and Radcliffe, Baker gained fame as the teacher of Eugene O'Neill, Edward Sheldon, Philip Barry, and Thomas Wolfe (Kinne 1).

However, Buck was also very much a product of the progressive society of her time, benefiting from her background and education. Her father, George Machan Buck, may have spurred Buck's interest in education, rhetoric, and social reform. George Buck was an attorney and judge in Kalamazoo, Michigan, where Gertrude Buck was born 14 July 1871. He was a Civil War veteran, a skilled rhetorician, and a "pioneer of Kalamazoo county, and for more than fifty years a member of [the] Kalamazoo bar . . ." (Dayton 58; "Death Call to Hon."). Less is known about Gertrude Buck's mother, Anne (Bradford) Buck, a descendent of Gov. William Bradford ("Buck, Hon. George M."). However, two of her poems about her mother, "An Epitaph: A.B.B." and "The Return," suggest a loving relationship (Ricks 3–4).

Buck received her bachelor's in 1894, master's in 1895, and doctorate in 1898, all at the University of Michigan, where she came under the influence of two powerful intellectual figures—John Dewey and Fred Newton Scott. In her dissertation, Buck acknowledges her debt to Dewey, "for the fundamental philosophic conceptions embodied in it . . ." and to Scott, "for much stimulus and criticism" in preparing her thesis (iii). As Rubin points out, Buck's acknowledgement of Dewey "was no frivolous compliment, but rather the key to her . . . political perspective" (12). Quoting Lawrence A. Cremin, Rubin adds that for Dewey and other progressive educators like Buck, the goal of education in a democracy is "'to make human beings who will live life to the fullest' by continuously enlarging their participation in society" (12).[6] Thus, education is not a neutral activity but serves the political function of creating a democratic society.

During this time, Buck also worked in Detroit with Scott's older sister, Harriet M. Scott, principal of the Detroit Normal Training School. Buck collaborated with Harriet M. Scott in the creation of *Organic Education: A Manual for Teachers in Primary and Grammar Grades,* published in 1897

(Scott, "Address" 4–5).[7] Fred Newton Scott emphasized the originality of the book, pointing out that "Professor Dewey and others who held with him or opposed him had not developed, at least in detail, the conclusions which were afterward set forth by them in so many ways" ("Address" 6). In 1897, Buck worked as an English teacher at Indianapolis High School, and she began her doctorate under Fred Newton Scott's guidance. In her dissertation, *The Metaphor: A Study in the Psychology of Rhetoric* (1898), Buck applied insights from contemporary psychology to her analysis of the metaphor.

While completing her doctorate, Buck was hired as an English instructor in 1897 at Vassar College and taught there for the rest of her life. (Wylie recruited Buck to Vassar after reading her dissertation.) Buck participated in the early progressive education movement, using her training with Harriet M. Scott, Fred Newton Scott, and John Dewey to respond to the significant pedagogical issues of her period.

At Vassar, Buck typically taught courses in composition, argument, rhetorical theory, literary criticism, poetics, English lyric poetry, and, toward the end of her career, drama. Much of her scholarly writing also focused on these areas. For Buck, the purpose of rhetoric and pedagogy was to foster the type of relationships that were inherent in a democratic society. This emphasis was evident not only in her approach to rhetoric and pedagogy but also in Wylie and Buck's collaborative administration of the English Department.

Buck taught at Vassar until she suffered a stroke in August 1921; she died after a second stroke on 8 January 1922 (Reed, "In Memoriam" 128–29). During her life, she authored and/or coauthored several books. Buck's individual publications include her master's thesis, *Figures of Rhetoric, a Psychological Study* (1895), her dissertation, *The Metaphor: A Study in the Psychology of Rhetoric* (1899), *A Course in Argumentative Writing* (1899), *The Social Criticism of Literature* (1916), and *Poems and Plays* (1922), a posthumously published collection of her poems and plays. Her coauthored books include *Organic Education: A Manual for Teachers in Primary and Grammar Grades* (1897) with Harriett M. Scott; *A Course in Expository Writing* (1899) with Elisabeth Woodbridge Morris, a Vassar colleague; *A Brief English Grammar* (1905) with Fred Newton Scott; *A Course in Narrative Writing* (1906) with Elisabeth Woodbridge Morris; and *A Handbook of Argumentation and Debating* (1906) with Kristine Mann, another Vassar colleague. She also edited an edition of John Ruskin's *Sesame and Lilies* and wrote numerous scholarly journal articles, many of which emphasized a democratic ethics and applied insights from progressive education and the new field of psychology to rhetoric and pedagogy.

Buck's Feminism and her "Social" Perspective

As noted, underlying Buck's efforts in pedagogy, rhetoric, administration, and drama was her "social" view of ethics. During this time, traditional Kantian ethics emphasized "putting aside" the personal and emotional side of experience to achieve objectivity and impartiality. This side of experience, the "subjective" realm, was viewed as opposed to reason (Pappas 81, 83). The ideal, or standard of value, also existed in a noumenal realm, viewed as "purely intelligible" and beyond the world of experience (Stumpf 309). This meant that morals typically were discussed without reference to human feelings, relationships, and experience. In contrast, Buck, like Dewey, viewed ethics as necessarily social, dependent on human interaction, and based in experience (Seigfried 224).[8]

There are significant parallels between Buck's ethics and feminine and feminist approaches to ethics of the late twentieth century. Rosemarie Tong draws on philosopher Betty A. Sichel's definitions to explain the difference between feminine and feminist approaches to ethics:

> "Feminine" at present refers to the search for women's unique voice and most often, the advocacy of an ethic of care that includes nurturance, care, compassion, and networks of communications. "Feminist" refers to those theorists, whether liberal or radical or other orientation, who argue against patriarchal domination, for equal rights, a just and fair distribution of scarce resources, etc. (4)

As Tong notes, although these two approaches differ, "they share many ontological and epistemological assumptions" (80). Namely, an individual supporting these ideas will tend to view the self as "an interdependent being rather than an atomistic entity. S/he will also tend to believe that knowledge is 'emotional' as well as 'rational' and that thoughtful persons reflect on concrete particularities as well as abstract universals" (80). These assumptions were central to Buck's ethics, which framed her approach to pedagogy, rhetoric, and drama. She held that moral experience is necessarily "social," that it begins with experience and concrete relationships and "not the traditional picture of an isolated moral conscience with duties and desires as her possessions" (Pappas 88). Thus, actions need to be considered in terms of their broader social implications.

With her focus on the primacy of concrete relationships, interdependence, and inclusiveness, Buck developed a women-centered alternative to traditional Kantian ethics that spoke "primarily to women about women's moral experience," something ignored by Kantian ethics (Tong 160). Her ethics was also a complex blend, including both feminine and feminist aspects. Like Carol Gilligan's and Nel Noddings's approaches to ethics, Buck's was feminine in that it emphasized an ethic of care built on cooperation and the centrality of relationships. However, her approach also included feminist aspects because it was specifically aimed at addressing traditional power imbalances. It was based, as noted, on the assumption that all should participate and benefit at a time when women were denied such opportunities, both socially and legally.

Since Buck viewed humans as inherently "social," she saw rhetoric as the means by which people could develop equality in their relationships. Her focus on the potential of rhetoric to promote community building was particularly evident in her emphasis on audience participation and invention. Her method contrasted with traditional argument's focus on the individual speaker and his abilities to use agonistic rhetoric to persuade others to his perspective. Instead, Buck stressed the role of the audience in the communicative process and viewed discourse aimed at manipulating the audience as "anti-social" because it was individualistic and "sanctioned only by that primitive ethical principle of the dominance of the strong" ("Present Status" 169). Instead, Buck believed that discourse should be social in its outcome, "leveling conditions between the two parties to the act . . ." (169). As Vickie Ricks points out, by focusing on issues of power and the need to equalize the communicative process, Buck's social view of rhetoric "raises hope for the oppressed of our own day as well as for hers, hope for those marginal groups—such as women, immigrants, blacks, children, and the elderly—who posit an alternative to the universal male voice" (6).

Buck's approach contrasted with dominant rhetorical theories in the late nineteenth century, which tended to be more mechanistic and structure based, guided by assumptions in faculty and associational psychologies. Instruction during the late nineteenth century was diverse, though, and the dominant approaches were not all identical (Kates, *Activist* 9). Faculty theories divided the mind into separate, innate faculties, such as memory, intellect, or taste. Part of the appeal of faculty psychology came from the analogy it drew between the mind and the body. Exercise was thought to strengthen the faculties as it does muscles. Drill and the rote learning of grammar rules were emphasized in the teaching of English grammar as a mental discipline. Faculty theories began losing their influence after 1850, but their ideas were not completely rejected by subsequent theoretical developments, which were based on associational psychology (Woods 23–25).

Associationism rejected the notion of innate first principles and static faculties and instead emphasized mental processes. It assumed that ideas derived from sense experience and memory were connected to each other according to "principles of association," which allowed the formation of more complex ideas (Crowley, *Methodical* 17; Woods 21). In terms of writing instruction, associationism, like faculty theories, promoted the memorization of grammar and rhetoric rules because memory provided students with "well-stocked" minds, thought to aid them in making mental associations (Woods 26). Memory recall was also assumed to be based on how closely ideas were related to each other. Efficient study, then, was "subject *specific*" because students' retention of knowledge was believed to be enhanced by the study of ideas that were closely related (Woods 27, emphasis in original). In addition, associationism emphasized a building-blocks approach to composition. In textbooks, this emphasis is evident in a parts-to-whole organization, which typically started with words and phrases and built up to more complex forms, such as entire essays. In writing instruction, this approach led to an emphasis on structure: "sentence structure, paragraph structure, and the arrangement of essays" (Woods 27). This focus, for instance, is evident in Adams Sherman Hill's *The Foundations of Rhetoric* (1892), which is divided into three sections: words, sentences, and paragraphs.

These more mechanical approaches to writing have been associated with "current-traditional rhetoric." Although current-traditional rhetoric has become a general label for virtually any theory that current practitioners view as negative, it typically has been used to characterize dominant approaches to pedagogy and rhetorical theory in the late nineteenth century. The term is primarily based on historians' analyses of rhetoric and grammar textbooks to understand the teaching of writing at men's eastern colleges such as Harvard, Yale, Amherst, and Michigan (Campbell, *Toward* xl). Current-traditional rhetoric emphasizes the formal aspects of writing over content, which "meant that students received little instruction in invention, wrote in the modes of discourse . . . , and received comments on the mechanical features of their prose rather than on their ideas" (Campbell, *Toward* xl).[9]

In contrast, Buck drew on insights from functionalist psychology, which meant studying the mind or consciousness as a part of nature, focusing on how it helped the human organism live in its environment. Functional psychology was based on a more organic, active view of the individual. Unlike the prevalent approach with its emphasis on rules and forms, Buck underscored writing as communication. In addition, rather than diminishing the role of invention, she stressed invention as a social, cooperative, community-building process, a way to make our relationships more democratic.

Buck's theory of rhetoric, which is investigated more fully in the next chapter, represents a direct response to the more agonistic, persuasion-oriented approach that Connors discusses in *Composition-Rhetoric: Backgrounds, Theory, and Pedagogy* (1997). With the entrance of women into higher education in the nineteenth century, Connors argues that the teaching of rhetoric became feminized, shifting from "a public, civic orientation" to "a more privatized, interiorized and even artistic orientation . . ." (23). However, articles first by Buck, then Fred Newton Scott, and later Mary Yost (a student of Buck and Scott) all discuss changes in argumentation from a perspective that differs from Connors's.[10] Instead of viewing the change as the loss of argumentation and debate, they see it as a positive: the rise of a more ethical approach to rhetoric and argumentation.

Similar to Buck, Yost contends that "the sophistic theory" has "held almost undisputed sway since the days of Aristotle, and to it may be traced much of the artificiality and insincerity of 'oratory'" ("Argument from the Point-of-View" 120). According to Scott, one outcome of this influence "has been to keep rhetoric within the limits of its earliest definition—the art of persuasion" ("Rhetoric Rediviva" 415). However, Buck contends that a Platonic approach to discourse is "at last coming home to the modern consciousness" ("Present Status" 172). According to Buck, discourse is "persuasion to the truth" for Plato, and knowledge of the truth is advantageous to both the speaker and the hearer because the interests of both are equally fulfilled.[11] Platonic approaches reappeared in the late nineteenth and early twentieth centuries because they provided an ethical approach to argumentation that was underemphasized in the agonistic tradition that Connors describes.

Gender is a key aspect of this shift because women had been left out of the rhetorical arena, which in itself is an ethical issue. Buck's more cooperative, egalitarian approach to rhetoric is a response to the transformation brought about by women entering higher education and the need for more ethical approaches to argumentation. This dramatic transformation challenged the values of an entrenched status quo, which, in turn, meant that the ethical dimension of rhetoric needed to be reexamined. In a broader sense, the shift can be seen as a response to Progressive Era insistence on more democratic forms of education.

Buck and Wylie and "Activist Rhetoric" Pedagogy

In addition to promoting a "social" perspective, Buck's approach to pedagogy reflects Susan Kates's notion of "activist rhetoric instruction." Kates discusses this pedagogical concept in her analysis of three student groups often excluded from traditional higher-education instruction: middle-class white women, African Americans, and members of the working class. According to Kates, activist rhetoric instruction is "characterized by three important pedagogical features": "(1) a profound respect for and awareness of the relationship between language and identity and a desire to integrate that awareness into the curriculum; (2) politicized writing and speaking assignments designed to help students interrogate their marginalized standing in the larger culture in terms of their gender, race, or class; and (3) an emphasis on service and responsibility" (*Activist* 1–2). She contrasts activist instruction with what she calls "mainstream pedagogies" (8). Kates emphasizes the diversity of instruction that did occur during the late nineteenth century and notes that mainstream pedagogies should not be viewed as "entirely uniform or monolithic" (9). However, she contends that more mainstream approaches "were *not* overtly politicized in terms of the features that characterize the activist curricula . . ." (9, emphasis in original). These were courses "in which instructors and students had no pressing needs to understand the politics, ethics, and social organization implicit in language acquisition and linguistic forms" (9). Kates's concept of activist rhetoric instruction resonates with the teaching of Buck and Wylie, whose pedagogy was politicized and highlighted service and responsibility. Like instructors that Kates examines, Buck and Wylie's goal was to democratize education.

Buck's stress on service and social responsibility was evident in her own activism. She was involved in the women's movement, particularly suffrage. Buck was a member of the Equal Suffrage League and later on the board of directors of the Women's City and County Club, a reorganized version of the suffrage party after New York women won the vote in 1917. She published two limericks, "Anti-Suffrage Sentiments," in *The Masses*, and she and Wylie participated in suffrage parades and activities. According to Vassar President Henry Noble MacCracken, Buck and Wylie's home "in the center of old Poughkeepsie became a rallying place for suffrage and for many other movements" ("Appreciations I" 150). After Wylie's death, the house that Buck and Wylie shared for so many years was purchased and dedicated as the headquarters of the Women's City and County Club.[12]

Buck's involvement in women's issues was supported through her relationship with Wylie. Their close personal and professional relationship was similar to that of many educated women of this period. As Lillian Faderman points out, during this time female relationships were not "yet widely stigmatized as 'lesbian,'" and the "female twosome was an accepted institution on the faculties of women's colleges in America in the late-nineteenth and early-twentieth century" (xii–xiii).[13] Their mutual devotion was evident in many ways, particularly in Wylie's establishment of a Gertrude Buck fund after Wylie's death in 1932. In her will, Wylie, who shared Buck's love for community theater, created a ten-thousand-dollar fund to "perpetuate friendly relations between the college and the city," achieved by Buck through her work with the Poughkeepsie Community Theatre ("Laura J. Wylie Dies"). Wylie also directed that "her body be cremated and the ashes buried in the grave of her friend, Gertrude Buck, in Woodlands Cemetery, Philadelphia" ("Miss Wylie's Will Probated"). As colleague Elisabeth Woodbridge Morris points out, "The coöperation of these two was unique, and it is impossible to separate their fields of achievement" ("Laura Johnson Wylie" 13).

Wylie was also active in women's issues throughout her life. She was the president of the Equal Suffrage League, and she founded and served as president of the Women's City and County Club from 1918 to 1928 ("Women's City and County Club" 2; "Laura J. Wylie Dies"). According to her obituary, Wylie was "instrumental in obtaining a membership of 500 from the city and county and was a leader among those who developed the organization into one of the best known of its kind in the country" ("Laura J. Wylie Dies"). Wylie devoted significant time to the club, and her leadership was integral to its success (Boice 43; "Laura J. Wylie Dies"). After her retirement, Wylie continued to be involved in women's issues, teaching at the Bryn Mawr Summer School for Women Workers in Industry. The school, which began the American workers' education movement, "drew its primary inspiration from the thriving women's social justice movement of the progressive era" (Heller, "Women of Summer" 4).[14] In her analysis of writing at the Bryn Mawr Summer School, Karyn L. Hollis argues that the school

> offers an important antecedent to the feminist and activist pedagogies we strive to develop today. The faculty practiced a nonhierarchical teaching style that relied extensively on the discussion method; the student-centered pedagogy focused on students' life experiences, and student input was sought in developing a meaningful and effective curriculum and administration. Interdisciplinary approaches prevailed, and a wide range of writing genres were taught, from poetry and labor drama to the expository essay, collaborative reports and autobiography. . . . women were encouraged to develop their confidence as speakers and writers and to seek leadership roles in the workplace. Most significantly, students and faculty believed education could be a catalyst for progressive social change. (*Liberating Voices* 11)[15]

Many of these pedagogical practices also characterized Wylie and Buck's teaching method at Vassar. For instance, the inductive approach advocated by Wylie and Buck represents an earlier version of the discussion method. (This approach will be explored in greater detail later in the chapter.) Students wrote in a wide variety of genres, practiced interdisciplinary approaches, and were encouraged to become effective speakers and participants in society. In addition, Wylie and Buck saw education as a vehicle for promoting social transformation. Hollis points out that there were close connections between the Bryn Mawr Summer School and the Vassar English Department. This connection came through Wylie's work as an instructor at the school. In addition, Helen Lockwood, a student of Buck and Wylie, taught at the school and shaped its curriculum in significant ways. In fact, Rita Rubinstein Heller places Lockwood among those teachers who had the "greatest impact" on the school during its first period (1921–1927). In 1939 the Bryn Mawr Summer School became the coeducational Hudson Shore Labor College, and Lockwood served as a teacher and was chair of the board of directors from 1943 to 1952 (Hollis, *Liberating Voices* 18–19; "Lockwood, Helen Drusilla").

This social and activist emphasis, which was central to Buck's life and work, was particularly evident in her work in drama. Toward the end of her career, Buck extended her work in rhetoric into the realm of drama and participated in the Little Theater movement. The movement developed in opposition to the commercial theater, which primarily featured melodramas, romances, and musicals but seldom addressed the significant social and political issues facing industrial America (Heller and Rudnick 5). In 1915–16, Buck took a leave from Vassar to attend Baker's "47 Workshop" at Radcliffe. Several workshop graduates became directors of Little Theater groups and teachers of university drama throughout the nation. This included, for instance, Buck at Vassar, Frederick H. Koch at the University of North Carolina, and Alexander M. Drummon at Cornell University (Fawson 2).[16] For Baker, the theater was able to break down traditional barriers, promoting a more democratic drama. Baker used a workshop or "laboratory" method that allowed students to "test out" their productions before a "sympathetic yet genuinely critical audience" ("English 47 Workshop").[17] The theater was no longer under the control of a theater manager and dependent on commercial success for its survival. The audience now helped to shape the productions, becoming an integral part of the dramatic process.

After returning to Vassar, Buck created a similar workshop, which gave its first production in 1916. Buck describes the workshop as "an extension of the classroom; and an indispensable means of learning practical play-writing" ("Vassar Workshop" 182). Buck's workshop soon produced successful results, and by 1919, eight workshop plays had been presented outside of Vassar. In addition, Edna St. Vincent Millay was among the first students of the workshop.

In 1920, Buck helped to establish the Poughkeepsie Community Theatre (Reed, "In Memoriam" 128–29). Colleague and friend Katherine Warren characterizes Buck's goal as the creation of a "democratic cooperative Community Theatre" ("Miss Buck" 34). Warren explains that Buck's idea was to form

> a true community activity, in which the people of the town, regardless of those racial or occupational differences which ordinarily separate them, should coöperate to produce artistic drama; and by this means should arouse among themselves the power to appreciate the best, awaken and stimulate the desire for self-expression, bring opportunity to talent, and through all develop the spirit of fraternity which is so fruitful a soil for all good growths. ("Miss Buck" 30–31)

Similar to her work in composition, rhetoric, and pedagogy, Buck's community theater project was based on her women-centered ethics. In addition, it directly responded to a concern of Buck's—the need to break down the barriers between the people of Poughkeepsie and the college.

During her leave, Buck also applied her ethics to literary criticism and the reading process. In 1916, Buck published *The Social Criticism of Literature,* in which she attempts to solve a battle among competing approaches to literary criticism by proposing her social, democratic model: "One must listen closely to hear, amid the jangle of conflicting theories as to what literary criticism really is, the still small voice of their harmonious relation to one another. Once heard, however, it cannot be disregarded" (16). As Rubin explains, Buck's social view of criticism "was a species of pragmatism: a book was 'good' if it 'worked.' One's assessments were only the results of a given 'experiment' with a piece of writing . . ." (11). Thus, no longer were judgments based on "conventional morality and supposedly timeless standards"; instead, the "test of great writing was whether it enriched the life of the reader" (Rubin 11).

Buck and Vassar's Approach to Teaching English

Buck's ethics was particularly evident in her approach to the teaching of English at Vassar. Her ethics is apparent when examining the required English curriculum from 1898 to 1903, which was offered to students during their first two years. The curriculum, based largely around Buck's textbooks, rejected faculty psychology in favor of a more functionalist approach, emphasizing human interests, the self, and thought. Feminine aspects of Buck's ethics and pedagogy were evident in her stress on process and induction, cooperation and equality, and her belief that teaching is facilitating and should be done with care. It's important to clarify, though, that I don't believe that there are essential "feminine" qualities of any kind. However, I don't think it's essentialist to demonstrate that during this particular period, women like Buck and Wylie were leaders in developing a more progressive approach to pedagogy. In addition, although Buck's approach shared many similarities with what could be considered "good teaching," her assumption of inclusiveness and her stress on leveling power imbalances gave her pedagogy feminist implications, since, at this time, women were denied the right to vote and socially oppressed.

The anonymous article "The Study of English on Psychological Principles—the Required Work at Vassar College" (1898; n.p.) underscores the psychological basis of Buck and the English Department's approach to the teaching of English. During the previous two years, the article explains, Vassar's English Department had "developed some features of marked educational interest, notably through the basing of both plan and method upon psychological principles." As a Vassar colleague points out, Buck came to Vassar in 1897, "the year in which Miss Wylie became head of the department and radical reconstruction began as the joint work of two women with a philosophic grasp of their subject and modern university training" (Reed, "In Memoriam" 128). The article describes the three required English courses students took during their first two years of study; this included a year of expository writing during the first year and a semester each of argumentation and English literature during the sophomore year. This requirement was in place from the 1898–99 academic year through the 1902–03 year (1898–1903 *Vassar College Catalogue*).

Two of the textbooks—*A Course in Expository Writing* (1899), coauthored by Buck and Elisabeth Woodbridge [Morris], and *A Course in Argumentative Writing* (1899), written by Buck—were most likely developed when Buck taught the courses at Vassar. Buck's stress on the interconnection of theory and practice reflected her rejection of prescriptive approaches in favor of inductive methods. Both textbooks emphasized an inductive approach. The inductive method had feminist effects because of its impact on the lives of Vassar students. While current feminist approaches to pedagogy differ, they typically involve strategies aimed at "bringing the learner to the center of the learning activity rather than positing the learner as the recipient of knowledge generated by authoritative others"

(Scarboro 1065). The objective of such strategies is to support the "devel-opment of voice and authority in the classroom" (Scarboro 1065). Like current feminist practices, the inductive approach placed the student at the center of the learning process by promoting dialogue, collaboration, and exploration, thus fostering student voice and agency.

According to the 1899–1900 Department Report, the publication of these textbooks benefited the department by allowing for greater program uniformity in the first-year and sophomore courses and by enabling new instructors to grasp more quickly the course material (qtd. in Campbell, *Toward* 257). In addition, the textbooks provided students with a "body of illustrative literary material, the accumulation and printing of which on our own account was previously a considerable drain upon the time and energy of the department at the beginning of each year" (qtd. in Campbell, *Toward* 257). However, following the national trend of colleges offering more elective courses, Vassar scaled back its required classes (Wozniak 118). In the 1903–04 academic year, one year of exposition was the only required English course, with the courses in argumentation and literature becoming electives (1903–04 *Vassar College Catalogue*).[18]

However, from 1898 to 1903 the required curriculum was more exten-sive. The first-year course was based on Buck and Woodbridge's *A Course in Expository Writing*.[19] Students learned exposition through studying description and definition, and they analyzed complex examples of ex-pository prose by authors such as Matthew Arnold, John Ruskin, Walter Pater, Emily Dickinson, and George Eliot.[20] In the course, students moved from "the description of simple or complex objects, through the interpretation of character from external manifestations, and of works of art, to the formulation of definitions and the exposition of qualities of style" ("Study of English on Psychological Principles").

In the preface, Buck and Woodbridge emphasize the need to make the composition process less artificial by having students write for a real audience and on subjects that are of interest to them and their audience. They stress writing as a process of communication, a way for people to con-nect and cooperate with each other. In addition, as Dana Hood Morgan points out, they urge compassion on the part of the teacher, particularly in terms of criticism (28–29). The authors explain that "criticism is apt to be discouraging because it considers too many things at once. The student has a hopeless feeling that he is all wrong, and he does not know which of his numberless vices to reform first" (vi–vii). Instead, Buck and Woodbridge ask teachers to move from higher- to lower-order concerns: "Beginning with the big things, the little things will many of them right themselves, and those that do not, can wait" (vii).

They also point out that by having a real audience of fellow students, writers can begin to develop their own sense of criticism, rather than relying solely on the teacher. Although such an approach encourages students to develop their critical skills, it is not always an easy process for students to learn, as most writing teachers know. This becomes evident when reading the following student's comment: "[I]n English we had to take the essay of some other girl and criticize it. . . . I like that sort of thing and I can always pick everybody else's essay apart whereas I can't my own at all" (letter, Helen D. Lockwood, 27 Oct. 1908, 1–2). The goal, though, is that students eventually will learn to apply these skills to their own writing.

In *A Course in Expository Writing,* students begin with the study of description, since the authors believe students must first understand their sense experiences before they can interpret them, which is what they do in exposition. According to the article "The Study of English on Psychological Principles," "This study [Buck and Woodbridge's textbook] is based on a brief investigation of the manner in which impressions are formed in the normal mind, on the principle that the reproduction of the process by which the writer has received a given impression is the most effective means for producing the same impression in the mind of the reader." From this passage, it is evident that Buck and Woodbridge's approach is based on the belief that communication requires cooperation and the interplay of ideas between the reader and the writer (Ricks 127). This belief is also apparent in a 1917 lecture Buck gave to the first-year students on "The Study of English." According to Buck, "We study English in all its forms to open the doors of the thoughts and feeling of others to ourselves and of ourselves to others. . . . All we get and all we give is through language" ("Study of English" 6). Language forms the basis of an individual's ability to communicate and to connect with others.

In addition, the authors believed certain thought processes were universal. The best way to communicate ideas to others is to study one's own process of perception to create the same concept in the minds of others. This belief in universal thought processes was central to much of Buck's work in rhetoric and pedagogy. Although this emphasis on universal thought processes was also the premise of rhetorics based on faculty and associational psychologies, the difference was the way the new functionalist psychology defined these processes. Faculty and associational psychologies viewed the activities of the mind in relative isolation from other individuals and the social context. In these theories, language served primarily as a conduit to transmit knowledge (Koch 32). In contrast, functionalist psychology meant studying the mind or consciousness as a part of nature, focusing on how it helped the human organism live in its environment. Knowledge for Buck was a communal and ethical construction. Rhetoric, then, was not a mere conduit; it was a form of knowledge.

In their textbook, Buck and Woodbridge ask students to practice experiments slowing down their process of perception so that they can trace the order and sequence of their observations and better understand these universal thought processes. According to the authors, the "order evidently proceeds from the vague to the definite, from the general to the detailed, and the impressiveness of the description lies in the accuracy with which the writer has recognized the characters and value of the different stages in perception" (11). Students are asked to complete an experiment in which they are exposed at brief intervals to "a bunch of leaves of various kinds" (12). After each exposure, students wrote down descriptions of what they had seen, with the experiment aimed at making them aware of the stages in their perception. In this way, the authors demonstrate how, for most people, perception moves from the indistinct to the detailed.[21]

In the first chapter of their textbook, Buck and Woodbridge encourage students to become aware of their own processes of perception through detailed exercises emphasizing the description process. For instance, students are asked to "Watch an approaching vehicle—a carriage, a horseman, a wheelman—and notice your impressions. Write an account of these, following as nearly as possible their actual order." And "Describe the way in which a black spot on the horizon resolves itself into detail as you approach" (*Expository Writing* 29). First-year students spent the first semester studying description (English A) and the second studying narration (English B).

As scholars have pointed out, Buck's application of contemporary psychology to writing made her work innovative for her time. However, some students were slightly amused by the approach. This becomes evident when reading the following student letter from Ruth Adams (Vassar class of 1904), who was the daughter of George B. Adams, a historian at Yale (Bohan, "Go to" 141): "We are having the most killing things to do in English you ever heard of. She flashes up some object behind a screen and you have to write down what you saw no. 1. Then she flashes it again and you write down the observations made the second time and so on. That is to make us notice what we see first in order to write good descriptions of things. It's very amusing" (Sept. 1900, 2). The cleverness of the following parody by F.A.H., 1905, titled "Some Suggestive Subjects for A English," is a backhanded demonstration of the significance of the method:

Characterize the acoustic properties of sound sleep.
Try to catch the spirit of wood alcohol, and describe exactly.
Discuss the fine art of the college breakfast, applying Pater's theory, "All art is but the removal of surplusage."
Visualize the melodious quality of quiet hours, and then if possible "recover the innocence of the eye."
Interpret in the style of Pater, "Cutie is Ruth, Ruth is cutie."

(319)

Similar to the students of today, Vassar women found humorous and playful ways to respond to their assignments, as is evident in the parody. Nonetheless, students also valued the course and Buck's teaching, as can be seen in this letter from a former student:

When I first went into Miss Buck's course in description, I thought it would be easy enough to make up the descriptions out of my head about things that I had seen before. But Miss Buck insisted upon truth to experience in our writing, and immediately detected infidelity of expression or falsification of experience. . . . Gradually we found that we could not make our writing beautiful by attending merely to the mode of expression, but we must learn to live differently, to react more vigorously and to perceive beauty more clearly. Not only did perception become more acute, but we learned to look deeper into meanings, to see subtle similarities, contrasts, distinctions and relationships existing below the surface. (qtd. in Warren, "In Remembrance" 186)

Buck's course was as much an approach to life as it was about writing. She pushed Vassar women to achieve deeper levels of thought and awareness.

As noted, the method used to teach exposition and English at Vassar was based on an inductive approach, although Buck and Woodbridge also characterize the course as "partly constructive and partly analytic" ("Study of English on Psychological Principles"). During this period, the new and preferred approach, particularly in the social and natural sciences, was the "scientific method," or inductive reasoning. Throughout much of the nineteenth century, deductive reasoning had been the dominant mode of gaining knowledge in U.S. colleges. An example of deductive thinking was the traditional rhetoric course at many all-male universities in which the teacher lectured and students typically read, memorized, and then applied the principles they had learned. Inductive reasoning offered a new method of learning. Rather than passively accepting received knowledge, an inductive approach emphasized investigation, discussion, and intellectual curiosity. By beginning with inductive reasoning, Vassar women were not simply accepting received opinion and thus preserving cultural authority. Instead, they were learning to think for themselves, to examine traditional assumptions. In using such methods, Buck was teaching her students to challenge unquestioning obedience to authority, including patriarchal authority.

Buck and Woodbridge's emphasis on the inductive method is evident in their focus on experimentation and observation. It is also evident in their description of how to teach writing: "[I]t may be suggested that it is always best, not first to tell a student how to write a thing, and then bid him to do it, but first to get him to do it, and afterwards to let him see how it was done" (vii). Buck and Woodbridge illustrate their point by drawing upon examples emphasizing "the various forms of the paragraph—the paragraph 'by method of specific instance' or 'by method of contrast'" (vii). They explain that the forms came about because "they were the best ones for the treatment of a given subject" and that most students will write these forms naturally (vii). In this way, students "will come to realize that writing is not made from rules, but rules are discovered in writing" (viii). Students also practice inductive methods in the analysis of their writing. According to the article "The Study of English on Psychological Principles," "By comparison of their own themes with those of others, and with selected passages from standard or current writers, they are led to discriminate between effective and ineffective methods and results, and thus discover for themselves the principles of composition." In this way, students will write not merely for the purpose of conforming to rules, but they will learn these principles through the process of communication.

In addition, Buck used an inductive approach in her own teaching practices. In a 1999 interview, Evalyn A. Clark, a noted Vassar historian and teacher who was in Buck's Composition and Reading class in 1920, discussed her experience in the required yearlong course. [22] According to Clark, who was ninety-six at the time of the interview, Buck's course was not a "routine question-and-answer" type class: "We never quite knew what we were going to be doing in class or what we were supposed to be doing outside of class. Because she [Buck] really assumed that we would bring up things we wanted to talk about and that is what would happen" (20 Mar. 1999). Clark later added, "I mean it was much more sort of unbuckled, the whole thing." Instead, Clark said the class of about fifteen students was based on the principle of student "self-organization": "You always had the feeling that it was up to you to take part in the conversation, and I never yet had a lecture when I was in the English Department, never listened to a lecture. And I mean that" (20 Mar. 1999). This stress on discussion and participation was central to Buck's teaching and the instructional practices of the broader department.[23] Students' humorous perception of the English Department's focus on the inductive method is evident in a composite picture of Laura Johnson Wylie in the 1901 student annual, the *Vassarion*. In the illustration, Wylie is holding a fishing pole with "inductive method" etched on the rod, suggesting that students viewed the exploratory nature of the approach as something akin to a fishing expedition.

Buck and Woodbridge's method also illustrated their innovative view of invention. For them, invention was learned through experimentation and practical application, and it was motivated by the desire to communicate with others. It was based on a theory of knowledge as a transaction among the writer, the reader, and the social context (Koch 14). Buck's emphasis on audience and social awareness is particularly evident in her textbook on argumentation in which oral debates complement students' written assignments. In *The Methodical Memory: Invention in Current-Traditional Rhetoric*, Sharon Crowley includes Buck among a lengthy list of authors who wrote current-traditional textbooks and defined invention "in terms of its focus on the private authoring mind" (xiv, 70). However, Crowley never specifically discusses any of Buck's texts to explain why she characterizes her as a current-traditional author.

Crowley traces current-traditional rhetoric's view of invention to eighteenth-century philosophical theories of the mind based on faculty and associational psychologies. This approach to invention "assumed that individual minds function in isolation from one another and that the knowledge they generate is derived either from empirical or logical investigation" (Crowley 86). From this perspective, knowledge is viewed as a *"commodity* capable of being possessed and transferred unchanged from one isolated mind to another" (Gage, "Towards" 5, emphasis in original). This view of knowledge led many late-nineteenth-century rhetoricians to reject invention, and to believe that "the content of discourse comes from the subject matter and not from rhetoric itself. Rhetoric conveys the results of thought, but is not a form of thought" (Herzberg 320). Rhetoric thus is reduced to a mere transfer medium for knowledge. However, invention for Buck was social, not the "introspective" process that Crowley discusses (xiii). This led Buck to teach writing as a communal, contextual activity that can change the way people think and act. Buck's approach to invention was based on the democratic assumption that all individuals were responsible and should be equally involved in the creation of knowledge.

During their sophomore year, students took a semester of argumentation. The course was based on Buck's *A Course in Argumentative Writing* (1899). Since Buck's approach to argumentation is discussed more fully in chapter 4, I will only briefly outline the key aspects of the course. As in the course in exposition, argumentation had an inductive emphasis. In other words, students discovered the principles of argumentation through discussion and analyzing their own reasoning processes, rather than simply learning formal principles of argumentation. According to the article "The Study of English on Psychological Principles," "[O]ne of the most interesting features of the course in argumentation is formed by the debates which take place almost weekly." During these debates, students discussed issues "of local or general interest" ("Study of English on Psychological Principles"). In her textbook, Buck asserts that the oral debates are "useful as complementary to the writing" (*Argumentative Writing* vii). Similar to her approach to expository writing, Buck underscores the importance of writing as communication, a form of human interaction.

Since her course was an approach to life, Buck's pedagogy reflected her feminism. In *Man Cannot Speak for Her: A Critical Study of Early Feminist*

Rhetoric (1989), Karyln Kohrs Campbell recovers the rhetoric of the U.S. women's rights/suffrage movement. In her analysis of women's persuasive efforts, Campbell identifies several recurring strategies, which she terms *feminine style*. She explains that many women speakers used these strategies in an effort "to reduce the hostility of audiences by appropriating traditional elements of femininity into their performances and presentations" ("Consciousness-Raising" 51). Although this style is not exclusive to women, Campbell explains that it reflects their learning experiences during this period (*Man Cannot* 14). Since women were denied formal education, instruction came in the form of craft-learning, in which women learned from each other "through a supervised internship combining expert advice with trial and error" (Campbell 13). According to Campbell, discourse produced from this rhetorical situation will be "personal in tone," because of the interpersonal nature of the craft internship, and it will be inductively structured because "crafts are learned bit by bit, instance by instance, from which generalizations emerge" (13). An inductive approach also "increases audience agency" (Campbell, "Consciousness-Raising" 51). Thus, the discourse will encourage audience participation and "efforts will be made to create identification with the experiences of the audience and those described by the speaker" (Campbell, *Man Cannot* 13). The primary objective of this discourse is "empowerment, a term contemporary feminists have used to refer to the process of persuading listeners that they can act effectively in the world, that they can be 'agents of change'" (Campbell 13). In her analysis, Campbell connects feminine style to what contemporary feminists call "consciousness-raising," which aims at empowerment through social change.

Although Buck's pedagogy and rhetoric included more social and political dimensions, various aspects of her teaching practices and those used by English Department faculty reflected "feminine style." This emphasis was evident in Buck's use of induction, so that students became more involved in the learning process; her focus on the communal nature of invention, so that the speaker and audience were sharing in the meaning-making process; and the faculty's belief in the importance of personal conferences in the learning process, so that the teacher-student connection was enhanced. Buck and the English Department faculty were empowering their female students to become agents of change. These aspects of feminine style are evident when exploring Vassar's writing courses.

The courses at Vassar required a significant amount of work from both students and teachers. In exposition and argumentation, "constant practice in writing is given," with students writing from "two to four themes" a week ("Study of English on Psychological Principles"). The themes were criticized in class through the students reading and commenting on each other's essays and in private conferences with the instructor. According to the article, "These interviews form an important feature of the work, furnishing a valuable supplement to the class study and giving the instructors opportunity for attention to individual needs." The English Department's commitment to student "interviews" is evident in the department reports. For instance, the first semester Department Report for the 1900–1901 academic year indicates that on a weekly basis, Buck averaged five hours in student interviews, three hours in written criticism of their work, and eight hours in department work. All told, she averaged eleven hours in classroom teaching and criticism and sixteen hours in department work per week. That semester, Buck taught four sections of argumentation (a total of ninety-four students), two sections of description (a total of fifty-seven students), and one section of the development of rhetorical theory (a total of nine students). Other instructors reported spending as much as ten hours in student interviews and twenty hours in written criticism per week.

The hours spent in interviews seem representative for the English Department based on department reports during this period. From the following letter to Vassar President James Monroe Taylor, Wylie's obvious concern that instructors may not be receiving credit for this significant and time-consuming work is evident. In her 1904 letter, Wylie emphasizes that looking at classroom hours alone "gives a very inadequate account of their work" (23 Nov., 1). She highlights the hours instructors spend in interviews and in preparation for interviews:

> By careful study of the reports sent in by each of them [instructors], supplemented by many inquiries, I find that the instructors of writing courses spend on the average as much or more time in the interviews as in class, and that preparation for their interviews takes about the same length of time as do the interviews themselves. Thus Miss Reed with three hours of freshman teaching spends about four hours a week in interviews with freshman, exclusive of office hours, interviews with other students, etc.;

Miss Dudley with nine hours of class teaching spends nine or ten hours a week in interviews. Miss Dudley, who carries only freshman work, thus spends at least eighteen hours a week in actual teaching, and reports for her interviews an amount of preparation at least equal to that necessary for offering a second course. This does not include general criticism of papers, but only such special study as is demanded for effective individual criticism. I have instanced Miss Reed's and Miss Dudley's hours because they represent almost exactly the average time reported. (23 Nov. 1904, 1)

For Wylie, the interviews were an integral part of the instructor's duties; thus, they should be considered equally with in-classroom teaching hours in determining the instructor's actual work within the department.

The interviews, similar to the English courses, emphasized communication, empowerment, and personal relationships. Based on their letters, many students seemed to appreciate the individualized attention offered in the interviews. In an article written in 1924, when Wylie retired from Vassar after twenty-nine years of service, friend and colleague Katherine Warren underscores the importance of conferences to Wylie's teaching: "But it was largely in private conferences that the clinching work of Miss Wylie's teaching was done; in the vigorous, unsparing but sympathetic criticism not only of class and written work, but if desirable, of attitude, mind and character" ("Retrospect" 91).[24]

According to the article "The Study of English on Psychological Principles," this extensive background in writing offered in exposition and argumentation "forms for the student a basis of criticism," providing a beginning for the study of literature. The benefit of such an approach is that "[t]he critical method thus acquired is applied" in the third required course, the Development of English Literature from *Beowulf* to Swift (1898–1903 *Vassar College Catalogue*). This background provides students with "both knowledge and method" for when they take "higher elective courses" during their last two years of study. Thus, at Vassar, rhetoric and literary criticism were closely related. This close connection is evident in the 1899–1900 Department Report, in which Wylie asserts that the study of rhetoric "maintains in all our courses a relation with the literature at once coequal and complementary" (qtd. in Campbell, *Toward* 260). The cooperative connection between literature and writing also reflected the close pedagogical ideas of Buck and Wylie: "The harmony between Miss

Buck's ideas and Miss Wylie's, and the completeness of their coöperation made the growth of an integral relation between their courses in literature and in writing a natural process, and formed a nucleus for similar relations in the department as a whole" (Warren, "Retrospect" 84).

Buck discusses the relationship between literary criticism and rhetoric in her article "What Does 'Rhetoric' Mean?" (1901). She reviews the findings of a recent report of the Modern Language Association (MLA) dealing with the subject of "'graduate study in rhetoric'" (197). The report, written by Fred Newton Scott, consisted of "sixty-three answers from teachers of graduate courses in English at American colleges" to these three questions (197): "Is rhetoric . . . a proper subject for graduate work? If so, what is the proper aim, what is the scope, and what are the leading problems of rhetoric as a graduate study? If rhetoric . . . should not be admitted to the list of graduate studies, what do you regard as the strongest reason for excluding it?" (197). As Donald C. Stewart points out, in asking such questions, "Scott was making the members of MLA face up to a basic question: were they willing to consider rhetoric in a modern and comprehensive sense, or had they relegated it . . . to little more than theme correcting in freshman composition and therefore of no intellectual substance whatsoever?" ("Fred Newton Scott and the Reform" 117). According to Stewart, although a majority of respondents agreed that rhetoric should include graduate work, "their opinion did not prevail at the MLA" (117).

However, Buck, like Scott, supported such a future for rhetoric. In her article, Buck contends that "we must look [to graduate students] for the development of the new science of rhetoric" (198). This new rhetorical theory is necessary because it "affords a field almost unworked by modern tools or with modern methods. It presents innumerable problems demanding solution on the basis of recently formulated psychological and aesthetic principles" (198). One of the findings of the report is that English specialists apparently see a close connection between rhetoric and literary criticism, "—subjects often set in different departments of our colleges, and jealously depreciated each by the other" (199). Buck adds,

> If the term rhetoric is once understood, however, in its new sense as a
> comprehensive study of communication by language, explanatory on psy-
> chologic grounds of all forms of written or spoken discourse, any sense of

antagonism between it and literary criticism straightway becomes impossible, not to say absurd. Both in material and in method the two subjects find meeting ground and opportunity for mutual re-enforcement. (199)

Rhetoric for Buck is a broad, interdisciplinary study of communication; it is also interconnected with literary criticism. Buck's emphasis on the interconnection of literary criticism and rhetoric was evident in the English Department at Vassar, where the teaching of rhetoric/writing and literature were valued equally and viewed as organically connected.

In examining Buck's "social" view of ethics and rhetoric, I have shown how she developed women-centered alternatives that diverged from traditional Kantian ethics and agonistic approaches to rhetoric. Her ethics shared significant ontological and epistemological assumptions with feminine and feminist approaches to ethics of the late twentieth century, including an emphasis on concrete relationships, interdependence, and participation. Buck's ethics was aimed at providing an inclusive method of dealing with conflict, one that stressed the significance of equality in relationships. In her approach to rhetoric, Buck challenged the dominant ideological stance by questioning the power basis of traditional argument. More specifically, by highlighting participation by all and fostering equality, Buck's approach to rhetoric underscored the unethical and individualistic nature of traditional rhetoric, and it provided an alternative accommodating to women and other marginalized groups.

In addition, I have demonstrated how these assumptions were central to Buck and the English Department's approach to the teaching of English. The department's inductive approach represents a significant precursor to the feminist approaches that are used today. From her psychology, Buck emphasized experimentation, organicism, and activity. She stressed discussion and viewed the student as an active participant in the learning process, not merely as a passive receiver of information. In addition, Buck highlighted the values of social activity and reform, compassion, and cooperation. She and members of the English Department sought to empower their students so that they could work as agents of change in society. These ideas formed the basis of her women-centered ethics, and they shaped her approach to rhetoric and pedagogy.

2

PROGRESSIVE EDUCATION, FEMINISM, AND THE DETROIT NORMAL TRAINING SCHOOL

> For the construction of an inner organic world, one which will enable him to live in organic relations with the outer world, the child's dominant interests must be noted, and as they appear they must be satisfied. Further, they must not only be satisfied but also organized, and this means a wide experience of his environment, wide enough to determine their most fundamental relations.
>
> —Harriet M. Scott and Gertrude Buck, *Organic Education: A Manual for Teachers in Primary and Grammar Grades*

> The main aim of education should be to produce competent, caring, loving people.
>
> —Nel Noddings, *Educating Moral People: A Caring Alternative to Character Education*

*B*uck began her professional career not at an elite institution but at the Detroit Normal Training School working with Harriet M. Scott, the school's principal and the older sister of Fred Newton Scott. Buck further developed her progressive ideas by coauthoring a textbook for teachers of primary and secondary grades with Harriet Scott. Unlike composition, which drew on the rhetorical tradition, normal schools, the postsecondary teacher-training schools of the nineteenth and early twentieth centuries, were influenced by European learning theories (Fitzgerald 244). In *The Young Composers: Composition's Beginnings in Nineteenth-Century Schools*, Lucille M. Schultz contends that school-based writing instruction "is a site where what we think of as personal or experienced-based writing began; it is a site where the democratization of writing was institutionalized; it is a site where some of our contemporary composition practices were prefigured; and it is a site where composition instruction, as we understand it today, began" (4).[1] Since the normal schools were instrumental in shaping the public school curriculum, they are a significant site to explore in terms of their development and implementation of democratic teaching practices. In addition, in examining Scott and Buck's textbook, significant overlap between their feminist approach and progressive education is evident. These similarities include a student-centered pedagogy that underscored students' interests and experiences, a focus on cooperation and inductive learning, and an emphasis on human relationships over abstract principles in the education of moral individuals. In particular, Scott and Buck's ideas anticipate aspects found in Nell Noddings's care ethics and her discussion of its significance to education. Scott's stress on cooperation and developing egalitarian relationships is also a significant aspect of Buck's feminist ethics. In addition, it is integral to Buck's understanding of the metaphor and her social theory of rhetoric, discussed near the end of the chapter.

Scott and Buck's efforts to democratize teaching practices parallel those of other women during this period. For instance, the collection *"Bending the Future to Their Will": Civic Women, Social Education, and Democracy* (1999) explores a group of women "who forged a distinctive tradition of social education from the late nineteenth to the late twentieth century, one that offered an alternative set of ideas about its means and ends to those propounded by mainstream educational theorists" (Crocco 1). Among the late-nineteenth-century women in the collection are Lucy Maynard Salmon, Buck's colleague at Vassar; Jane Addams of Hull House; and Mary Sheldon Barnes, who, like Salmon, advocated the inductive use of sources to teach history. Collection coeditor Margaret Smith Crocco explains that she uses the term "social education" to indicate that education concerned with democracy has occurred not only in universities but in various settings including "women's clubs, settlement houses, and activist and professional organizations" (1–2). In defining *social education*, Crocco explains that it "seeks to address the issue of what skills and knowledge individuals need to live effectively in a democracy, the definition of which we borrow from John Dewey, who considered democracy 'a mode of associated living'" (1). Like the women in this collection, Scott and Buck were part of this tradition of social education, which stood in contrast to mainstream educational approaches of the times. Scott and Buck's goals focused on developing "social individuals," or individuals possessing a deeper understanding of the interconnected nature of society. These individuals would then use this knowledge to improve society.

Gendered Histories and the Normal Schools

One significant reason the contributions of the normal schools and the efforts of women like Scott and Buck have been marginalized is because of the gendered nature of the traditional histories of education and rhetoric. As Crocco argues, "Across the social sciences as well as in history, women's contributions have been ignored, underestimated, or marginalized" (8). This marginalization is evident in the work of Buck and Harriett Scott as well as that of the normal schools. As noted, Buck's efforts often have been overshadowed by or viewed only in relation to those of Fred Newton Scott. Similarly, the work of Harriet Scott has been virtually ignored. This pattern of neglect also appears true for the normal schools, which have been largely overlooked by traditional histories of composition and rhetoric. The focus has tended to be on males at elite eastern and coeducational universities, rather than on females in the normal and public school settings. Select women's eastern colleges, like Vassar, also have garnered scholars' attention.

Despite this neglect, the normal school is "a site that turns out to harbor rich intellectual, methodological, and political implications for composition's tradition" (Fitzgerald 225). In her analysis of Midwestern normal schools, Kathryn Fitzgerald emphasizes two striking differences between normal schools and "the elite Eastern colleges," which have been the primary focus of historians (224). The first major difference is in terms of their objectives. Fitzgerald contends that normal schools "were intended to be inclusive, democratic institutions that focused on professional rather than academic preparation" (244). The second is that normal school faculty "had access to an intellectual tradition completely outside of rhetorical theory—the tradition of European pedagogy" (226). Fitzgerald contends that these factors contributed to a "unique normal school ethos," and that a significant aspect of this ethos was "the active integration of theory and practice" (244).

These elements are apparent in Scott and Buck's work in Detroit. For instance, Fitzgerald, Schultz, and Beth Ann Rothermel all argue that the pedagogical theories of Swiss teacher and reformer Johann Heinrich Pestalozzi were "embraced" by nineteenth-century American normal schools (Schultz 57). In fact, in *Archives of Instruction: Nineteenth-Century Rhetorics, Readers and Composition Books in the United States,* Schultz, in her chapter on composition books, contends that Pestalozzi (1746–1827) was "[t]he most powerful influence on the nineteenth-century composition book for young students . . ." (Carr, Carr, Schultz 153). Pestalozzi emphasized that "education's aim was to 'fit,' or adjust, all children to society and that all learning begins with the child's sense perceptions" (Fitzgerald 231). Scott and Buck also drew on the work of Pestalozzi in framing many of their pedagogical practices, and, like other normal schools, the Detroit school was "grounded in a very different intellectual perspective from the rhetorical tradition of composition" (Fitzgerald 231). Some of the key concepts introduced by this tradition include a more developmental approach to education, an emphasis on starting learning with the child's interest, and a focus on instruction "organized inductively from the familiar and concrete toward the unfamiliar and abstract" (Fitzgerald 231).

One important reason the European pedagogical tradition may have been "embraced" by the normal schools was the gendered nature of the normal and public schools (Schultz 57). As Sandra D. Harmon emphasizes, from 1850 to 1900 "more than half of all women enrolled in schools beyond secondary level were students in normal schools" (84). Quoting an article in the 1894 Illinois State Normal School student newspaper, Harmon points out that "nationally 65.5 percent of public-school teachers were women" and that this figure was similar to the percentage of women at the Illinois school, the focus of her article (88). However, she notes that this was unusual for eastern normal schools, "where the percentage of male students was generally lower, especially toward the end of the century" (88). Thus, in terms of sheer numbers, women were in the majority both nationwide in common schools and in eastern normal schools. Various teaching strategies used at the normal schools challenged the traditional emphasis on memorization and recitation. Instead, several pedagogical practices used by the normal schools reflected Karyln Kohrs Campbell's discussion of "feminine style," including a more personal emphasis, a focus on induction, and a goal of empowerment (*Man Cannot* 12–13).

Although not all women may have embraced such approaches, many may have applied feminine style and feminist practices to their teaching because it coincided with their experiences as women.

The Educational Context in the 1890s

In exploring the educational setting, important connections between Buck and Scott's feminist pedagogy and those advocated by progressive educators emerge, particularly the focus on student interest and social transformation. According to Lawrence A. Cremin, "[P]rogressive education began as part of a vast humanitarian effort to apply the promise of American life—the ideal of government by, of, and for the people—to the puzzling new urban-industrial civilization that came into being during the latter half of the nineteenth century" (viii). In other words, progressive education started as a movement aimed at furthering democracy in the face of rapid industrialization.[2]

In bibliographical notes, Cremin traces the start of progressive education to 1892 (358–59). That was the year Joseph Mayer Rice, New York pediatrician turned investigative journalist, published his controversial series on schools in *The Forum* (3–4).[3] Rice's aim was to learn about different methods of instruction and the management of schools across the nation. From 7 January to 25 June 1892, Rice traveled to thirty-six cities where he observed some twelve hundred teachers and visited twenty teacher-training schools. According to Cremin, Rice's series "bore all the earmarks of the journalism destined to make 'muckraking' a household word in America. In city after city public apathy, political interference, corruption, and incompetence were conspiring to ruin the schools" (4). For example, Rice opened his series with a telling description of New York City schools because they represented conditions that were typical in larger cities.

Rice reports that at one New York City primary school, the principal advocated the maxim: "Save the minutes." He adds, "Everything is prohibited that is of no measurable advantage to the child, such as the movement of the head or limb, when there is no logical reason why it should be moved at that time. I asked the principal whether the children were not allowed to move their heads. She answered, 'Why should they look behind when the teacher is in front of them?'—words too logical to be refuted" (31–32). In such schools the emphasis obviously was not on the interests of the child. Instead, it was on control and the desires of the teacher. The approach closely resembled turn-of-the-century business models, in which the focus was on maintaining a daily schedule and not wasting resources and time.

Progressive educators opposed this more traditional educational system, with its lack of concern for the child and emphasis on filling the mind with facts. In *The School and Society* (1899), Dewey summarizes such an approach by stating that "the center of gravity is outside of the child" (47). However, he contends that changes in education are resulting in a shift to a new center of gravity: "It is a change, a revolution, not unlike that introduced by Copernicus when the astronomical center shifted from the earth to the sun. In this case the child becomes the sun about which the appliances of education revolve; he is the center about which they are organized" (*School and Society* 47). Dewey viewed these changes as dramatic in scale, having the potential to revolutionize the school and society.

For people like Lucy Maynard Salmon, such changes indicated deeper societal transformations. A history professor at Vassar, Salmon completed her bachelor's and master's degrees at Michigan and thus like Buck was among a group of women who obtained progressive education at Michigan (Bohan, "Lucy Maynard" 49). In "Progress in Education at Vassar College" (1919), Salmon contends that education characteristically has been conservative and slow to recognize "the possibility of doing more than accepting a body of formulated knowledge and passing it on unchanged . . ." (1). However, she argues that a "profound change" has spread throughout society and even has influenced education: "A new principle antagonistic to authority has come into political, social, and industrial society and education has not been unaffected by it, although it has been long in responding to it. This new principle is that of intellectual curiosity, investigation, and research—three developing phases of a force that has controlled all progressive movements" (1). For Salmon, this opposition to authority represented a new reform spirit evident in diverse movements across the nation.

The "profound change" in education manifested itself in many forms during the 1890s and the early decades of the twentieth century. As Melvin C. Baker points out, the period was one of "unusual vigor, novelty, and enthusiasm in educational speculation and programmatic change" from the kindergarten to the college level (86). Among the various educational movements of the time were the American Herbartians, the Kindergarten Movement, the Child Study Movement, the Manual Training Movement, and W. T. Harris and "Traditional Education" (M. C. Baker 86).[4] Diverse educational issues were debated; however, according to D. G. Myers, two sides who staked out opposing positions were the "humanists and developmentalists" (104). The humanists viewed the learner in terms of faculty psychology, which, as noted, typically depicted the mind as consisting of various mental abilities or faculties that needed to be disciplined and trained. The developmentalists, on the other hand, were the supporters of education "as an unfolding of a child's *interest,* who embraced the Rousseauistic conviction that the 'human heritage' had too often meant a bridling of the child's true nature" (Myers 104, emphasis in original).

Dewey sought to resolve the conflict between the two groups by blending self-activity (effort) with interest (Myers 104). He saw the learner biologically; in other words, he saw learning as part of a "natural process of seeking, inquiring, purposing or looking for means to realize ends" (Beck 83). In Dewey's "Interest in Relation to Training of the Will" (1896), he presents his theory of interest as he critiques then-current doctrines of interest and of effort.[5] The opposing positions Dewey examines include those who believe in "interest" and those who discount interest, arguing students need to exert themselves mentally at tasks that may be boring or even disagreeable (Beck 84). The two approaches represent clashing sides in debates involving interest and moral training. The first represents the American Herbartians, who gained influence in the 1890s, while the second reflects a Kantian approach based on faculty psychology.[6]

The flaw with both approaches, according to Dewey, is that they assume that the "object or idea to be mastered, the end to be reached, the act to be performed" is external to the student (EW 5: 117). For both, knowledge is some container lying outside the student, which needs "to be made interesting by artificial methods or had to be mastered by jaw-tightening activity" (Myers 105). Dewey contends that interest "marks the annihilation of the distance between the person and the materials and results of his action; it is the instrument which effects their organic union" (EW 5: 122). For Dewey, interest provides the bridge that allows individuals to fully integrate the end of action with the means. Thus, interests are not passive things to be "fed" or rejected. Instead, for Dewey interests already exist within children; they are active projections of the self. The

PROGRESSIVE EDUCATION AND FEMINISM

role for the teacher is to recognize the connection between students and their interests and to use interest to guide education (Beck 84).

The underlying psychology of Dewey's ideas is closely connected to his democratic ideals. According to Dewey, the American Herbartians view interest as a "passive reflex," an "outcome," not an impulse or desire on the part of the student (EW 5: 140). Dewey contends that such an approach is not democratic: "It is not the psychology of a nation which professes to believe that every individual has within him the principles of authority, and that order means co-ordination, not subordination" (EW 5: 141).

Dewey's version of interest extends beyond the walls of the classroom to shape an ideal society. It is aimed at developing individuals suited to democracy—governments that maintain social order through coordination, not subordination, of individual interests. This emphasis on individual interests and the need to develop moral citizens was integral to Buck's work with Harriet Scott.

Harriet M. Scott

As mentioned in chapter 1, discussions of Buck's work often emphasize the influence of Fred Newton Scott; however, scholars have not focused on how Harriet "Hattie" Maria Scott (1854–1906) shaped both Fred Newton Scott's and Buck's ideas. Several factors explain why Harriet Scott's contributions have been largely ignored by traditional histories of rhetoric and composition. The focus, as noted, has tended to be on male teachers at elite eastern and coeducational universities rather than on females in the normal and public school settings. In addition, as Crocco emphasizes, the "gendered nature of the social sciences and education has positioned women's contributions as low-status 'practice' rather than high-status 'theory'" (3). This gendered positioning, Crocco explains, is evident in the fact that Jane Addams's contributions typically are associated with "social work rather than 'sociology'" (3), and Vassar's administration viewed Salmon's research "of domestic service as inappropriate for serious academic inquiry and found her support of woman suffrage unsuitable for a female professor" (3). Although Crocco is discussing the field of social sciences, her analysis also applies to histories of rhetoric and composition. Traditional histories have tended to focus on textbooks on rhetoric and rhetorical theory rather than on teaching manuals and actual classroom practices. One result of this focus is that the work of Harriet Scott and other important women teachers has been rendered invisible.

However, in exploring Scott's efforts at the Detroit Normal Training School (now Wayne State University College of Education), it is evident that her ideas were influential to the works of Fred Newton Scott and Gertrude Buck. Born in Terre Haute, Indiana, Harriet Scott was educated at home through a governess and in the public schools (Scott, "Biography" 1). In 1870, she was enrolled in the first class at the newly opened Indiana State Normal School (now Indiana State University) (Stewart and Stewart 8). She was also among the first graduates in 1872;[7] she took an advanced course from 1874 to 1876 and later taught at Indiana Normal (Hanawalt 111; Lynch 44, 67). In 1893, she moved to Detroit at the urging of Amanda Parker Funnelle, who had been Scott's former teacher and mentor at Indiana Normal and now was the principal at the Detroit Normal Training School. After Funnelle resigned in 1886, Scott became the school's principal, holding that position until 1899. That year, Scott "resigned her position in the midst of controversy over her principles of instruction" (Stewart and Stewart 8). She moved to Pasadena, California, where she died in 1906 at the age of 52 (Sosnowsky 1; Scott, "Biography" 3).

Fred Newton Scott "greatly admired" his sister, who was six years his senior, and "may have been profoundly influenced in his thinking about the nature of education by her" (Stewart and Stewart 8). As noted, Harriet Scott was the principal of the Detroit school, and the ideas she developed at her school are significant in terms of understanding both Scott's and Buck's ideas. According to Donald and Patricia Stewart, Harriet Scott's "insistence on education being an organic process, developing naturally out of a child's interests, suggests the whole notion of organic conceptions which one finds in the mature work of [Fred Newton] Scott" (8–9).

Organic Education

Harriet Scott's work in Detroit seems equally important in understanding the development of Buck's ideas. At a memorial meeting for Buck in 1923, Fred Newton Scott discussed how he suggested to Buck that "she go to Detroit, live with my sister, visit the school, and collaborate in the production of the book" ("Address" 5). The collaboration resulted in *Organic Education: A Manual for Teachers in Primary and Grammar*

Grades (1897), which was based on Scott's work at the Detroit Normal School, "an institution that was garnering significant attention for its creative and innovative ideas in both the education of students and the preparation of teachers" (Stewart and Stewart 8). In Fred Newton Scott's biography of his sister, he asserts that the Detroit school "became a center for those who were interested in a certain type of educational thought and experiment, and many well known students of education came to visit it. It is not too much to say that for a period of years it was a distributing point of the best educational thought" (3). He adds that the educational ideas that Harriet Scott developed at her school were "clearly set forth" in *Organic Education.*

In preparing to write *Organic Education,* Fred Newton Scott notes that Buck "read through everything that had been written upon this phase of education. I think nothing was neglected. It was one of the most thorough bits of research, I believe, in her entire career" ("Address" 5). Through researching and writing *Organic Education,* Buck's feminist and progressive education ideas were more fully developed, more specifically, her emphasis on cooperation, interest, relationships, and reconstruction. These ideas not only were central to Buck's later approach to administration and education but also were evident throughout much of her work.

This emphasis is apparent when examining *Organic Education.* Scott and Buck's approach resembled the "culture-epoch" theory of education, which viewed child development as a "repetition in little of the history of civilization" (4). However, Scott and Buck emphasize that the curriculum's origin was based on "meeting certain observed conditions of child-life" and that theory was "an afterthought" (9). As the authors explain, "Every expansion, retraction, or modification of the work has been made at the initiative of the children, and the coherence, if the system may claim any, is the coherence of the naturally developing organism, rather than that of the artificial structure" (10). Scott and Buck's words underscore the need for a flexible curriculum, one that is based on specific observation of children's interests, not a preconceived, rigid theory.

The curriculum for primary and secondary levels moves students through different grade levels relating to their interests and supposedly matching the "progress" of civilization, or "certain period[s] of race development" (13). The program, for example, begins with Hiawatha the Indian Boy, moves through to Cleon the Greek Boy, Horatius the Roman

Boy, Wulf the Saxon Boy, and Gilbert the French Boy, only to end with the study of Puritans and the development of America. According to Gail Bederman, within the context of public perceptions of Darwinism in the late 1890s, "civilization was seen as an explicitly racial concept. It meant more than simply 'the west' or 'industrially advanced societies.' . . . Human races were assumed to evolve from simple savagery, through violent barbarism, to advanced and valuable civilization. But only white races had, as yet, evolved to the civilized stage" (25). This racialized view of civilization is evident in Scott and Buck's curriculum, which includes no mention of African Americans and places white Anglo-Saxons at the top of the civilization ladder.

In her article on the Detroit school "Another Phase of the New Education" (1896), Buck explains the purpose behind the culture-epoch theory: "The history of the world's progress as a whole was then summarized for the purpose of disclosing the principle of coöperation, which has been more or less explicitly recognized throughout the grades as the underlying principle, not only of political but also of industrial and social development" (383). This emphasis on cooperation is underscored at the article's conclusion. At this point in the article, Buck tells Scott that she is unsure whether to call the school "'the apotheosis of the story, or a gigantic philosophy of coöperation.' 'Either will do,' she [Scott] responded; 'coöperation is the idea, and the story is our method'" (384). As George M. Fredrickson points out, during this period, some of the originators of the new field of sociology viewed society as "evolving toward higher forms of cooperative endeavor" (312). This perspective, according to Fredrickson, represented a reaction against "the rugged individualism of the social Darwinists" and their notion that society is built on survival of the fittest (312).[8] Like these early sociologists, Scott and Buck worked against the social Darwinist emphasis on conflict and competition and instead viewed cooperation as "an underlying principle" of society. Scott's approach was viewed as fostering this existing principle.

In titling their book *Organic Education,* Scott and Buck meant "education that was unified, integrated, and coordinated" (Hanawalt 121). The approach, according to the authors, is based on differentiating a specific period into "all its various interrelated activities, industrial, artistic, scientific, mathematical, political, social, religious, and then, by comparison with other periods, unif[ying] it again into what seems to be its fundamental idea or central principles, which as such has always an ethical bearing" (13–14). As Leslie L. Hanawalt notes, Scott and Buck's emphasis reflected "the Victorian faith that a basis of ethics and morality could be inculcated by the schools" (122). The book's stress on ethics is evident in the fact that the outline for each grade encourages students to compare their character traits and ethical aims to the "type-character" and period they are studying (61–62). For example, when children are ages six and seven, they study Darius, the Persian Boy and Persian civilization. The authors contend that at this age, children's "military spirit" starts to emerge, and their character traits include wanting to "be noticed, to conquer, to control" (117). In terms of ethical aims, Scott and Buck assert that "[t]hese instincts should be utilized by the teacher, turned into healthful channels, that the character may be enriched by them. Individual self-assertion must be tempered and directed through obedience, in which alone coöperation becomes possible" (117).

Scott and Buck's association of certain character traits and ethical aims to supposed periods of race development is obviously racist and fosters stereotyping. Their ideas, though, reflected the pervasive nature of racialized and racist discourse in America during this period. In the late nineteenth century, the culture-epoch theory or recapitulation theory, as it was also called, was "scientific orthodoxy among most American biologists" (Bederman 92).[9] As David Gary Shaw notes, Herbert Spencer's social Darwinism was influential in terms of supposedly explaining the "natural" superiority of certain cultures, and these ideas received further justification by evolutionary theory: "Building on well-developed notions of race and racism, the new theory seemed to offer, with startling finality, a nearly religious vindication of the hierarchy of peoples long assumed by educated Europeans and the superiority of elites demanded by class systems. In America and Europe in this century, evolutionary thought helped to breed a nasty fascination with eugenics as social policy" (2). Shaw's words highlight the embedded and ideological nature of such "scientific" frameworks and how they have been used "with sometimes disastrous effects" (Shaw 2).

While Scott and Buck participated in the discourse of racial domination prominent during this period, it's also important to try to understand the assumptions behind their ideas. Scott and Buck embraced a Westernized and racialized view of civilization that favored differentiation over wholeness. Within such a framework, certain civilizations are thus rendered "primitive" while others represent "advancement." These assumptions are evident in Scott and Buck's curriculum. For example, they note that in first grade, children tend to view their "world as one undivided whole, not distinguished even from [themselves]" (69); therefore, at this level, they study Hiawatha, the Indian boy, since this period "most adequately [represents] the mental status of the child just entering school" (71). This belief that consciousness begins with a whole that through a process of differentiation becomes more complex is central to Buck's organic view of life and thought development, as will be shown later in the chapter. Like the principle of cooperation, Buck viewed this movement from the simple to the complex as an underlying law of mental and social life.

Feminine Style and Feminist Assumptions

As mentioned, feminine style and feminist assumptions were apparent in Buck's pedagogical practices at Vassar. They also are apparent in Scott and Buck's book, particularly their emphasis on interest. They sought to resolve the conflict between those who supported student interest and those who discounted it by blending self-activity with interest. In addition, they stressed the role of the teacher in recognizing the vital connection between students and their interests and the importance of using this interest to guide their education. More significantly, Scott and Buck viewed interest as closely connected to the question of the relation between the individual and society and the education of moral individuals. People gain shared common values through their mutual individual interests. These interests bond humans together, eliminating the gap between the individual and the social. While Scott and Buck still favored their own class and race, they also believed that having shared common interests helped to build relationships between individuals, breaking down class distinctions and other differences that can separate people.

Scott and Buck viewed interest and discipline not as opposing forces but as complementary factors in purposeful activity. The authors contend that they cannot "['create] an interest' in a certain subject," nor can they continue to deny student interest (16–17). As discussed in the previous chapter, traditionally, education had valued memorization and the learning of formal principles. Student interest, grounded in emotion and desire for pleasure, was believed to prevent students from gaining moral motivation through reason (Feffer 123). The problem with such an approach was that concrete experience was excluded from shaping students' moral motivations. So, instead of drawing upon interest as a motivating force, students were asked to act out of duty or discipline. However, according to Scott and Buck, following student interest "enriches both teacher and pupil an hundred fold more even than the denial of nature has heretofore impoverished them" (17).

As will become evident in chapter 4, Buck's theory of interest was central to her approach to argumentation. It was also of key importance to *Organic Education*. In fact, Scott and Buck characterize their overall approach as the

> progressive organization of the child's interests. And this means nothing less than life itself. Education is the widest and deepest living possible at any given moment. Or it is the most highly developed interrelation of life—on the one hand the life of the individual, on the other that of the social organism. And the relations of organism to individual are, from the standpoint of the individual, his interests, physical, economic, social, artistic, religious. Hence it is plain why education, which is, in the universe-sense, life itself, may be, from the practical side, defined as the progressive organization of individual interests. (16)

The social and political implications of Scott and Buck's principle of interest are evident in this passage. In asking students to draw on their own interests, the authors wanted to develop individuals suited to democracy—governments that maintain social order through coordination, not subordination, of individual interests. By widening individual interests, or concern for and interest in others, the individual extends and broadens the development of the self. Hence, by having a direct interest in others, the individual and social good become interconnected.

Buck's Later Focus on Interest in Educating Women

This view of interest remained central to Buck's pedagogy throughout her life and career. This focus becomes evident when examining correspondence from Buck to Vassar President Henry Noble MacCracken. In a letter dated 18 November 1918, Buck emphasizes the key importance of interest in women's education in the twentieth century:

College education for women after the war should make them capable of
a greater degree of initiative and constructive intellectual activity than
heretofore. This means a change, not in the subjects studied, but in the
methods of studying them. The self-generating initiative of the student
must be made use of in every course and in every recitation. (See *Education by Dynamism*, Jul. of the Assoc. of Collegiate Alumnae, Dec. 1917).
[Article reference is part of Buck's letter.]

Dynamism in education demands far more of the student, and in-
finitely more of the teacher (though, at first glance it seems to demand
less of the teacher.) It means real understanding of the student's point of
view, and a utilizing of his genuine motives. We have used this principle
for years in our writing courses here, and this year I am definitely trying
it in *Literary Criticism*. (letter to MacCracken 1–2)

Buck believed that women needed to be capable of greater intellectual
freedom and responsibility in the wake of World War I. In other words,
they needed to be educated in a different capacity and have a different
authority in the postwar years. Buck argues that education needs to
change to emphasize "the self-generating initiative" of her women students through the development of their interests or "genuine" motives.
Buck's ethics and feminist ideals were apparent in her confidence in the
intellectual potential of women. This perspective is evident in the fact
that this more challenging pedagogical approach already had been used
in Vassar's writing courses. Buck also seemed confident that women could
be challenged even further. For Buck, participatory democracy required
this higher level of intellectual freedom.

In the article she recommends to MacCracken, "Education by Dynamism," Frederic Burk, president of San Francisco State Normal School,
argues that "[t]he advance of civilization has been from the primitive principle of external force toward the use of self-generated dynamism within the
individual" (218). However, Burk contends that most schools still operate
by using external force and that the current school system is basically a
"replica of the military monarchy," which was used for training serfs:

It is a strange anachronism that the schooling mechanism for training
men to be serfs, should have been passed down, unchanged by tradition,
to become the schooling system of American democracy for the training

of free born, thinking, self-responsible, government-making citizens of the twentieth century. Yet this fact stares at us complacently in nearly all forms of our schooling from the kindergarten through the universities. (219–20)

In the school system, Burk contends the student is "little more than a mechanical automaton" and that the system produces what the student seeks—"units" (220). In addition, Burk argues that "memorizing is the limit of possibility" in terms of education (220). He calls for "radical reconstruction" of the education system and forwards several recommendations (223). Key aspects of his recommendations include a proposal to use "the dynamic energy within the student" for educational purposes (223). He also argues that educational methods should be rethought, moving away from "the artificial contrivances which have been used to compel education in the absence of sufficient propelling force" (224). In place of such methods, Burk advocates the "indirect guidance" of student interest from its initial "crude, self-centered" form to "the higher channels of modern civilization" (224).

Buck similarly believed that schools must move from external to internal authority. For Buck, a democratic country rejects subordination to external authority; instead, it depends on cooperation and interest, or the widening of shared concerns among individuals. However, this was not apparently how Buck thought President MacCracken interpreted the article. In a long letter to MacCracken, Buck further detailed her interpretation and her approach to pedagogy. Buck writes that she does not accept Burk's comments *"in toto,"* since he "entirely disregards" or may be "ignorant of" the work colleges already do in applying "education by dynamism" (letter to MacCracken, 27 Nov. 1918, 1). However, Buck openly and outspokenly explains to the president why she disagrees with his interpretation of Burk. Buck's words are given in full to provide a deeper understanding of her pedagogy and the points of disagreement with MacCracken:

> . . . I do not think you read him rightly in conceiving his suggestion to be that of leading the student to believe the educational enterprise to be his own through choice and discovery, when it is not actually so. The phrase, "indirect guidance," taken out of its context, can be made to mean this, but the context destroys this interpretation. In the preceding

sentence Mr. Burk speaks of the "artificial contrivances, which have been used to compel education in the absence of sufficient propelling force," and states that "this goal" (that is, the student's own motive for learning the particular material at hand) "in most cases will need transformation through indirect guidance." This means, as I take it, that while we must use the student's own real motives for acquiring information or power, (and use them honestly, not merely pretend we are doing so), we must not regard these motives as fixed, or ultimate. They are usually, as Mr. Burk explains in this same paragraph, motives too personal and too trivial to be more than a starting point, but by using them "for all they are worth," as the slang phrase goes, they are tested out and usually replaced by deeper-lying, and *more social* motives, which have been actually acquired by the student, not foisted upon him by external authority. The phrase "indirect guidance" applies *only* to this process of transforming motives, not at all to the various enterprises of the class-room [*sic*]; and I am sure Mr. Burk would be as astonished and shocked to find that you credited him with fooling the student about the part he is playing in the initiation of class activities, as I am to have you suppose that I would approve of or practice such deception. As you say, any such attempt would be as fruitless as it is dishonest. And Mr. Burk could hardly be so stupid as to overlook this patent fact. I imagine that you read the article very hastily or you would not have gotten such an idea from it. (letter to MacCracken, 27 Nov. 1918, emphasis in original, 1)

From Buck's letter, it is evident that the conflict focused on the meaning of the words *indirect guidance.* Buck suggests that for MacCracken, "indirect guidance" may be a masked form of teaching by external authority. However, Buck agrees with MacCracken that such an approach would be "as fruitless as it is dishonest" (letter to MacCracken, 27 Nov. 1918). Instead, Buck contends that teachers need to start with the student's own interest or motives. By testing them out, Buck argues that the student often replaces these original motives with "deeper-lying, and more social motives" acquired through the education process (letter to MacCracken, 27 Nov. 1918). The student becomes more aware of the interconnection between the individual and the larger community.

In later correspondence, Buck reveals her disappointment with Mac-Cracken because of his interpretation of Burk and potentially her teaching practices:

I am sorry that you continue to misunderstand Mr. Burk—and me. I can only assure you once more that I have never dealt doubly in the slightest degree with a class and never expect to do so, and that Mr. Burk's article has not been understood in this way by anyone but yourself, so far as I know, though I have discussed it with several people <who have read it>. (letter to MacCracken, 2 Dec. 1918, 1)[10]

MacCracken responds by clarifying his own position:

I should be sorry if my earlier letter to you were interpreted as even hinting that you engaged in double dealing with a class; I think that it would be twisting my meaning to get this out of my letter. I think we are not very far apart on what seems to me the essential principle which is that the student gains most from an educational program whenever she feels that she has a vital share in the enterprise. Whether it is necessary, as a general principle, that the student should be made to feel that she has arrived at a certain motive for conducting her work entirely by herself when, as a matter of fact, this motive has been supplied by indirect guidance, is the question I tried to raise. My experience up to the present time in education makes me answer this question in the negative, but this is very far from placing me in the category of those who teach either by military discipline or by traditional authority. (letter to Buck, 9 Dec. 1918, 1)

From the exchange of letters between Buck and MacCracken, it is clear that Buck believed passionately in student interest and "indirect guidance," since these principles were integral to her own approach to pedagogy. She strongly defended such practices even if that meant clashing with the president of the college over her teaching principles. It's also evident that Buck's focus on the significance of student interest was deeply influenced by her work with Harriet Scott and Scott's belief that education is an organic process, emerging naturally from children's interests and motivations.

Developing Relationships and Social Transformation through Education

Buck's focus on student interest leads naturally to another major aspect of her pedagogical theory—education as socialization. Buck believed that students needed to deepen and widen their individual interests to gain a better understanding of the social relationships that connect people and society. In the late nineteenth century, the negative effects of industrialization on workers and the increasingly harsh conflicts between capital and labor furthered the fragmentation of the classes and of the individual and social life.[11] During this time, many individuals no longer worked for themselves, but for major corporations. This dramatic increase in industrial mechanization led to what a Knights of Labor member called the "degradation of labor": "The men are looked upon as nothing more than parts of the machinery that they work" (qtd. in Painter xxxiv–xxxv). One response to this view of labor as a commodity was a number of strikes, which sharply illustrated the class conflicts throughout the nation. Scott and Buck responded to these consequences by arguing for a more integrated view of society.

In *Organic Education,* Scott and Buck's approach to education as socialization, like their approach to interest, emphasized synthesis through reconstruction and balance. The authors contend that schools typically are isolated entities, "not, in any practical sense, responsible either to the individual child or to the social structure for its policy or its methods" (18). In response, educators have recently emphasized individualism. Scott and Buck contend that these two theories of education are now in conflict: the "old institutional conception of individualism" in which the individual exists for the institution and a "newer theory of individualism," in which the institution exists for the individual (18). However, Scott and Buck argue that out of the "clash" of these two battling theories, a new "truer" ideal is developing—"social individualism," "reconciling institutionalism on the one hand with private individualism on the other" (20). Borrowing the term from Dewey and James, Scott and Buck use it to explain the interconnection between the individual and society (Ricks 124). The authors contend that this ideal is reflected in the saying of Dewey, "Education is not preparation for life it *is* life," and in the words of Col. Francis W. Parker, a Chicago educator and innovator, "The common school is the central means for preserving and perpetuating the true democracy" (19–20, emphasis in original). According to Scott and Buck,

> Such expressions as these recognize the fact that the individual is, indeed, the centre of every rational educational system, not however the individual as such, in the limited sense, but the whole individual in all his relations;

that is, the social individual. They involve the philosophical conception of the individual as a specialized or focussed functioning of society, and, conversely, of society as the whole functioning of the individual. The individual is society acting in a certain direction. He is a focussed activity of the entire social organism, just as the eye is the whole body directed toward the end of seeing. Society for its part is the complete activity of each individual. (19)

Buck and Harriet Scott's emphasis on education as socialization was closely connected to their dynamic, organic view of society. The authors point to the functioning of the human body as an example of the organic social relationships they advocate. The body is a complex, fully integrated, adaptable system. Although each organ has an individual function, the parts work together for the life of the entire organism.

This concept of an interconnected, mutually responsive organic whole was central to Buck's view of education. Under the "old," static view of education, teachers basically taught students to adjust to their environment. However, Buck and Harriet Scott's approach emphasized the transaction of students with their environment and other individuals. For Scott and Buck, an essential aspect of education was to make students aware of the interconnected nature of life. This emphasis is evident in the curriculum advocated in *Organic Education*. For instance, the authors contend that under the "old curriculum" the student would study

reading, spelling, grammar and composition, arithmetic, natural science, United States history, civil government, writing, drawing, and vocal music under the one as under the other system. But the new plan further provides him with systematic instruction in the history of civilization, sociology, literature, art, and ethics, which subjects are at present only incidentally and fragmentarily, if at all, touched upon in primary and grammar grades. (20)

The authors believe students would gain a wider understanding of social relationships and the perspectives of others by studying sociology, art, and ethics. They contend that their curriculum meets the artistic and expressive interests of the child at each stage of his or her development. Similarly, they argue that the study of sociology is necessary for social individualism:

The relationship between the individual and the social organism cannot be wholly effective until it has come to self-consciousness—of which self-consciousness sociology is the scientific expression. The social development of the individual is not complete without a knowledge of the science of society, and under the hypothesis of social individualism, the social development of the individual is the end proposed to education. (26)

Through studying sociology, students would become more self-reflective of their social environment, the goal of their approach to education. In addition, the authors contend that their method furthers the "natural ethical development of the child" (26). This development is central to their approach because the

child gains the invaluable habit of pursuing his ideals into the stage of conduct, reflecting upon the conduct, as its consequences return upon him, and thus modifying or reconstructing the old ideal in accordance with the new light. And it does not seem extravagant to say that if only this one habit were deposited from the tide of school life,—as it assuredly may be, under the organization plan,—the years of primary education would have been well spent; for it is this alone which renders a life at once morally free and morally responsible. (26–27)

By deepening students' understanding of social relationships, Scott and Buck's pedagogy encouraged students to consider the ideas and viewpoints of others in their moral reasoning process. Thus, in comprehending how they are part of a larger social whole, students could potentially improve education and society through reflection and modification of their actions. As noted, Buck's ethics, with its emphasis on the affective, experience, and relationships, contrasted with the dominant male-biased approach of her times. This approach was central to *Organic Education*.

Besides their approach to curriculum, Scott and Buck's view of how schools must change reflected their emphasis on education as the social development of individuals. In fact, the authors declare that their discussion anticipates the transformation of the school under their method: "In general, it may be prophetically described as a treasure-house of the art, literature, science, and industry of the world, a laboratory of civilization, a busy cell or ganglion in the social system, a real segment of a real world" (28). Schools were to function like social systems or small communities.

In Buck's work in composition and rhetoric, this focus on making schools a "laboratory of civilization" was evident in her "laboratory" approach to education. As will become apparent, it was also featured in her approach to drama, in which she stressed that the dramatic workshop was "to serve as an experimental laboratory for the play-wrights of Vassar College" ("Primer of the Vassar Dramatic Workshop").[12] Student ideas or plays were completed through putting them into practice. In addition to allowing for the testing and reformulating of ideas, a laboratory or workshop approach prepared students for future social life by having them work together in cooperative, communal activities. In this way it mirrored the organic view of society Scott and Buck advocated in *Organic Education*.

As noted, an organic view of life not only was central to Buck's view of social development but also was central to her approach to the growth of thought. Buck was influenced by Jamesian psychology and idealist organicism, and she believed that the mind begins with a vague impression that, through differentiation, develops into a more complex consciousness, or perception.[13] In her work with Harriet Scott, this view of the development of perception was central to the notion that education should move inductively from the familiar to the unfamiliar, from the simple to the complex. This concept, for instance, was evident in the curriculum's movement through the supposed stages of civilizations. Buck's view of the development of perception also reflected her organic view of life. This focus is evident in her article "The Sentence-Diagram" (1897), in which Buck reacts against more "mechanical" or "artificial" approaches to composition and instead argues that sentences are the "natural outcomes of psychological or social conditions" (251). She strongly opposes the popular use of the "straight-line, Reed-Kellog diagram," contending such diagrams fail to represent the true anatomy and organic nature of a sentence—the fact that sentences are "live growing things, warm from the speaker's mind" (255). Buck argues that mechanical diagrams lead students to believe that a sentence is a "fixed and bounded thing," and that the main concern is to know that it can be "chopped up into small pieces" for use in diagrams (250).

Buck contends that our thoughts do not grow from isolated parts into a whole, an approach prevalent in rhetorics based on associational psychology.[14] Instead, Buck argues our thoughts grow by "successive differentiations from a homogenous whole" (252–53). Buck uses an amoeba-

PROGRESSIVE EDUCATION AND FEMINISM

like diagram to show how a child's thoughts start as a "jelly-like mass of feeling," a "nebulous, ill-defined consciousness," and then divide as separate thoughts emerge (253, 255). She contends her amoeba drawings are more accurate than the straight-line diagrams, adding that it is "high time that this idea of growth, now dominant in other fields of investigation, dawn upon the darkness of grammar" (259). For Buck, the straight-line diagram inadequately represented the organic growth of thought as a normal development of psychological and social conditions. Such an approach failed to emphasize the social individualism, how individuals and their thoughts are interconnected with the social world.

The Metaphor and Buck's Social Theory of Rhetoric

An organic view of thought development was also central to Buck's approach to the metaphor. In her dissertation, *The Metaphor: A Study in the Psychology of Rhetoric* (1899), Buck presents an organic view of the metaphor, based on then-recent developments in psychology. She challenges the philologists' theory that the radical metaphor developed as a consequence of the "poverty of language," and rhetoricians' belief that the poetic metaphor "comes into being as the result of a desire to beautify or to energize speech" (19). Buck rejects both positions and instead explains the origin of the metaphor based on the development of thought. For Buck, consciousness grows from "simplicity to complexity, from homogeneousness to differentiation" (8). This growth pattern is what Buck calls the "theory of the progress of intellectual experience" (8). She sees this theory as applying to all of life, from the development of ideas to the growth of social organizations.

Buck's description of the development of thought reveals how she viewed the growth of mental life as basically paralleling that of physical life. This similarity is apparent in Buck's description of the development of an idea, which resembled the growth of an amoeba: "The definition of an idea is a long and gradual process, much like that by which a formless sprawl of protoplasm becomes a firmly articulate creature" (7). For Buck, radical and poetic metaphors represented different stages in the development of the writer's perception.

Besides being based on her organic view of life, Buck's approach to the metaphor, like her approach to pedagogy, emphasized the interconnection of the social and the individual. In her dissertation, Buck contends that rhetoricians "of the old school" tended to emphasize persuasion as the aim of discourse. Consequently, their focus was on the hearer: "Their precepts were all directed to producing a certain effect upon the hearer. Do this in order that you may conciliate him; do that to win his confidence; attempt by a third device to make him think well of himself. Seldom was it recommended 'Say this because you feel it to be true; only express yourself'" (23). As a result, the cause or origin of the metaphor has been explained as a conscious creation of the speaker designed to produce some specific effect on the hearer. According to Buck, the problem with this approach is that it "makes the act of metaphor so mechanical, so crude, so essentially cheap and tawdry that the sensitive reader of literature can hardly suffer serious consideration of its truthfulness" (27). Buck then points out the effects of such an approach in student writing:

> And few are the happy teachers of English composition who have not thus explained to themselves the existence of many a metaphor in student essays. The boy who speaks of Hawthorne as "the queen-bee in American literature," and the girl who characterizes reading as "the indispensable nectar of existence" present us no insoluble problem as to the metaphorical process which has gone on in their minds. Clearly it was somewhat like this: A figure is necessary to any well-regulated composition. Therefore let us have a figure. Since we are writing about Hawthorne, we may as well say that Hawthorne was something besides what he really was. Hawthorne was. . . . . Hawthorne was. . . . . What was Hawthorne, anyhow? He was awfully important in American literature, the teacher said. Well, what else is important to something? Perhaps a bee wings across the field of vision just at the moment of despair and is frantically clutched as by the despairing mind. Oh I guess Hawthorne was the queen-bee in American literature. And the successful author beams with satisfaction over the way that expression will "hit" the teacher. (27–28)

For Buck, the result was a mechanical and formulaic approach to metaphor creation aimed primarily at pleasing the reader. She argues that such an approach has resulted in what she calls "metaphoraphobia," or a "distrust of the figure, amounting almost to fear" (30). Thus, the "practical man" views metaphors "much as the old saints regarded women—as charming snares, in which he may be too easily entangled" (30). Similarly, "[p]hilosophers, logicians, and scientific men" tend to "exhibit a healthy scorn for metaphor" (31). Buck challenged this view by emphasizing the role of the speaker and the hearer in the metaphor-making process.

She refers to this recent approach as the "communication theory of discourse" and uses it to support her organic and psychological view of the metaphor:

> This theory is that known as the communication theory of discourse, which has, in the later rhetorical systems, largely superseded the one-sided theories of discourse as persuasion and as self-expression. The theory that discourse is self-expression has reference only to the speaker; the hypothesis that it is persuasion makes the hearer all-important. When discourse is regarded as communication the two factors in the process are equally emphasized. (30)

According to Buck, discourse as persuasion focuses on the hearer, while discourse as "self-expression" highlights the speaker. The communication theory of discourse, in contrast, focuses on both the speaker and the hearer. Built into Buck's view of the metaphor was her emphasis on the social-individual, or the way that the metaphor, like language, was created by the relationship between the speaker and the hearer, or the individual and the social.

In investigating Buck's involvement in the progressive education issues of her time and her prior collaboration with Harriet Scott, it is evident that her goal was to develop social-individuals—individuals who considered the perspectives of others and who saw themselves as part of a larger social whole. Since Buck viewed the individual and the social as interconnected, her principle of interest was central to this process. Traditional education had emphasized discipline, memorization, and the acceptance of received knowledge. However, Buck viewed the learner as active, creative, and self-reflective. For Buck, the development of such individuals was necessary to foster the growth of a more democratic society, one modeled after her dynamic, organic concept of society. The aim of education was to help students develop their sense of social individualism so that they could become aware of the concrete relationships between individuals and the broader social community to which they belonged.

Scott and Buck's focus on the primacy of relationships and the need for education to develop individuals who care about each other resembles Nel Noddings's care ethics and its significance to moral education.

According to Noddings, the purpose of school is not to focus only on developing children's intelligence but also to educate them in terms of their emotional needs and morality: "The primary aim of every educational institution and of every educational effort must be the maintenance and enhancement of caring" (*Caring* 172). In *Educating Moral People: A Caring Alternative to Character Education* (2002), Noddings specifically discusses how individuals can be educated to be moral by applying her care ethics to the educational process. Like Scott and Buck, Noddings underscores the role of interest and motivation over the learning of abstract principles in moral education. She explains that Kantian ethics "subordinated feelings to reason. He insisted that only acts done out of duty to carefully reasoned principle are morally worthy. Love, feeling, and inclination are all supposed by Kant to be untrustworthy. An ethic of care inverts these priorities" (14). However, the "prescriptive use of principles" has been ineffective since "[m]oral people rarely consult abstract principles when they act morally" (1). Instead, Noddings argues that "[i]t is feeling with and for the other that motivates us in natural caring" (14). She clarifies that a care ethics also uses logic and reasoning, but it begins at the emotional level with relationships: "I am arguing here about the power (or lack of it) of principles. Care theorists might accurately describe carers as operating so as to 'establish, maintain, or enhance caring relations'" (8). An inversion of traditional Kantian priorities and an emphasis on the power of relationships and "our ethical interdependence" also are central to Scott and Buck's pedagogical approach (Noddings 9).

By teaching students to discover their broader social relationships, Buck believed it was possible for them to improve their environment by learning to see it as part of a larger organic whole. Scott and Buck believed their approach led to the "natural ethical development" of children because it taught them mentally to test out and reflect on their conduct, to see it in terms of its broader social relations and the perspective of others, and then to reconstruct their actions.

Buck's focus on interest, socialization, and reconstruction is evident in her article "Recent Tendencies in the Teaching of English Composition" (1901), written four years after the publication of *Organic Education*. In the article Buck discusses four "movements" in the teaching of composition: the "revolt" against teaching writing based on formal rhetorical principles, the shift toward deriving writing topics from the student's interests and experience, the emphasis on directing student writing toward an actual audience, and the movement toward criticizing student writing based on "the ultimate ends of discourse" rather than prescriptive rules. Buck contends that although the movements may seem disconnected, they actually have a "common basis": "Each aims at securing better writing from the student by furnishing more natural conditions for that writing" (371). Buck believed that the purpose of writing was not to complete formal exercises but to communicate to another individual. At this time, several eastern male universities focused on eliminating error in their introductory composition classes (Stewart and Stewart 2).

Buck concludes her article by underscoring the benefits of the recent changes in composition teaching:

> The trend of every recent reform in composition-teaching has been toward a responsible freedom for the process of writing—a freedom from laws apparently arbitrary and externally imposed, a responsibility to the law of its own nature as a process of communication. Thus free and thus responsible, composition becomes for the first time a normal act, capable of development practically unlimited. ("Recent Tendencies" 382)

Since Buck viewed writing as a social act, she saw broad potential for these changes in terms of their ability to foster the ethical development of social individuals and the democratic transformation of society.

In addition, Buck's stress on a broader social perspective and reconstruction is apparent in her article "The Present Status of Rhetorical Theory" (1900), which represents the "clearest statement of her rhetorical theory: discourse should aim for the further good of the social organism" (Campbell, *Toward* 45). In her article, Buck contends two concepts of discourse, inherited from antiquity, are still vying for dominance in modern rhetorical theory—"the social conception of Plato and the anti-social conception of the Sophists" (168). Buck argues that the "Platonic theory of discourse is at last coming home to the modern consciousness" (172). For Buck, the Platonic theory is in agreement with "the rising modern rhetorical theory" in that both are aimed at promoting equality and social cooperation (174). Buck argues that such a theory is "rich in implications" because it "shall complete the social justification which rhetoric has so long been silently working out for itself" (174). Rhetoric has the potential to function socially by "leveling conditions" between the speaker and the hearer, which furthers social cooperation (169). Buck's new social theory of rhetoric closely resembles the "communication theory of discourse" she refers to in her dissertation.

According to Buck, the Sophist rhetor "pays great deference" to the hearer, but the Sophist does this "simply that he [the hearer] may the more completely be subjugated to the speaker's will" (168). The hearer is of little value in the discourse, and his or her views are often attacked. Buck calls such discourse "anti-social," since its goal is individual and thus morally backward. Such discourse is "purely predatory" and "sanctioned only by the primitive ethical principle of the dominance of the strong" (169). Furthermore, Buck argues that the discourse is antisocial in its results: "Instead of leveling conditions between the two parties to the act, as we are told is the tendency in all true social functioning, discourse renders these conditions more unequal than they were before it took place" (169). For Buck, "all true social functioning" is democratic in process, equalizing conditions between the speaker and the hearer. In her article, Buck graphically represents this view of discourse by showing how the speaker's mind and conclusion veer off in a forty-five degree angle, rather than transacting with the hearer's mind and conclusion.

Buck contends that Plato was the first to protest against the Sophists' antisocial discourse. For Plato, the speaker has certain responsibilities, "not perhaps directly to the hearer, but to the absolute truth . . ." (171). Discourse is "persuasion to the truth," and knowledge of the truth is advantageous to both the speaker and the hearer (171). The interests of both are equally fulfilled; thus, the speaker and the hearer "stand on a footing of at least approximate equality" (171). Buck adds, "In fact the ultimate end of discourse must be, from the Platonic premises, to establish equality between them" (171). Buck represents the Platonic view of discourse by showing the speaker's mind and conclusion and the hearer's mind and conclusion transacting along the same line.

Buck argues that many current textbooks contain descriptions of discourse similar to the Sophists'—"a conception which regards discourse as an act performed by the speaker upon the hearer for the advantage of the speaker alone" (172). However, she says the Platonic theory of discourse is "at last coming home to modern consciousness" (172). But Plato's approach is not perfect either. For Plato, the end of discourse was to proclaim absolute truths to another. Buck jokingly points out that "we are not now-a-days on such joyfully intimate terms with absolute truth as was Plato" (172). However, she says that even Plato allowed the subject of discourse to be the speaker's "own vision of the absolute truth, thus individualizing the abstraction until we cannot regard it as fundamentally alien from our modern conception of experience, in the largest sense of the word" (173). For Buck, the subject of discourse has a clear connection to the writer's mental process and experience.

Buck then shows how self-expression has become a part of modern rhetoric. She explains that the "rising modern rhetorical theory" largely agrees with Plato's theory but differs in viewing rhetoric as a less self-conscious process. Instead, discourse is seen as emerging from the speaker's desire "for closer relations with his environment, rather than from any explicit desire to communicate his own vision of the truth to another" (174). According to Buck, "Both the Platonic and the modern theory of discourse make it not an individualistic and isolated process for the advantage of the speaker alone, but a real communication between the speaker and hearer, to the equal advantage of both, and thus a real function of the social organism" (174). Buck's modern theory of discourse responds to Progressive Era insistence on furthering democracy by fostering communication that benefits all individuals in the community.

As noted in chapter 1, Fred Newton Scott and Mary Yost also discuss the reappearance of Platonic forms of discourse. Like Buck, they contend that rhetoric has been defined narrowly in terms of persuasion. Scott, for instance, discusses how Western rhetorical theory was first based on the persuasion-oriented rhetoric of Korax. This narrower view of rhetoric then became the basis of Aristotle's *Rhetoric*, "which determined the course of rhetorical speculation for more than 2000 years" (Scott, "Rhetoric Rediviva" 414). According to Scott, "The influence of Aristotle, then, has been to keep rhetoric within the limits of its earliest definition—the art of persuasion" ("Rhetoric Rediviva" 415).

However, Scott and Yost contend a more social perspective is emerging. Like Buck, they stress the ethical implications of Platonic forms of discourse. According to Scott, Plato's approach "takes what we should now call the social or sociological point of view" ("Rhetoric Rediviva" 415). In the following quotation, Scott draws on Plato's *Gorgias:* "The value of any piece of discourse, or mode of communication, is to be measured by its effect upon the welfare of the community. Good discourse is that which by disseminating truth creates a healthy public opinion and thus effects in Plato's words, 'a training and improvement in the souls of the citizens'" ("Rhetoric Rediviva" 415).

Like Buck, Yost and Scott emphasized the ethical implications of rhetoric and the Progressive ideal of building more democratic communities. Buck's democratic theory of rhetoric directly responded to more agonistic, persuasion-oriented approaches. In addition, all three saw it as a positive development—the rise of a more ethical approach to argumentation. All three seemed to be responding to Progressive Era insistence on more democratic forms of education and communication. It is also evident that women and men were involved in creating alternate approaches to rhetoric and argumentation. A significant reason for this democratic turn was that it provided an ethical approach to argumentation that was missing in the older agonistic tradition.

In exploring Buck's work with Harriet Maria Scott at the Detroit Normal Training School and the broader educational context of the 1890s, it is apparent that their feminist approach was closely interwoven with many of the ideals of progressive education. Buck's work with Scott at the Detroit School, for example, introduced her to European pedagogical theories, "a very different intellectual perspective from the rhetorical tradition of composition" (Fitzgerald 213). This background included significant points of intersection with Buck and Scott's feminist approach, such as an emphasis on student interest and a developmental and child-centered approach to education. It was also evident in their stress on relationships in the moral education of children. A key aspect of Buck's focus on individual interests and socialization was her goal of social individualism, or her emphasis on the interplay between the individual and society. Although Scott and Buck still privileged their own class and race, their organic perspective was aimed at breaking down barriers among people, which were prevalent during the Progressive Era. More significantly, Buck believed that expanding the social aspect of education made it possible for individuals to improve education and society by seeing both as part of a larger whole. By becoming aware of the interconnection between the individual and the social, individuals were learning a practical ethics aimed at encouraging them to consider the ideas of others in moral reasoning and social transformation.

Ultimately, Buck's pedagogy promoted her social, organic view of society. Because of her transactional view of the relationship between the individual and the social, Buck, like Dewey, believed that "the quality of our character depends on the quality of our relationships and vice versa" (Pappas 89). Her focus was on the type of relationship built through the education process. This concern with developing democratic relationships was key to her feminist ethics, and it was integral to her work in rhetoric and composition. It was also evident in Buck's approach to the metaphor, which emphasized the figure as a construction of both the reader and the writer, instead of just one or the other. Similarly, Buck's new social theory of rhetoric emphasized cooperative relationships that promoted equality between the speaker and the hearer. Buck's focus on building democratic relationships was also evident in her work within the English Department with Laura Johnson Wylie. I will now turn to and more fully explore Buck's administrative work with Wylie, showing how Buck applied her feminist ethics to this context.

3

THE "ADVANCE" TOWARD DEMOCRATIC ADMINISTRATION

Here were two women [Wylie and Buck] of the highest distinction, either one of whom, alone, would have made an English
department, in the same sense that Mark Hopkins alone, as it
was said, would have made a university. Together, they achieved
something which I believe was quite without parallel, then or
perhaps since, in the field of American college English teaching;
something, moreover, which has lived on as a sound and creative
influence, through the students who have gone out to become
leaders in many corners of the country.
        —Elisabeth Woodbridge Morris,
        "Laura Johnson Wylie 1855–1932"

In addition to her work with Harriet Maria Scott, Gertrude Buck's
life at Vassar with Laura Johnson Wylie profoundly influenced her view
of rhetoric and pedagogy. A key aspect of Buck's and Wylie's professional
lives was their application of feminist principles not only to the classroom
but also to the administrative domain. As scholars have noted, "The closer
we come to women-centered enclaves in the university, the more dominant
the ethic of care appears to be" (Clark, "Argument" 95–96). Although not
always the case, this statement seems true for Vassar's English Department,
which was predominantly made up of women.[1] For twenty-four years, Buck
and Wylie worked together and crafted a feminist model of administration
that encouraged members of the English Department to take an active role
in running the department. As chair of the English Department, Wylie
oversaw literature while Buck coordinated rhetoric and writing. (The
department also included the study of language and eventually grew to

include spoken English and drama.) Wylie and Buck viewed the teaching of literature and rhetoric/writing as equally important and organically interconnected, which typically was not the case within other English departments across the nation (Connors, "Overwork/Underpay").

This chapter begins with an overview of Wylie and an examination of her article "What Can Be Done about It?" (1918), in which she underscores the political and pedagogical reasons for why teaching writing is so difficult. Three issues she raises—the conflict between the demands of business and those of democracy and the need for small classes and better working conditions—are echoed in her department reports. The second part of the chapter investigates Wylie's ideas about the growth of democratic administration at Vassar. This context provides the backdrop for a discussion of how Wylie and Buck developed a collaborative model of administration that was inextricably connected to its Progressive Era context.[2] The progressive ideals of cooperation, freedom of thought, and equality were integral to Buck's social theory of rhetoric. These democratic ideals were also central to Wylie and Buck's approach to administration and their feminism.

In addition, the chapter examines how Wylie and Buck enacted their ideas in the administration of the English Department and how they responded to clashes with the administration during tight budgetary times. It demonstrates that although the administration of a writing program and college may seem to share similar goals, they often can be in direct conflict with each other. At the same time, this analysis shows how Wylie and Buck's model anticipates current approaches, such as those advocated by Jeanne Gunner.[3] One difference, though, is that Gunner's model advocates a decentered writing program, whereas Wylie and Buck's approach demonstrates a collaboratively administered English Department, with equal literature and writing components. Gunner contends that the most powerful support for a decentered model is political: "[I]t is a democratic model. It places power in the hands of *all* faculty, giving them the means to influence the direction of the program they form . . ." (14–15, emphasis in original). Gunner concludes that a centralized model "will not only not solve the professional problems that face us, but will actually continue the system of oppression that we ostensibly are trying to overcome" (15). Like Gunner, Wylie also felt that the strongest argument for her model of administration was the fact that it was democratic. She also saw it as a way of alleviating the potentially oppressive outcomes of the traditional hierarchical system of administration.

Laura Johnson Wylie

To better understand Wylie and Buck's approach to administration, it is helpful to know something about Wylie's life. Laura Johnson Wylie came from a less privileged background than Buck. Wylie (1855–1932) was the daughter of William Theodorus Wylie and Sarah Murray Johnson. Similar to his Scottish father, Samuel Wylie, William was a "Covenanter" minister for the Presbyterian church.[4] After graduating from the Covenanter Theological Seminary in Zelianople, Ohio, William traveled to Philadelphia and served as a tutor for the family of L. Johnson, who apparently "had made a fortune, large for those days, as a printer, and was the first maker of stereotype in that city" (Woodbridge, "Laura Johnson Wylie" 4). Sarah was the eldest daughter in the Johnson family, and William Wylie soon married her. The Wylies had two children, Laura and Samuel; however, when Laura was four and her brother two, her mother died of cancer. Several years after the death of his first wife, William married Eliza Watson, and they had a daughter Margaret, to whom Laura was devoted (6). (Her father subsequently married a third time and had a second son, Walter.)

During Wylie's early years, her family moved frequently; thus, she attended school on an irregular basis. Much of her education came from her father and his tutoring, particularly in Latin, and "through her own enthusiastic efforts" (Woodbridge, "Laura Johnson Wylie" 7). However, there were "gaps" in her education: "[Wylie] once said that when she entered college she could not spell, knew almost no geography, and was ignorant in many subjects quite familiar to her classmates" (7). Despite her educational gaps, Wylie attended Vassar and graduated as Valedictorian of the class of 1877. At college, she studied English with Truman J. Backus, who later became the principal of Packer Collegiate Institute in Brooklyn and who was also a favorite teacher of Harriot Stanton Blatch's (Vassar class of 1878), the daughter of Elizabeth Cady Stanton (Gordon 130; Woodbridge, "Laura Johnson Wylie" 8).

After graduating, Wylie taught briefly (1882–83) at a boarding and day school for girls in Cincinnati (1913 *Vassarion* 20). However, she left the school to care for her half sister, Margaret, who subsequently died of consumption. Backus then invited Wylie to teach at the Packer Institute, and she taught there from 1884 to 1892 and 1894 to 1895 (1913 *Vassarion* 20). While at Packer, Wylie also felt "very deeply the appeal of the new social movement of which the Rivington Street College Settlement was an arresting and to her a challenging embodiment" (Woodbridge, "Laura Johnson Wylie" 11). She apparently debated working for the settlement, which was founded by graduates from Vassar, Smith, and Wellesley (Gordon 130). Wylie finally decided to pursue teaching; however, "the decision was a difficult one, she never ceased to feel the pull of the other calling, and never wholly turned from it" (Woodbridge, "Laura Johnson Wylie" 11–12).

Wylie took time off from the Packer Institute to study at Yale University from 1892 to 1894. She was among the first women to receive her Ph.D. from Yale, and her dissertation, *Studies in the Evolution of English Criticism* (1894), was "the first woman's thesis published by Yale" (Gordon 130; "Wylie File"). Wylie began her career at Vassar as an English instructor in 1895; two years later, she became the chair of the English Department and remained chair from 1897 to 1922. Most of her energy focused on her administrative and teaching duties, rather than publishing. Thus, she was not as prolific a scholar as Buck. According to Elisabeth Woodbridge Morris, Wylie was "[f]ull of racy speech herself, and enjoying picturesque language as she enjoyed color everywhere, she was continually making vivid statements and as continually modifying them. She was a talker rather than a writer, because she was never wholly willing to let her ideas stiffen into the printed phrase" ("Pioneer and Humanist" 68). Personal communications and teaching were her preferred mediums. However, even with her heavy teaching and administrative load, Wylie did publish. In addition to her dissertation, her publications include *Social Studies in English Literature* (1916) and "What Can Be Done about It?" (1918). She also edited *Poems and Plays* by Buck (1922), and she edited school editions of the following texts: *The Winter's Tale, Adam Bede,* and *The Sir Roger de Coverly Papers from* The Spectator (Woodbridge, *Miss Wylie* n.p.).

In addition to her teaching and scholarship, Wylie was active in women's issues throughout her life. As mentioned, she was a leader in the Poughkeepsie women's suffrage movement, and she founded and served as president of the Women's City and County Club ("Women's City and County Club" 2; "Wylie File"). She also served as a faculty vice-elector and an honorary member of the Vassar College Chapter of the College Settlement Association (1898 *Vassarion* 94). After her retirement in 1924, Wylie continued to be involved in women's issues, teaching at the Bryn Mawr Summer School for Women Workers in Industry.[5]

As Lynn D. Gordon points out, "Wylie combined teaching with community volunteer work and a commitment to suffrage and social reform" (130). This interconnected view is evident in the comment of a former student: "Every aspect of her nature was social. Even to our undergraduate minds there was a realization that it was her social spirit that integrated and unified the English department" (E. F. Johnson 101). Wylie's social emphasis was particularly evident in the cooperative nature of the department.

Because historians have rediscovered Buck's work in rhetoric and composition, she is now much better known within the field than Wylie. However, in her time and within the community at Vassar, Wylie, who was sixteen years older than Buck, was admired and recognized for her work as an administrator and teacher. After Wylie's death in 1932, her former students, friends, and colleagues wrote and published *Miss Wylie of Vassar* (1934), a tribute to her efforts as an outstanding individual, teacher, and administrator. According to Vassar Economics Professor Herbert E. Mills, Wylie's dominant characteristic was "an ever present struggle for human freedom . . ." ("Appreciations II" 152).

"What Can Be Done about It?"

Wylie's commitment to promoting democratic values was present in her varied activities, from suffrage to educating women workers, to her work in the English Department, which will be explored later in the chapter. These same ideals and their influence on her approach to writing are evident in her essay "What Can Be Done about It?," published in the *Vassar Quarterly* in 1918 and republished in *Miss Wylie of Vassar*.[6] Wylie's title is taken from the concluding questions in a letter printed in the *Atlantic Monthly* the previous year: "What can be done about it? What on earth can be done about it?" ("Higher Education Again" 572). Wylie explains that the letter, focusing on the "futility of English teaching," was written by a history of literature teacher at an elite northeastern university, "based on the experience of a single vivid hour spent in reading the examination papers of a class of sophomores" (Woodbridge, "What Can Be Done about It?" 131).

She also suggests that the abundance of evidence he presents would "seem amply to justify his impatience and despair" (131). In the article, though, Wylie underscores the complexity of the issue, demonstrating that the problems in teaching writing are both political and pedagogical.

According to Wylie, the privileged young men discussed in the letter wrote "pages of stereotyped information" and even more disheartening was their "meaningless grandiloquence" (132). Wylie asserts that these "chosen youths, the flower of American society," are "suffering from the blight of unreality in their task" (133). Although the "disease of unreality in writing" has spread widely, it is treatable, according to Wylie. She notes different attempts to respond to the sickness, including efforts by teachers to have students draw on their own experiences in their writing: "[I]n the last decade of the nineteenth century, the Daily Themes course, in which the student was asked to see and think for himself, was established at Harvard; and at about the same time the University of Michigan, by calling attention to the social nature of the writing process, opened the way to a fuller understanding of its scope and significance" (134). She adds that the principles behind these efforts have been supported in the research of philosophers and psychologists and that Dewey's contention "that not preparation for life but actual living can alone truly educate" has been particularly influential (134).

Wylie asserts that the concept behind these different efforts—"the right of every child to the training that will make him a useful and happy member of the community into which he has been born, the right of every community to such training for its children—is neither new nor radical" (134–35). Noting that the principles trace to Plato, Wylie explains that in trying to apply these ideals "to an education essentially democratic and involving problems so complex," teachers are only now becoming aware of the depth of the issues they face (135). A significant problem, according to Wylie, is that the demands by business for productive workers conflict with the democratic ideals of educating all children to be active, thinking citizens:

> [T]he American people, democratic in little more than name, have at least, till very lately, been in the main satisfied with an ideal of democracy as superficial as shortsighted; have considered its workmen chiefly as "hands" and have seen in its workmen's children future employees rather than future citizens. So long as we were content to measure efficiency in terms

of immediate material output rather than in increase in vital productive power, it was impossible for the community to understand the nature and conditions of good teaching. (136)

To highlight her point, Wylie notes that the request by English teachers for "classes small enough to be really taught looks strangely chimerical to certain business men,—especially when provision for such classes inevitably doubles or triples the salary roll. . . . English has suffered peculiarly from such penny-wise economy" (136–37). To further support her case, Wylie draws on the 1913 report *The Cost and Labor of English Teaching*, published by the Modern Language Association and the National Council of Teachers of English. According to Wylie, the report demonstrates that "[o]vercrowded classes, insufficient equipment, and the consequent slavery of routine have made a practical situation peculiarly difficult for the English teacher to meet" ("What Can Be Done about It?" 137). This document evolved into a larger, more comprehensive report, completed in 1923 by Edwin Hopkins (Popken 7). According to Randall Popken, Hopkins's purpose in writing the report was to use "data to demonstrate the deplorable conditions endured by writing faculty" (8). In her department reports, Wylie also uses statistical data to argue for improved working conditions for her writing teachers.

In the article, though, Wylie emphasizes that the problems are not all "external" ("What Can Be Done about It?" 137). A more significant internal dilemma has to do with the way writing is taught. A "certain professional bias" encourages "teachers as a class to overestimate clarity of presentation as compared with reality of understanding," Wylie notes (137). Many teachers, in other words, have adopted a mechanistic and formalistic view of language and learning that conflicts with the complicated human process of learning (Bergon 10). As is evident from the 1913 report, one reason teachers may have embraced a more formalist approach was because of the demanding workload, which left little time for investigating alternate approaches. Wylie asserts that teachers need to understand "the natural processes of learning" and to trust in the "capability for growth of the younger generation" ("What Can Be Done about It?" 139). The task of the teacher, then, is not to impose understanding upon students but to "[stimulate] our students to the exercise and discipline of such powers of thought or imagination as they actually possess" (140). Wylie's democratic values are evident in her insistence that teachers need to foster students' independent thinking skills and reject more formulaic approaches. She also, though, was keenly aware of the shallow nature of American democracy and the demands of business, which further complicated the process of teaching writing. These issues of overcrowded classes and "penny-wise economy" are apparent in the situations she faced in her work administering the English Department with Buck.

Wylie's democratic ideals were put into practice in the department's administration. Wylie and Buck revised the traditional power of the chair by developing a collaborative model that emphasized the role of department faculty in the administrative process. In this way, the department became more inclusive and democratic. Wylie's ideas about democratic administration are evident in the following talk to the Vassar alumnae.

"Experiments in Democracy"

In a June 1921 presentation at the fiftieth anniversary of the Vassar Alumnae Association, Wylie discussed "the advance toward Democratic Government at Vassar" (Speaking on the Topic 12). Wylie traced this advance from the late 1870s, when she was a student at Vassar, to her return to the college in 1895, to the present in 1921. If asked to summarize the changes at Vassar, Wylie explains that she "should call them experiments in democracy, experiments in democratic government . . ." (12). In her presentation, Wylie does more than simply trace this advance. She constructs Vassar's identity as a college that has a long history of developing a democratic consciousness. More specifically, she discusses different stages in this movement, emphasizing that it is a positive and continuing development at Vassar. In addition, she suggests that this advance toward democratic government did not just involve Vassar but was the ultimate question for Progressive Era society. She concludes with a strong argument for this movement's importance: "Educationally, it means free power. . . . It means that better people are going to come to teach, if they have a chance to shape a larger teaching policy themselves" (23). For Wylie, the development of a democratic consciousness in administration is much more consequential than "even that most important and essential question of bread and butter" (23). Wylie's presentation is significant because it gives us insight into her own "democratic consciousness" and her belief in cooperative forms of administration.

Wylie's introduction, similar to her conclusion, echoes the significance of this advance: "[A]s in the world around us, the achievement of some sort of real Democratic administration of life, in whatever form we take it, is the supreme question, so I believe in college to-day [*sic*] the establishing of a truly democratic sentiment, of a truly democratic administration is the crucial point" (12). She establishes her credibility to speak on the topic by linking the issue of forming a more democratic administration at Vassar to the broader question of creating democratic relationships within society. Wylie sees this as "the supreme question" facing Progressive Era society, affecting everyone.

In this movement toward democratic administration, Wylie asserts that the major challenge is no longer simply having "a voice" (13): "It wasn't so very many generations ago when we thought that a voice was enough, if we could say what we wanted, and if enough of us said it, we were fairly sure to get it. We don't feel that way now. We know that besides the voice, we have to have the technique, the method" (13). Wylie recognizes that a voice without power is as meaningless as no voice at all. The problem, then, was gaining the influence to create organizational structures that foster democratic relationships. This situation is still a challenge that administrators face.

In the early years at Vassar, Wylie notes that the college was largely cut off from broader society and, as a consequence, "[w]e were not very conscious of ourselves" (14). However, in assessing the early days, Wylie contends that "the thing that I can see that we got toward that democratic consciousness which has underlain our later progress was that tremendous sense of solidarity" (15). During this early period, Wylie asserts that the college was "a solid family" in which the president lived on campus, "and we all lived around him, and almost all the members of the faculty, and almost all of their children lived in Main Building . . ." (14). In many ways, Wylie contends that the isolation was extremely negative, but, on the other hand, "it tremendously concentrated our group feeling toward the college. And I think one reason was that we didn't have any sense of class or sub-groups within it, we were a single unit" (16). One result of this isolation was a lack of awareness of how radical the college was:

> We didn't feel our radicalism very much because we didn't know that we
> were radical. It is really amazing, when I look back on it, to think that

THE "ADVANCE" TOWARD DEMOCRATIC ADMINISTRATION

we were not very far from reaching, when I was in college, what I suppose ought to be the most radical venture, the thing that was going to do much, to do more than any other thing to change the position of women in the economic world. We didn't think about that. We thought the world was all right, and we would live just the same and the world would be just the same when we were educated. If anybody had told us what was going to happen, we would simply have scouted the idea. (16)

This isolation allowed the college to carry out "the most radical venture" of educating women without much outside interference. Wylie emphasizes how radical educating women truly was in the 1870s and how this education could, in turn, dramatically alter society.

Wylie then discusses changes she noticed at Vassar when she came back as a teacher in 1895: "[I]t was a new world that I came into, absolutely different from the one that I had left" (17). In this advance toward democratic government, Wylie singles out two developments as significant. First, "the group consciousness" remained strong but "developed into a perfect class consciousness" (18). Second, the faculty had become more aware of the students' needs (18).

During this period, Wylie points out that the "administrative machinery of education" had become more advanced, closely paralleling the growth of American business (18–19). So, when Wylie first became the chair of the English Department in 1897, she and other chairs "were all given free hands" (19): "We were to be managers and we were told explicitly that we were to be managers. It was our business to manage our departments. It was our business to know the advanced thought in our departments, it was our business to organize and be responsible for the work" (19). Chairs "managed" their departments using a top-down approach similar to the ways businesses were managed during this period.

The formation of distinct departments at Vassar is significant because it meant the development of a new administrative layer in the educational process. In her description of Vassar from 1870 to 1880, Mary Augusta Jordan (Vassar class of 1876) emphasizes that during this period

there was a marked absence of rigidity in administrative order. Vassar illustrated easily the best aspects of what may be called academic quantivalence. Teaching Greek did not unfit an officer for usefulness in the library, and the instructor in gymnastics might teach German. The watertight compartment treatment of learning, or even of scholarship, would not have seemed dignified to the aspirant for culture in those days. (57)

Ada F. Snell, a Mount Holyoke English professor who completed an unpublished history of the college's English Department in 1942, notes similar changes brought about by departmentalization in the late nineteenth century (Mastrangelo, "Stories of a Progressive Past" 94): "Previous to this period, as for all colleges, each subject had been a single course; now each subject unfolded into many courses clustered in departments administered by highly specialized instructors" (qtd. in Mastrangelo, "Stories of a Progressive Past" 111). Departmentalization resulted in dramatic changes in how learning and the curriculum were conceived and administered and in the level of specialization required of its instructors.

Wylie's report notes that during the 1890s, the different classes within the university also became more distinct: "There was the faculty feeling among the groups at the top. There was the faculty group of workers who were under the group at the top" (Speaking on the Topic 19). Wylie asserts that she is discussing the class distinctions that developed only to emphasize

> that this group consciousness into which the college was at that time largely divided was an inevitable thing in the course of progress. It was on a parallel with the outside world. It was the thing that, for efficiency, had to be. And I think it led us farther and better than could possibly have been done by any other method at that time. And when you talk of the democratic consciousness, it was not excessively democratic, it was the strengthening of feeling, it was a heightening of responsibility at different points; it was not inclined to draw the community very much closer together. (19–20)

Wylie views the managerial stage in department administration as a necessary step in the seemingly inevitable "advance" toward a more democratic administration. This phase allowed for certain efficiency in moving departments forward in the early years. However, with the development of separate classes within the college came "a very keen sense of the need of a closer co-operation" (20). According to Wylie, a recent change was the belief that "the whole college should be represented and people who live here should appear in the political life. That went through a few weeks ago, and there wasn't [a] ripple, nobody minded that employees of the college had a chance to be members of the political life. Yet, when I came to the college it was only spoken of with bated breath, behind closed doors" (21). She suggests that this change is significant in terms of the movement toward democratic administration.

A second major change occurred at the department level:

> Quite a number of us found that, if our positions allowed us to be bosses, we rather were guilty of benevolent despotism and we found that that didn't go far in getting departmental teachings done. We found, if we were going to have good departments, if we were going to have good teachers, we simply had to have democratic organizations. And so gradually the departments in many cases made their own experiment toward a real and genuine democratic government. (21–22)

Here, we get a sense of Wylie's own philosophy in terms of chairing the English Department and how she viewed the department administration as an "experiment" in democracy.

According to Wylie, the "third very hopeful sign outstanding was the first joint-committee," when President Taylor asked certain students, faculty members, and student representatives to meet "to talk over that burning question [of] how we could simplify social life at Vassar. . . . I didn't realize at all at the time that that was really the beginning of the solution that is going on so well to-day [*sic*]" (22). In each administrative level of the college, Wylie emphasizes this movement toward more cooperative and inclusive organizations.[7]

Wylie concludes her presentation by discussing what Vassar had become in 1921. Wylie suggests that the ideas that were developed in the 1890s and early twentieth century are continuing. For the past two years, Wylie contends that all sectors of the university

> have been working at the very center to try to get at that question of how we can get together. Educationally, it means free power. . . . It means that better people are going to come to teach, if they have a chance to shape a larger teaching policy themselves. It isn't only lack of money, it isn't only poverty that has made teaching for the last ten years in a great majority of cases a rather lean profession. It is because people have been placed in positions where they don't control their lives, their own activities, and this working out of a democratic government and democratic consciousness seems to me far and away more important than even that most important and most essential question of bread and butter. (23)

The leanness Wylie describes was felt at Vassar. The 1921 "Report of the Department of English" states that the tight budget at Vassar meant "the failure of five members of our department to get the promotion, with corresponding increase in salary and intercollegiate dignity, to which long and recognized service should have entitled them" (1). The current budget constraints hindered this advance toward democratic government and subsequently made the need for it all the more apparent.

Democratic Organization and the English Department

In her discussion of feminist leadership in writing program administration, Hildy Miller explains that "[t]o lead, then, is not to dominate but rather to facilitate, to share power, and to enable both self and others to contribute" (81–82). The records of the English Department indicate Wylie enacted many of the ideas she discussed in her 1921 presentation, and they resemble Miller's "feminist vision of personal power" (81). Although Wylie was nominally the chair of the English Department, it is evident from department reports that in the first twelve years, Wylie and Buck collaboratively administered the department. However, in Wylie's last twelve or so years as chair, the faculty took an even more active role in the department's administration. In the 1911–12 "Report of the Department of English," for instance, Wylie writes that "the general administrative work of the department has been more effectively done than ever before <I think> because the members of the department have done more of it and taken more responsibility in it" (3).[8] Wylie details the different duties of faculty members: scheduling department lectures, overseeing the commencement essays, supervising tutors, attending meetings with the Poughkeepsie teachers of English, reexamining students needing "special attention," running a "special spelling class weekly," managing the English Book Club, and arranging department and journal club meetings (4).

Although Wylie's aim was a democratically run department, her actual practices may have emphasized responsibility and "efficiency" over personal freedom, as is evident in the following quotation from President Henry Noble MacCracken:

> She [Wylie] was not a radical as the term is generally understood. She liked organization. A born commander, this advocate of personal freedom expected and obtained a willing obedience and service from all her

associates. The members of the Department of English were her loving aids long after her resignation from active work, yet her training was really a training in freedom and in administrative efficiency, and every teacher in the Department of English was given some executive responsibility. ("Appreciations I" 149)

Despite this apparent contradiction, a key aspect of the department was an interconnected view of literature and writing. In "Retrospect, 1924," written upon Wylie's retirement, Katherine Warren describes the organic philosophy that was central to the department's organization:

The ideas upon which this [the development of the department] rested were definite, and original both in themselves and in their application. Chief among them was her conception of the field of English as a single territory of art and scholarship, the "branches" of which were not separate, but were merely different aspects or approaches, emphasizing one or another element without detaching it from the rest. From this it inevitably followed that the department itself should be an organic whole in the main trend and character of its teaching . . . (83–84)

This interconnected view of the department was central to Wylie's understanding of society and her belief in the "advance toward democratic organization." This perspective was also foundational to Buck's approach to rhetoric and pedagogy and is evident throughout her textbooks.

This organic philosophy was particularly evident in the collaboration between Wylie and Buck. For instance, in the 1905–06 "Report of the Department of English," Wylie emphasizes Buck's significant value to the department in asking that she be appointed to a full professor: "Miss Buck's arduous service for the college both as a teacher and as an administrator imperatively demand this recognition, while her standing outside the college and her influence with the students add possibly less weighty reasons for it" (4). Wylie reiterated her request in a 1906–07 report, and Buck was appointed a full professor in 1907, according to the 1921 student yearbook, the *Vassarion* (15).

The joint significance of their efforts within the department also became evident in their salaries. In the 1908–09 Report, Wylie asks that Buck's salary be equal to hers (2). Here again, Wylie underscores Buck's role in administering the English Department, emphasizing the benefits this collaboration has for the college:

This [the salary increase] has for some time seemed just to me, because of the size, and consequent administrative work of the department of English. Of this administrative work, Miss Buck does her full share, relieving me entirely of a great deal of it. Indeed, if we did not work to-gether [*sic*] in entire harmony, it would be necessary either for me to do considerably less teaching, or to divide the department, as has been unfortunately done in many places, into the departments of English or Rhetoric, and of Literature. The present union of the two subjects in a single department, [*sic* comma in original] has many advantages of economy and efficiency, and it seems unfortunate that in order to preserve these, one of the people concerned should suffer serious and permanent financial loss. (2)

Wylie stresses the inherent unfairness of the current salary scale, given Buck's department responsibilities. She also highlights how this collaboration benefits the college since it would be much more costly to have two separate departments. This issue has not gone away; today, departments still struggle over potential Rhetoric/English sectional splits.

In addition, as Barbara E. L'Eplattenier points out, the collaboration of the women is visually evident in several of the department reports and draft reports. Wylie and Buck often were involved in drafting them, even though they are signed "Respectfully submitted" by Wylie. For example, the 31 January 1908 "Report of the Department of English" is typed, and both Buck's and Wylie's corrections are evident throughout the report. As L'Eplattenier explains, "Open, sweeping, rounded and bold, Buck's handwriting is easily recognizable and clearly different from Wylie's tight, scrawling chicken scratch" ("Investigating Institutional Power" 83). Wylie and Buck also probably discussed the reports and their contents since they lived together for many years. Another indicator of their close working relationship is the fact that Buck served as the chair during the 1913–14 academic year, when Wylie was on leave. The department documents demonstrate the close collaboration between Wylie and Buck.

The collaborative nature of the department is particularly evident in the 1920–21 "Report of the Department of English," submitted by Wylie on 2 May 1921. A committee consisting of Wylie, Alice Snyder, and Amy Reed wrote the report, and then a draft was read to the entire department and "had the benefit of much suggestion and criticism" (13). Wylie's emphasis on democratic organization and budgetary constraints, evident in her earlier presentation, is echoed in this document. This report is important because it was Wylie's last before stepping down as chair; she resigned as chair shortly after Buck's death in January 1922. In the 1921–22 report, Amy Reed, who became the department chair, explains the significance of the document, noting the report is "in some sense a summary of accomplishment during her [Wylie's] administration, and an analysis of needs for the future" (1). Reed notes that Buck's death "meant a revolution for the Department" (2). JoAnn Campbell points out that Wylie's 1920–21 report "differs in tone considerably, for she [Wylie] holds nothing back in giving [President] MacCracken her opinion of the way finances have been handled by the college" (*Toward* 253).

The report was written in response to President MacCracken's request that the English Department "consider plans and methods in relation to the budget, with a special view to retrenchment wherever such retrenchment was possible" (13). However, according to Wylie and the members of the department, the "financial pressure" had increased over the past five years to the point "where there must be not merely amelioration of a bad situation, but a radical change in administrative policy towards the department, involving a considerable enlargement of our resources" (1). They explain, though, that it is "in no spirit of rebellion" that they present their findings, but instead so that the President and Trustees' Committee on Faculty and Studies "should have a chance to know what seem to us the educational issues involved in [the] present retrenchment" (1). The first part of the reports details how the department is "suffering from a long-continued pressure of overwork, with little prospect of relief" (7). The remaining pages "prove the fallacy of the current impression that the Department of English is among the most expensive in the college" (8). The department demonstrates this fallacy through a statistical analysis of the "student-hours per teacher" (8–9), which shows that the department "not only rank[s] fourth from the lowest in money spent, but that only five departments carry a larger number of students, or of student-hours, per teacher" (9).

The report also includes a table showing the number of students per teacher within the English Department from 1898 to 1921. During the 1920–21 year, teachers taught an average of 150.2 students per year and 75.1 students per semester. Based on the number of students taught, Wylie and the other department members contend that they are being asked "to work a fifth harder than we did six years ago, when we, for the first time in our history, even approached our early estimates as to numbers,—an estimate which, as we were even then convinced, was too high for truly efficient teaching" (10). The situation at Vassar was not unusual. For instance, according to Wellesley's 1895 President's Report, Sophie Chantal Hart (who became chair of the English Department) and a "Miss Weaver" "were responsible for the theme writing of 200 students apiece. Weaver, in addition, taught another twenty-six students in a course in Theme Writing" (Mastrangelo, "Stories of a Progressive Past" 145). Hart's heavy workload apparently continued and was the primary reason she resigned her chair position in 1935 (Mastrangelo, "Stories of a Progressive Past" 157). Similarly, at Harvard, the average first-year class size had increased to more than 200 students by 1870; the class size jumped to more than 600 students by 1903. In many colleges, the average first-year class was 200 plus students, and similar to Vassar, many teachers were required to meet individually with students to discuss their work (Connors, "Overwork/Underpay" 112). At Vassar, teachers devoted an average of three or more "interviews" to each student each semester, and the interviews typically lasted twenty-five minutes ("Report of the Department of English," 1911, 2).

Calling the budget situation "the present regime of drastic retrenchment," the report emphasizes some of the major consequences: the failure of five department members to gain promotions and salary increases (1). The budget crisis was made worse by World War I and the fact that members of the department and faculty "have been giving liberally of our time and strength to help the college bear the financial burdens inevitable in time of war" (2). Instead of relief, though, the workload had become even heavier than it was during the war:

> We are also keenly aware that the budget for labor and for material equipment has been exceeded again and again. In other words, the administration will face a deficit to meet material, but not spiritual or intellectual, necessities; and it would seem that a co-operative spirit on the part of teachers makes them inevitable victims of retrenchment when coal dealers or hand workers get their price. (2)

Wylie and other members of the department felt that the administration had taken advantage of their cooperative nature for its own cost-cutting benefits. In her analysis of feminist approaches to power in writing program administration, Miller explains that feminist leadership may be "misinterpreted from a masculinist point of view" because of ideological differences (83). As Miller asserts, "Leadership can appear weak if receptivity is mistaken for passivity" (83). Wylie's words emphasized her awareness of these ideological conflicts, particularly the ways they played out in terms of differences in priorities.[9]

Because of this "educationally precarious situation," the report outlines the key principles of the department, with specific references to budget issues (2). The first department principle is that "English is primarily an art, and that, whether considered from the point of view of literature or of writing, it should be so studied and taught" (2). One outcome of viewing English as an art is that "it must be taught as individually as possible and must concern itself with the imaginative and perceptive hardly less than with the intellectual training of the student" (3). Thus, the department had "made every effort to have small classes, and to allow opportunity for individual teaching" (3). Class teaching and individual conferences were emphasized. As President MacCracken notes, "This basic and simple face-to-face relationship . . . formed the basis of training for generations of Vassar writers such as Margaret Culkin Banning, Constance Rourke, Edna St. Vincent Millay, Mary McCarthy, Elizabeth Bishop, Eleanor Clark, and others" (qtd. in Daniels, *Bridges to the World* 58). According to the report, the key difference, though, between Vassar and Princeton, which had used a preceptorial system since 1905, and Harvard, which adopted a tutorial plan for its class of 1917, was that the same teacher did the classroom teaching and conferences (4). This difference was because the department held the "conviction that all our teaching must be done by the best people" (5).

Wylie then emphasizes why the department needs "the best" teachers:

The need of an experienced staff is the more important because the second article of our educational creed is the co-operative or democratic organization of the department.

From 1896 at least, we have worked co-operatively whenever co-operation was possible. Matters affecting the interests of the whole group have in every case been made subjects for joint discussion, and whenever it was practicable have been jointly determined. (5)

In other words, because the department is democratically organized, the department needs experienced faculty. In practice, "the best" often meant middle- and upper-class white women like themselves, with several being former Vassar graduates. Their actions suggest that while they were committed to democratic ideals, they still thought in terms of hierarchy, viewing their own class- and culture-based values as "the best."

Later in the report, Wylie contends that the "co-operative management of the department, though at first sight remote from questions of budget, is in fact intimately bound up with it" (7). She then clarifies the direct connection between democratic management and budgetary issues. In the early years, Wylie explains that "the English staff co-operated rather in carrying out policies outlined by Professor Buck or me than in initiating activities or modifying those suggested" (7). However, in the past twelve or more years, department faculty members

> have increasingly taken a vital share in the management of the department, with the natural result that, while I carry less personal responsibility than formerly, the other members carry considerably more. Such departmental organization as ours seems to me to be just now especially necessary if Vassar is to advance towards the democratic government rapidly developing in most of our colleges and universities. Democratic government—i.e. general departmental and faculty control of educational policies—is possible only when the members of the faculty share in ultimate educational responsibility. Such responsibility requires time and energy as well as interest; and if the college is to benefit by the best services of its faculty, the work involved in joint management of common business must be recognized as an integral part of the teacher's task. Such work can assuredly not be done by people exhausted by excessive demands whether of the classroom, of the additional conference-hours made necessary by sections that are too large, or of an over-burden of administrative detail. It is true, too, that these more general activities, essential as they are both to the well-being of the college and to the teacher's grasp of large educational polities, ordinarily meet with scanty recognition either administrative or scholarly. (7)

Wylie's anger and frustration at the administration's lack of understanding of the "time and energy" required to create more democratic organizations is clearly evident. She sees the current budget crisis as severely hindering this movement because the faculty is "exhausted by excessive demands." Here, similar to her presentation, Wylie emphasizes this democratic movement is happening beyond Vassar and that the college needs to keep up with this "advance."

In this chapter, I have shown how several of the political and pedagogical issues that Wylie outlined in her 1918 article were apparent in conflicts between the English Department and the administration. Contextualizing Wylie and Buck's democratic approach to administration within the Progressive Era also demonstrates how both women were influenced by a strong sense of social responsibility felt by many upper-class white women during this period. Throughout their administrative practices, Wylie and Buck emphasized the importance of democratic government. Although the contexts are markedly different, the situations that Wylie and Buck faced anticipate current administrative circumstances. Issues such as teaching load, pay, promotion, and ideological clashes between decentered and hierarchical administrative structures still are central to English departments and writing programs. While these issues are evident at virtually all universities, they are particularly still prevalent today in small, private teaching institutions. Questions about whether rhetoric and composition programs should be in English departments or separate and how to gain recognition for the kinds of service so often involved in writing programs also are relevant. Wylie and Buck's administrative efforts remain vital to us because their work can be illuminating to today's administrators grappling with similar concerns.

As Cheryl Glenn reminds us, inherent in each effort to remap the history of rhetoric "is the necessary historical inquiry that empowers political action . . . , for historical inquiry helps people situate problems in a broader context and discover the available means of persuading their communities to act from their shared historical experiences and needs" (17). How might Wylie and Buck's story serve to "empower political action" today? The lean budget times they faced severely hindered their efforts to foster democratic organizations. As Wylie emphasizes in the 1921 "Report of the Department of English," such efforts take time and money and they "ordinarily meet with scanty recognition either administrative or scholarly" (7). Although Wylie is talking about a situation seventy-five years in the past, her words seem prophetic, given today's tight economic situation. Efforts toward more democratic administration will, no doubt, be difficult. This situation makes the need to gain recognition for such efforts that much more necessary and the analysis of prior models and alternate means of persuasion all the more significant. Although many priorities vie for importance during tight times, as Wylie reminds us, the development of more democratic administration is more important than even the "most essential question of bread and butter" (Speaking on the Topic 23).

George Machan Buck, Gertrude Buck's father, a Civil War veteran and a judge and attorney in Kalamazoo, Michigan. Courtesy of Kindred Roots Genealogical Society.

Gertrude Buck's mother, Anne Bradford Buck, a descendent of Gov. William Bradford of Plymouth. Courtesy of Kindred Roots Genealogical Society.

Gertrude Buck's picture
and signature (*Vassarion*,
1903). Courtesy of Special Collections, Vassar College Libraries.

Undated picture of
Gertrude Buck. Courtesy of
Kindred Roots Genealogical Society.

Sketch of Gertrude Buck, professor of English at Vassar College 1897–1922 (Warren, "In Remembrance"). Courtesy of Special Collections, Vassar College Libraries.

Detroit Normal Training School graduating class of January 1898 with Harriet M. Scott, principal of the school (center). Courtesy of the Walter P. Reuther Library, Wayne State University.

Laura Johnson Wylie (composite) holding a fishing pole labeled "inductive method" (*Vassarion*, 1901). Courtesy of Special Collections, Vassar College Libraries.

Laura Johnson Wylie, a member of the English Department at Vassar College from 1895 to 1924 (Woodbridge, *Miss Wylie*). Courtesy of Special Collections, Vassar College Libraries.

Laura Johnson Wylie and
Gertrude Buck with one
"among the long suc-
cession of 'little ones'"
(Warren, "112 Market
Street" 143). The pic-
ture is featured in Evert
Sprinchorn's "Stagestruck
in Academe: Acceptance
of Theater as a Liberal
Art Was No Overnight
Success." Courtesy of Special
Collections, Vassar College Libraries.

Gertrude Buck and Laura
Johnson Wylie (Laura
Johnson Wylie Biographi-
cal File Box 4). Courtesy of
Special Collections, Vassar College
Libraries.

Laura Johnson Wylie and students (Laura Johnson Wylie Biographical File Box 5). Courtesy of Special Collections, Vassar College Libraries.

Debate: 1908 committee at work (Simpson, "Helen Lockwood's College Years"). Courtesy of Special Collections, Vassar College Libraries.

Wellesley-Vassar Debate

APRIL 25, 1903

Question

Resolved: "That economically, it is not advantageous for the United States to possess territory in the tropics."

Debaters and Alternates

SUSANNAH JANE MCMURPHY, 1903   ANNA P. STEARNS, 1904
KATHARINE M. MORGAN, 1903   JEANNETTE S. TAYLOR, 1904
CHARLOTTE L. RUDYARD, 1904   HELEN E. TRUE, 1904

Committee

CLARA MILDRED THOMPSON, 1903
ELEANOR BUCHANAN CONKLIN, 1903   MARY GERALDINE FOLEY, 1904
MENETTA WHITE BROOKS, 1904   DOROTHY LEWIS, 1905

Wellesley-Vassar Debate, 25 April 1903 (*Vassarion,* 1903). Courtesy of Special Collections, Vassar College Libraries.

Picture of Mary Yost included with the article "The Need of the Community-Mind: In Which the Dean of Women Says Some Things That Every Stanford Man and Woman Should Think About," published December 1921, three months after her arrival at Stanford. Courtesy of Stanford University Libraries, Stanford, California.

Portrait of Helen Drusilla Lockwood (Swain, "Helen Drusilla Lockwood"). Courtesy of Special Collections, Vassar College Libraries.

4

THE SUFFRAGE MOVEMENT AND BUCK'S
APPROACH TO ARGUMENT AND DEBATE

In Sophomore Argumentation
Our training's been simply great;
And now before the public
We challenge in debate.

—*Vassarion* (1900)

The democratic ideals that were central to Gertrude Buck's feminism and her approach to administration and pedagogy were integral to her view of argument and debate. Buck believed democracy was an achievable ideal and that the goal of education was to prepare individuals to participate in democracy. Throughout her work, she resisted late-nineteenth-century mechanical and patriarchal approaches to rhetorical theory by presenting an alternate view of rhetoric and the individual. In so doing, Buck redefined rhetoric, argumentation, and the role of women in a participatory democracy. She applied her feminist ethics to argumentation and broke down the claims of the domestic sphere by encouraging Vassar women to take a more active and public role in both college and society. Buck's work in argumentation and debate complicates claims that with the entrance of women into higher education, the teaching of rhetoric became "less contestive and more interiorized, even personalized" (Connors, *Composition-Rhetoric* 66). In significant ways, Buck's revision of argumentation also anticipates efforts by contemporary feminists to challenge the traditional focus on persuasion and develop alternative forms of argument. It is important to emphasize, though, that Buck developed her approach to argument almost one-hundred years before these efforts.

Buck's notions about an ethical approach to argumentation in a participatory democracy were put into action in encounters between suffragists and the college administration. These encounters demonstrate how suffrage became intertwined with debate, issues of individual freedom, and the nature of democracy. Buck's textbooks and debating activities at the college encouraged Vassar women to think about women's issues, and her approach to argumentation, with its emphasis on social action, communal interests, free inquiry, and equality, ultimately had feminist effects.

Suffrage Issues at Vassar

To better grasp Buck's approach to argumentation and debate, it's helpful to understand the Vassar context in the early decades of the twentieth century. Buck's ideas about argumentation were not limited to her classroom but were practiced in clashes between suffragists and the college administration. Suffrage uprisings in 1908 and 1909 at Vassar brought out several significant questions, particularly concerns relating to personal freedom versus institutional authority. These issues were especially prominent during the presidency of James Monroe Taylor, who served from 1886 until 1914. According to his successor, Henry Noble McCracken, Taylor "literally was the life of the campus. . . . His gay laughter pervaded the whole college" (*Hickory Limb* 22). On a personal level, Taylor was respected and well liked by many students: "We all loved President Taylor. I say 'all.' I don't know anyone who didn't. We all thought he was the most charming man and very capable," said Gladys E. Hull Hopkins (Vassar class of 1913) in a 1981 interview (qtd. in Daniels, *Bridges to the World* 70). Although committed to offering women the same intellectual opportunities as men, Taylor was a conservative in terms of women's rights (Herman 315).[1] Taylor believed that students should be able to pursue their studies without interference from various political or social reform movements ("'Conservatism'"). So, although Vassar students were allowed to argue about suffrage in their debate clubs and to discuss it among themselves, they were not allowed to form a suffrage club on campus (Daniels, *Bridges to the World* 65–66).

According to MacCracken, Taylor supported the ideal of the "'well-rounded'" Vassar woman. Graduates were to be "cultured but human, not leaders but good wives and mothers, truly liberal in things intellectual but conservative in matters social" (MacCracken, *Hickory Limb* 24). When suffrage and other issues began to enter the protected realm of Vassar more frequently, Taylor drafted a policy limiting public discussion of such issues on campus (Daniels, "Suffrage as a Lever" 32).[2] However, a request by M. Carey Thomas, president of Bryn Mawr College, to have Jane Addams speak at Vassar on suffrage brought the issue to the foreground. Taylor's strong stance concerning his policy and his opposition to suffrage as a form of "propaganda" is apparent from the correspondence that ensued.

In October 1907, Thomas informed Taylor that a Committee on Equal Suffrage Lectures before Women College Students had been formed so that suffrage concerns could be "properly presented to the women college students of the country" (letter to Taylor, 30 Oct. 1907, 1). The committee had secured Jane Addams as the speaker for the year, and she was scheduled to present at Smith, Wellesley, Radcliffe, Mount Holyoke, and Bryn Mawr. In her letter, Thomas asks if Addams can also speak at Vassar on the "workingwoman's need of the ballot" and if Taylor would serve on a college advisory board to the newly formed committee (letter to Taylor, 30 Oct. 1907, 1–2; Daniels, *Bridges to the World* 66).[3] In a private response to Thomas, President Taylor declines both offers, asserting that he is

> confirmed in [his] feeling that it is best not to allow a propaganda of any kind whatever to enter this college. That is not due to want of sympathy with certain of these causes, but to a general principle which stretches far beyond a matter of suffrage. I have found the principle a good working hypothesis in regard to socialistic matters, and some questionable forms of missionary effort, <and extreme temperance agitators,> as well as regarding this question of suffrage. (letter to Thomas, 4 Nov. 1907, 1)[4]

In explaining his reasons for declining to serve on the advisory board, Taylor writes that by accepting he would associate himself with supporters of suffrage. Although publicly Taylor insisted he was neutral on the question of suffrage, in his private letter to Thomas, Taylor admits he opposed "the larger circumstances involved in a great extension of suffrage for either men or women" (letter to Thomas, 4 Nov. 1907, 2; Daniels, *Bridges to the World* 66). Taylor agrees with Thomas that it is important for students to understand both sides of the issue. However, he contends this already happens at Vassar, where there "has been a great deal of discussion of the matter from time to time though I do not think for the sake of any particular practical interest" (letter to Thomas, 4 Nov. 1907, 2). He concludes that he is "unwilling to have the College, as such, represented on the·Board" (letter to Thomas, 4 Nov. 1907, 2).

Taylor clarified his stance toward "the progressive movements of the day" in a speech titled "The 'Conservatism' of Vassar" presented in 1909 before an annual meeting of the alumnae and later published as a pamphlet and distributed nationally. In the speech, Taylor emphasizes that he does not specifically oppose any one cause but that he is concerned that such movements are potentially exploitative of students: "Suppose now that every explorer of new views and every adherent of new isms have [*sic*] a chance at will to attack these young and comparatively inexperienced minds. What results will you look for?" Reiterating what second Vassar President John Howard Raymond had said in 1875, Taylor asserts that "'the mission of Vassar College was not to reform society but to educate women.'" Thus, Taylor contends that "plain old-fashioned preparatory education, opening up all of these questions but under the influence of the spirit of teaching and investigation, and not of agitation, has some claim upon the undergraduate mind. . . ." Furthermore, Taylor argues the college "does not love notoriety for the undergraduate, and declares it to be unhealthful, intellectually and socially." Instead, he asserts that the college "affirms its belief in the home and in the old-fashioned view of marriage and children and the splendid service of society wrought through these quiet and unradical means."

Despite Taylor's speech and his opposition to suffrage as a "movement" or form of "propaganda," the issue did not go away. The situation escalated with a major clash occurring in June 1908. In accordance with Taylor's policy regarding suffrage, a number of Vassar suffragists were prohibited from organizing and meeting on the college campus during commencement activities. To circumvent his policy, some forty students left campus and held a suffrage meeting in a cemetery located next to the college. Inez Milholland, then a Vassar undergraduate who went on to become a lawyer, a socialist, and a charismatic suffrage leader, led the revolt. Suffragist speakers at the "graveyard rally," as it was later named, included Harriot Stanton Blatch, Charlotte Perkins Gilman, Helen Hay, corporation counsel for the Equality League of Self-Supporting Women, and Rose Schneiderman of the Cap Makers Union. During the meeting, the speakers urged the students to become involved in suffrage. According to reports, Stanton Blatch, "in order to allay the fears of any member of the faculty who might chance that way, bore aloft a yellow banner on which was inscribed in large black letters, 'Come let us reason together'" (Ellis 43). The suffragists also disregarded Taylor's opposition to "notoriety for the undergraduate student" ("'Conservatism'"). The women brought a reporter to cover the meeting, and the rally attracted the attention of several New York City newspapers.[5] Laura Johnson Wylie organized the Woman's Suffrage Party of Poughkeepsie as a direct result of the graveyard rally ("Snyder Describes Difficulties" 4).

In March of 1909, Milholland was involved in another suffrage incident that included several faculty members and raised questions concerning individual freedom. Milholland requested a room for a suffrage meeting. President Taylor agreed to the request so long as the meeting was private and did not involve outside speakers. In a report written two years after the event from notes at the time of the meeting, Taylor asserts that he was given the impression that "both sides and students only would have a talk over the issue" (Report: In re Faculty discussion 1). However, Taylor later found out that the meeting was "presided over and addressed by members of the faculty, and that only those favoring suffrage were invited to speak" (1).

On 19 March 1909, a contentious faculty meeting followed this incident. In his later report of the meeting, Taylor writes that he realized that faculty had participated in the meeting because of a "misconception" concerning the permission given (1). However, he emphasizes that such participation appeared to disregard his position opposing discussion of controversial issues on campus as stated in his recent alumnae address. Taylor stresses that suffrage is not "at issue" but that a "principle" is involved. He argues that "we are bound to restrain our own views when by their public expression we are liable to seem to commit the college to them and when especially the issues are those of a highly excited time or party. The college, it seemed to me, should be first" (2). According to Taylor's report of the meeting, "[a] section of the faculty very strongly opposed this [Taylor's position] as an attack on individual freedom" (2).

Taylor sent a letter reiterating his position to "a number of the leaders in the discussion," one of whom was Wylie (Report: In re Faculty discussion 2). In this letter, included in his report, Taylor contends that the issue "involves more than the vital question of personal liberty. It includes as well the proper restraint imposed on that liberty by considerations of the larger welfare of the college . . ." (Report: In re Faculty discussion 3). He advises faculty members to put aside personal opinion for the betterment of the college—to put "the college above ourselves" (Report: In re Faculty discussion 3). Furthermore, he underscores his position that suffrage is an effort of propaganda, which also includes "socialism, temperance, and other allied questions" (Report: In re Faculty discussion 3).

Taylor's memorandum drew a number of replies. As Elizabeth A. Daniels points out, the response of Mary W. Whitney of the Astronomy Department underscored a major question involved (*Bridges to the World* 67):

> I am afraid that if we do not come to a clear understanding of the difference between propogandism [*sic*] and freedom of discussion, that rumors of repression will get abroad. . . . Suppose in this unfortunate case, the instructors when asked had said, "The policy of the college forbids my speaking," the result that has so disturbed you would have been avoided, but a far greater danger in my opinion would have been incurred. Don't you think. . . that we might well frame a resolution, stating what propogandism is and what equal discussion is? (letter to Taylor, 7 Apr. 1909, 2–3)

For Whitney, the difference between Taylor's definition of free speech and propaganda was not black and white, as he seemed to assume. She suggested the president's position could be viewed as a significant challenge to individual freedom.

In reviewing this period, it is evident that several issues became interconnected, revealing not only Taylor's position but also the repressive atmosphere of the college. In his correspondence, Taylor conflated suffrage with several separate reform efforts that he labeled as "new isms," including socialism, temperance, and religious movements. For Taylor, these "progressive movements of the day" were to be regarded with suspicion, "propaganda," something that should not be on campus. Several of the movements had progressive social agendas that clashed with Taylor's view that Vassar's purpose was to affirm "its beliefs in the home and in the old-fashioned view of marriage and children." In quoting the words of Vassar's former president, Taylor reminded his audience of the college's traditional orientation. Taylor's more conservative views were also evident in his notion of protecting his female students' "comparatively inexperienced minds," which reflected a paternalistic attitude toward women. This attitude was also evident in his argument that faculty, instead of following their individual ideas, should be obedient to a "general principle" and "put the college above ourselves." Thus, like students, the faculty should obey rather than question this principle. Taylor's arguments and actions demonstrated his attitudes toward democracy, basic freedoms, and individual rights. They revealed his discomfort with the notion that the women over whom he had charge might be given the right to participate in deciding issues that affected their own and even his life.

Buck and Women's Issues

Buck's involvement in women's issues started before her years at Vassar. In fact, her participation is evident beginning with her early college days at the University of Michigan. Buck served as the editor of a symposium in the senior literary magazine, *The Inlander,* which asked forty-three American authors to respond to the following question: "What do you think of athletic education for women?" The aim of the project was to raise money for a women's gymnasium, with proceeds from the sale of the magazine and the authors' autographs contributing to the fund. Twenty-six authors responded to Buck's question, including William Dean Howells, Brander Matthews, Mary Hallock Foote, and Harriet Prescott Spofford. In his response, Edmund C. Stedman compared Buck's distinctive handwriting to his own, suggesting her penmanship was indicative of the "modern" or "New Woman" of the period: "When I contrast the modern woman's spacious hand writing [*sic*] (your own, for instance) with my lesser scrawl, I feel that her 'athletic education' shows itself even in correspondence!" ("Athletic Education for Women" 293).[6]

Buck's participation in the debate concerning athletic education for women at Michigan suggests she may have been involved in the discourse on the "New Woman" of the period. Buck grew up at a time when concerns about women's exercise and dress were beginning to be raised by educated women and some doctors. During this time, the bicycle also created the opportunity for the reformists' philosophies to be realized. In a practical sense, this realization came in the form of less restrictive clothing and greater mobility. However, more significantly, the changes in middle-class women's roles meant freedom from traditional feminine stereotypes (Caffrey 42). In the 1890s, the changes were reflected in magazines with the emergence of the "New Woman," who was generally defined by her "independent spirit and athletic zeal" (Rosenberg 54).

Buck's involvement in women's issues continued throughout her years at Vassar. However, perhaps out of respect for Taylor and his policy, Buck did not seem to pursue actively suffrage issues on campus. Her full teaching load and her scholarly writing may also have left little time for her to be involved in such issues.[7] Buck's activism, though, did appear to benefit from her friendship with certain members of the Vassar faculty during this period. In his description of the faculty, President MacCracken details what he labels the characteristics of the "creative" group:

> They left the protection of college rooms, and lived in town, where they participated strenuously in civic life. They worked for suffrage, against child labor, against economic inequality and other forms of injustice. It was whispered of one of them that she had defended the right of an unmarried woman to bear a child and rear it. One or two, it was darkly hinted, were socialists. . . . Dangerous women, all of them. They rejoiced in every conflict of ideas. The times were ripe for change. (*Hickory Limb* 70)

MacCracken's description accurately characterized women like Buck and Laura Johnson Wylie. Buck and Wylie considered adopting a child, and Buck had been a member of the Socialist Party of New York State.[8] They also left the confines of Vassar to live in Poughkeepsie, they were active in civic life, and they devotedly worked for suffrage and social justice.[9]

As mentioned, Buck was a member of the Poughkeepsie Equal Suffrage League, and she served on the board of directors of its successor, the Women's City and County Club. Based on a 1920 report, the club was involved in a variety of public welfare issues such as improving poor housing, providing civic education, monitoring state legislation, and opposing the "re-election of Senator [James W.] Wadsworth, on the ground that we did not deem his social conscience sufficiently awakened to the needs of the present day" ("Condensed Report 1920" 6). A Republican, anti-suffragist candidate, Wadsworth was running for reelection to the U.S. Senate (Sharer 117).[10] As mentioned, Wylie had served as the first president of the Woman's Suffrage Party of Poughkeepsie, which replaced the older Poughkeepsie Equal Suffrage League (M. P. Whitney 122). She also founded and served as president of the Women's City and County Club ("Women's City and County Club" 3). Moreover, Wylie and history professor Lucy Maynard Salmon became "great allies as the years went on, as they saw eye to eye on many subjects" (Brown 182).

In addition, Buck was active in suffrage issues during this time. In 1913, Buck published two limericks entitled "Anti-Suffrage Sentiments" in *The Masses,* a magazine that reflected a socialist viewpoint:

> A delicate Angora cat
> Had whiskers; but, pray, what of that?
> "I don't want to vote."
> To a friend she once wrote:
> "My place is at home on the mat."

> "Let me hold the umbrella, my dear,"
> Mrs. Hen said to kind Chantecleer.
> "'Tis man's privilege, love."
> And he held it above
> His own head, so it dripped in her ear.
>   (qtd. in Campbell, *Toward* xxvii–xxviii)[11]

In both limericks, Buck challenges the traditional patriarchal hierarchy and advocates broader rights for women. In the first limerick Buck suggests that without the right to vote, a woman's position in society is equally as restrictive as a cat "at home on the mat." She also implies that women may be participating in their own oppression. In the second, she shows how "man's privilege" often is at the expense of women's rights.

Buck and Wylie also seemed particularly active in suffrage activities during this period. A 21 November 1911 *Poughkeepsie Courier* article reports that Wylie, as president of the Equal Suffrage League, presided over a meeting whose speakers included Milholland, no longer a student but now "an ardent advocate of equal suffrage both in the United States and abroad" ("Equal Suffrage Meeting"). In correspondence dated 30 April 1912, Wylie talks about going to New York City to "march in the parade" (letter to Fanny Hart, 1). In later correspondence, she mentions how both she and Buck enjoyed the day: "Miss Buck went all the way and was rested rather than tired by the expedition. . . . I really felt freshened and made over by it; partly because the weather was so lovely and partly because I gave up the whole day to do a thing I wanted to do" (letter to Fanny Hart, 9 May 1912, 1). In addition, on 21 December 1912, Buck and Wylie were among those who met and had lunch with a group of suffragists marching from New York City to the state capitol in Albany. As president of the Equal Suffrage League, Wylie gave a presentation during the lunch ("Suffragists Reach Rhinebeck" 5). The suffragists marched to Albany "to petition Governor-elect Sulzer to further 'the cause' of equal suffrage" ("Suffragists in Waiting for Sulzer" 1). In correspondence dated 18 January 1913, Wylie mentions how suffrage activities keep her occupied: "We are busier than I can tell with my teaching, suffrage meetings and the play, but everybody exclaims on how well I am looking and I really do not feel the least particle tired" (letter to Fanny Hart, 1).

Both Buck and Wylie's feminist ethics can be viewed as a response to, among other things, the suffrage movement. Both viewed suffrage as "inevitable" because they strongly believed that democracy was the ideal toward which society was moving. The goal was to further, not to hinder, this movement. These ideas are evident in a speech of Wylie's in a 5 February 1913 meeting before the city's Mothers' and Teachers' Association in Poughkeepsie.[12] In her presentation, Wylie gave three reasons why women should be interested in suffrage: First, "it is inevitable and must be prepared for beforehand" ("Address on Woman Suffrage" 5). Wylie points out that after women won the vote in California in 1911, suffrage had "become a fact to be respected even by politicians . . ." ("Address on Woman Suffrage" 5). (New York was set to vote on the question in 1915.) Second, now that women work outside of the home, Wylie contends that they "must have the vote to protect themselves and improve their conditions. Men cannot know women's needs or legislate them alone"; and the "final reason for suffrage is its democracy. We believe today that every one [sic] must be free to develop and govern himself or herself" ("Address on Woman Suffrage" 5).

In significant ways, Buck's emphasis on the principles of freedom and equality in her democratic theory of rhetoric and pedagogy can be seen as a response to the struggle women faced concerning suffrage. Buck and Wylie argued that suffrage was necessary because they believed society was moving toward democracy, and they wanted to foster this movement at every level of social existence.

A Course in Argumentative Writing

Buck's approach to argumentation helped to prepare young women for a more active and thoughtful social role. As mentioned, her pedagogy can be viewed as a reaction to the issues raised by the suffrage movement—questions relating to individual freedom and the broader nature of democracy. These issues were important to Buck because she and other women were struggling to achieve more expansive rights in their everyday lives and on a broader national level. These issues were also central to her approach to argumentation. By promoting these values, Buck's pedagogy had feminist effects in terms of its influence on the lives of her students. Buck's approach encouraged young women to question received opinion, to evaluate critically their own thought processes, and to act in a way that promoted equality and cooperation.

For instance, in Buck's textbook *A Course in Argumentative Writing* (1899), a central concept is the idea that students should learn argumentation inductively from experience and practice rather than starting deductively from principles of formal logic. According to Buck, such an approach is "at once more difficult and more stimulating" than the typical method (iii). This is because the student is "not asked simply to accept certain logical formulae on the authority of text-book or teacher . . . ; but first to quarry out these formulae from his own writing and then to use them for such modification of that writing as may seem necessary" (iii). For Buck, the inductive method was consistent with her feminism, and it equated with the "laboratory" or experimental method of inquiry (154). Such a thought process, highlighting the exploratory side of knowledge rather than reliance on tradition or principle, was also consistent with and necessary for a democratic society.[13]

In her textbook, Buck emphasizes beginning inductively rather than deductively; however, she clarifies the relationship in Appendix B of her book. Buck explains that "the processes of induction and of deduction arise side by side out of the chaos of the child's earliest consciousness" (160). For Buck, induction and deduction are dialectically related. They both are "two phases or aspects of the same process of thought, each involving and each resting upon the other" (160). Although Buck viewed inductive and deductive reasoning as interdependent processes, her emphasis on starting with inductive reasoning can be seen as a reaction against patriarchal and conservative approaches. By starting with inductive reasoning, Vassar women were not simply accepting received knowledge and, in so doing, preserving cultural authority. Instead, they were learning to examine traditional assumptions and think for themselves.

Buck's approach also ran counter to the "old idea of education," in which students were given abstract generalizations and, as Buck points out, told "only [to] apply them to particular cases" (153). Under the old method, students were not expected to think for themselves; instead, they were expected to memorize previous conclusions or generalized rules. Based on reports, such an approach seems to have been the preferred method of President Taylor, who taught ethics at Vassar: "His [Taylor's] ethics course was dry-as-dust and we had to learn by memory. Taylor was an old-fashioned school-teacher type. I kept away from the overlords as much as I could," writes Gabriella Forbush, president of the class of 1912 in a 1981 interview (qtd. in Daniels, *Bridges to the World* 73). Under such an approach, knowledge is restricted, bound by tradition and existing conclusions. Education means accepting a body of knowledge and passing it on basically unchanged. Buck's approach to argumentation, with its emphasis on the interrelation between inductive and deductive processes, does not completely negate tradition. However, by promoting personal observation and freedom of thought, Buck's more democratic approach challenged the conservative, patriarchal emphasis of traditional methods.

A Focus on Student Interest

A second major tenet of Buck's book is that the subject for argumentation should mirror the student's interests (iv). As noted, *interest* is a key term in discussions of education and psychology of the time. Buck's emphasis on interest reflects her work with Harriet M. Scott and the belief that education is an organic process that should develop naturally from a student's interests. In "Recent Tendencies in the Teaching of English Composition" (1900), Buck contends that students have difficulty writing when the subject is remote from their interests. She argues teachers "often are reminded" that students have little to say about "'The vice of ambition' or 'Autumn thoughts'" (373). However, she contends that all students have interests, which to them are worth communicating. Highlighting student interest not only makes it easier for students to write. By encouraging students to draw on their interests, this focus also helps to break down barriers between academic work and the life of the student. In this way, Buck's pedagogy allows students to bring issues such as suffrage into the classroom.

Logic and Argumentation

The third tenet of Buck's argumentation textbook is the connection between the logical structure of argumentation and its substructure based in psychology. Buck contends that while the logical basis of argumentation is "an old world philosophy," it has been overlooked in works on argumentation (v). Buck argues that "cut off from its deepest roots, logic has come to seem rather like a dead tool than like a living expression of thought" (v). In her book, Buck emphasizes that the logical and psychological structure of each argument is revealed to the student, "so that the maxims and formulae, usually regarded by the learner as malign inventions of Aristotle, represent to our student rather the ways in which real people really think" (v). In her pedagogy, she encourages Vassar women to critically evaluate their own thought processes rather than rely on formal principles or tradition.

Buck stresses the importance of logic in argumentation, emphasizing its practical benefits. She explains that she uses the "syllogistic brief" to analyze arguments because "it brings into clear relief the actual structure of an argument, which the ordinary brief so often allows to be forgotten" (v). According to Buck, the purpose of learning such methods of analysis is that "nothing is more indispensable than this to a mastery of argumentation as a practical art" (vi). For Buck, the syllogism provides a way to think through and to illuminate the basic structure of an argument. In this way, it has practical application to the everyday problematic situations of life. In showing individuals how to analyze their own thought processes, they, in turn, can better understand the thought processes of others (Ricks 153). As discussed, Buck's approach was novel, because traditional theories of knowledge and ethics, such as Kantian ethics, typically were removed from everyday life, locating the object of knowledge in a transcendent realm of fixed absolutes. Logic tended to be formal and abstract, rather than informal and practical.

For Buck, finding a "train of reasoning" that will lead another person to a given conclusion basically means "looking into one's own mind and noting the series of ideas which there have actually established the conclusion for one's self" (4–5). A student can "feel assured" that the "train of reasoning" will lead to the same conclusion in another's mind "simply because in his own it has already done so" (5). According to Buck, this is not an unreasonable assumption given "that the mental processes of all normal people follow the same general laws" (5). For Buck, logic is "knowledge of those typical activities of mind common to all thinking people" (5). Here again, Buck emphasizes freedom of thought, rather than reliance on abstract rules or tradition. Her approach to argumentation was aimed at preparing women who were capable of critically evaluating their own thought processes, women unaccepting of blind obedience to authority, and, most important, women suited to democracy.

Critical Reasoning, Egalitarian Behavior, and Sympathy

In addition to Buck's three major tenets, her definition of argumentation reflects her feminist ethics. Buck's definition underscores her emphasis on the audience and its active thought process and critical reasoning ability. She also stresses that argument itself must be a cooperative, egalitarian activity. Buck defines argumentation as the "act of establishing in the mind of another person a conclusion which has become fixed in your own, by means of setting up in the other person's mind the train of thought or reasoning which has perviously [sic] led you to this conclusion" (3). Since Buck believes certain mental processes are universal, she encourages students to examine the chain of reasoning in their own minds to understand how it will lead the audience to a similar conclusion. As Vickie Ricks points out, the argument "'acts as a guide,' setting up a line of reasoning in someone else's mind, not merely a conclusion" (161).

In Buck's cooperative approach, knowledge was something people did together.[14] Argumentative knowledge must engage the mind of the speaker and the hearer in a reasoning process in which both identify with each other's thought processes. For Buck, argumentation was not something a speaker did to the passive mind of the hearer. Instead, it was a more egalitarian process involving a speaker and an active, thinking auditor. Underlying Buck's approach was her organic concept of society, which emphasized a reciprocal relationship between the social and the individual. This focus was evident in her view of the connection between induction and deduction. For Buck, personal observation and induction were formed in relation to deduction or the broader social context (Ricks 153). The interplay of the individual and the social was also evident in her use of the syllogistic brief. The substructure of the syllogism reflected the dynamic relationship between a writer's assertion and a premise shared by the audience. It reflected the fact that both contribute to the argumentative process.

The importance of the audience and its critical reasoning process is particularly evident in Buck's discussion of debate in Appendix C. According to Buck, the main difference between argumentation and debate is that debate involves three participants and argumentation two. Debate includes the speaker, the audience, "but also a representative of the resisting element in the mind of the audience—the speaker's opponent" (162). According to Buck, the opponent "embodies and expresses the opposition felt by the audience to the speaker's conclusion, as the speaker embodies and expresses its acquiescence. The two opposing debaters, then, represent each a distinct movement of the mind of the audience toward or away from a certain conclusion . . ." (162). Unlike a "simple argument," then, the speaker does not merely convince his or her opponent. The speaker ultimately must convince the audience. To do this, the speaker needs to bring to articulate and reasonable expression the "formless tendencies" in the audience's mind (163). As mentioned, Buck's notion of "formless tendencies" was based in contemporary psychology and reflected her belief that ideas develop from a whole through successive differentiations. In addition, the speaker not only must deal with the direct objections of the opponent but also must detect all the potential objections of the audience. Debating for Buck is equivalent to "an explicit presentation on each side of the implicit movement of the mind of the audience toward or away from a certain conclusion . . ." (164). Thus, according to Buck, successful debating depends on the "clearness with which each speaker divines the unspoken reasonings of the audience" and on the "force with which these [the audience's] reasonings are presented" (164). In debating, then, as opposed to argument, debaters embody opposing positions in the mind of the audience. Debaters uncover the "formless tendencies," the yet unrecognized arguments in the audience's mind, and they express them as fully formed reasons and conclusions (Ricks 160). Buck's focus on audience encouraged speakers to have a broader social consciousness. In debate, speakers must respond to the larger needs of the audience, not just their fellow debaters. Buck's approach to debate, with its emphasis on audience and broader social responsibility, thus differed significantly from the agonistic, individualistic approach that scholars have emphasized.

Besides her focus on audience, Buck's egalitarian emphasis is particularly evident in her article "The Present Status of Rhetorical Theory" (1900), which was discussed in chapter 2. Buck synthesizes two competing rhetorical methods to reconstruct a new democratic theory of rhetoric aimed at promoting equality and cooperation. She justifies the synthesis by arguing that all "true" social functions are egalitarian in action, "leveling conditions" between the speaker and hearer. Hence, the goal is not the persuasion or coercion of the hearer to the speaker's position. The hearer must first reenact the "train of reasoning" of the speaker and then make his or her own decision on the matter in question.

Buck's more cooperative, transactional idea of argumentation is also evident in her view of how people think through arguments. According to Buck, in complex arguments a sympathetic imagination may be required. Sometimes an individual may refuse to accept "the train of reasoning" of the other person. In this instance, the individual "must put himself imaginatively in the place of the person he addresses, and then come, by any way he logically can, to the conclusions he desires to establish" (7). For Buck, sympathy, or the ability to put oneself in the place of another and consider alternate perspectives, is key to resolving difficult situations. Furthermore by using imagination, an individual can experimentally test out different possible options before applying them in the real world.

In the appendix of her textbook on argumentation, Buck contends that the "bibliography of argumentation is as yet meager" (204). Contemporary rhetoricians who were first to publish in argumentation, like George Pierce Baker and E. J. MacEwan, disagree over the significance of logic to argumentation. In addition, the standard traditional sources tend to emphasize persuasion, and modern rhetoricians have continued this emphasis. Buck argues that much of Aristotle's and Quintilian's work in rhetoric was "devoted to 'persuasion,' in which argumentation was regarded as a factor of varying importance" (204). She adds that George Campbell and Richard Whately had a similar emphasis and that contemporary rhetoricians have devoted "scant space, or none at all, to argumentation, and those who consider it have thrown little light upon its problems" (204). [15]

In her textbook, Buck revised previous treatments of argumentation by her male counterparts, from the time of Aristotle through the late nineteenth century. Instead of viewing argumentation in terms of persuasion, which she viewed as coercion of the hearer to the speaker's side, Buck redefined argumentation as an interactive reasoning process aimed at building democratic relationships. She did this by approaching argumentation inductively from practice instead of the dominant approach, which stressed memorizing formal rules and principles. In so doing, she redefined logic as "the explicit formulation of the typical modes of thought" (204). By emphasizing the psychological basis of logic, Buck offered fresh insight into the part that logic plays in argumentation.

Buck's argument that rhetoric has been associated with persuasion anticipates criticism of traditional rhetoric by contemporary feminists. In a 1979 article, for example, Sally Miller Gearhart connects rhetoric with persuasion and contends that "any intent to persuade is an act of violence" (195). Gearhart views persuasion as unethical because it is based on a "conquest/conversion model" (195), which is associated with invasion, violence, and "the conquest of the victim" (196). However, Gearhart notes that contemporary communication theory is moving toward more transactional approaches and suggests that communication be viewed "as a *matrix*, a womb" (199, emphasis in original). A matrix would create "an atmosphere in which meanings are generated and nurtured" (200). Like feminism, it would also foster "new forms of relationship which allow for wholeness in the individual and differences among people and entities" (200). Gearhart's interconnected matrix is strikingly similar to Buck's organic perspective. Both models are based on a transactional epistemology, and both emphasize the new types of relationships that could be developed through a more equitable communicative process.

In 1991, Catherine E. Lamb contends that most individuals have been taught and most scholars write "monologic argument," which emphasizes persuasion and antagonism. Lamb advocates mediation and negotiation as an alternative to "the self-assertiveness of monologic argument" (287). In her essay, Lamb argues that feminist approaches to writing have tended to emphasize "the writer's ability to find her own voice through open-ended, exploratory, often autobiographical, writing in which she assumes a sympathetic audience" (281). Lamb's goal is to broaden the scope of feminist composition to include argumentation. Rather than beginning with particular genres, which can be limiting, Lamb asserts that individuals need to examine the variety of power relations available to writers and their readers. Then they can determine "which are consistent with the emphasis on cooperation, collaboration, shared leadership, and integration of the cognitive and affective which is characteristic of feminist pedagogy" (281). Lamb also intentionally avoids associating monologic argument with classical rhetoric, emphasizing scholarship that challenges the assumption that its goal is persuasion. Although Buck does associate classical rhetoric with persuasion, she, like Lamb, sees the need to provide a feminist alternative to monologic approaches to argument.

Buck's revisioning of logic and argumentation, though, seems to be something that other scholars have not fully appreciated. For instance, Gregory Clark and S. Michael Halloran contend that Buck's argumentation textbook "made no mention at all of persuasion, treating argument as applied logic, pure and simple" (22). Part of the reason Buck may not have mentioned persuasion was because she believed that argumentation had traditionally focused on persuasion in the negative sense. She was specifically working against the older, agonistic tradition. By defining logic in terms of common mental processes, Buck revitalized the role of logic in argumentation. She encouraged students to become more aware of their own mental processes, so that they could better understand the thought processes of others. Argumentation, then, is not a coercive activity but a cooperative reasoning process.

Although Buck may seem to be reacting against the rhetorical tradition, in the preface of her book she emphasizes that she is instead bringing out something from within the tradition. She explains that her book was developed out of "certain beliefs concerning the study of argumentation which, tho perhaps not wholly novel, have as yet found no recognition in the literature of the subject" (iii). In *A Course in Argumentative Writing,* it is evident that Buck was introducing a more democratic approach to argumentation. By doing so, Buck also encouraged Vassar women to challenge received opinion, to deal with issues of personal interest, and to critically evaluate their own thought processes. Since Buck viewed language as moral action, she was also encouraging them to act in a way that promoted equality and cooperation.

Buck's view of argumentation and its important social influence seems to have been an idea her students supported. For instance, a student editorial entitled "College Debating" in the 1907 *Vassar Miscellany* argues that intersociety debating is healthy because "both societies have the common function of drawing together all the members of the college" (106). The article continues, underscoring the importance of cooperation:

> So it happens that our debating societies connect rather than break up our
> college organization. And now why is this last function of debate work so
> important to the college? It is simply because union means cooperation

and it is only through cooperation that we can accomplish the highest social good. So let us give more of our energy to debating, not only that we may obtain perfection in that line, but that we may encourage a spirit of enthusiastic cooperation throughout the college. (106)

Another student editorial entitled "Socialized Speech" in the 1909 *Vassar Miscellany* argues that "[w]e need to realize that our habits of speech are powerful forces in the furthering or retarding of that community of understanding to which we look as the necessary basis of all social progress" (335). The goal is to benefit the broader community. The article's conclusion echoes Buck's words:

> The way to socialize our speech, to precisely adapt it to the listener while completely expressing ourselves, lies neither in oversensitiveness to others' opinion, nor in overconsciousness of our own, but in the concentration on the idea itself. If we think our own thoughts through, we shall see them in all their relations to the thoughts of others, in all their possibilities of intimate, convincing expression. If we can learn,—and it lies within the power of every one of us, to say precisely what we see, we shall be on the way toward making our speech social, that is, *communication*. (335, emphasis in original)

Buck's social theory of discourse was not merely something she wrote about in her textbooks. Based on these student editorials, it seems to be a concept that Vassar women internalized and were applying in their own lives. So, though Buck's approach may not have been intentionally feminist, by promoting communal interests, equality, and freedom of thought, Buck's social theory of discourse did have feminist effects, particularly in terms of its influence on her students.[16]

Buck's interest in women's issues and social reform was not limited to her public activities but entered her classroom at Vassar. Educational materials provided by the National College Equal Suffrage League state that "[e]ducation in suffrage among the other undergraduates may be promoted through debates with student opponents of Woman Suffrage, suffrage plays and addresses by outside speakers." In Buck's classes, suffrage was debated by her students, based on the assignments in her textbooks. For instance, in *A Course in Argumentative Writing,* students are asked to write specific kinds of arguments leading to the following conclusions: "Women will be allowed to vote on all questions in all States" (125); "Freedom of thought is essential to intellectual growth" (150); "Every woman should be able to earn her own living"; and "Women who desire to do so should enter the profession of medicine" (151). Appendix E includes the following among a list of propositions for argument: "Women should receive the same salaries as men for the same work" (199); "Women's clubs are a positive influence for good upon the community" (200); "Bicycle-riding is physically beneficial to women" (200); "The short skirt will ultimately be adopted by women for all street wear" (201); and "The life of women in the nineteenth century is extremely complex" (201). In addition, students are asked to analyze arguments that include claims such as "Shakespeare has no heroes—he has only heroines" and then to consider that "[t]he catastrophe of every play is caused always by the folly or fault of a man; the redemption, if there be any, is by the wisdom of a woman . . ." (36–37). Although Buck's textbook also includes examples that place women in more traditional roles, many encourage Vassar students to consider women in a positive and powerful light and to envision themselves in ways that extend beyond the domestic sphere.

The progressive ideals of cooperation, freedom of thought, and equality were at the heart of Buck's approach to argumentation and her social theory of discourse. These democratic ideals were also central to the suffrage movement.[17] For Buck, suffrage was necessary because it was democratic; it promoted equality and individual freedom. By emphasizing these goals, Buck's textbook prepared Vassar women for a more vocal and public social role.

Buck's Method Compared to Her Contemporaries

This focus is significant when viewed in terms of other more widely used turn-of-the-century rhetoric and argumentation textbooks. For instance, in *The Foundations of Rhetoric* (1892), Adams Sherman Hill uses a few examples drawn from women authors, namely Elizabeth Barrett Browning, George Eliot, and Jane Austen.[18] However, Hill tends to use those authors, particularly Austen, to show examples of writing styles to avoid—all four of the selections drawn from Austen's work illustrate negative examples. For instance, Hill writes that one of the "sins against good use" is the practice "of making a plural pronoun represent a singular noun, a fault of which Miss Austen is frequently guilty" (139). Similarly, Hill contends that one example sentence taken from Austen's work "lacks unity in every respect and from every point of view. It fell from the lips of Miss Bates,—a character in Jane Austen's 'Emma,'—who is as slipshod in mind as she is tedious and confusing in speech" (281). As JoAnn Campbell points out, Hill also used men writers to show examples of writing styles to avoid, but his biting critique of women authors would be particularly discouraging to women students (*Toward* xxxiii).

One notable exception among the prominent male theorists of this period is *Composition-Rhetoric: Designed for Use in Secondary School* (1897) by Joseph V. Denney and Fred Newton Scott. In Appendix C of the book, "Materials for Analysis and Reproduction," Scott and Denney provide an extensive and impressive list of sources for teachers to draw upon. Many articles deal with current social issues, including those related to women. For instance, the "Essays, Speeches, Sketches" section includes articles titled "Coöperative Womanhood in the State," "Women Wage Earners," "Universal Suffrage in France," and "Trade Unions for Women." Appendix C provides a list of articles showing women in roles that extend beyond the traditional domestic sphere. Although Buck's textbook differs from some of the dominant male theorists of her time, she was not alone in providing students with examples of women in nontraditional roles.

Buck was also not the only individual attempting to design alternative approaches for women studying rhetoric during this period. Susan Kates, for instance, argues that Mary Augusta Jordan's *Correct Writing and Speaking* (1904) "makes a contribution to the history of a feminist rhetoric because of its critique of the dominant pedagogical ideals of the writing and speaking instruction of the period" ("Subversive Feminism" 501–2).[19] Kates shows how Jordan challenged typical views of the social meaning of language use by devoting significant attention to alternative conventions and forms of communication. According to Kates, Jordan's focus is significant when viewed in terms of the dominant theorists of the time. Kates asserts that unlike Jordan, theorists such as Adams Sherman Hill, Franklin Genung, and Barrett Wendell "never address the issue of language and identity and the barriers for rhetorical study posed by issues of difference such as race, class, or gender" ("Subversive Feminism" 502).

Although Buck was not alone in her efforts, she was one of only a few women writing college textbooks on argumentation during this period.[20] Her approach also seemed more feminist compared to other argumentation and rhetoric textbooks written by women at this time. While there probably are others, one book that I found is *An Introductory Course in Argumentation* (1906) by Frances M. Perry of Wellesley College. In her book, Perry critiques the dominant pedagogy of the time, as do Buck and Jordan. Like Buck, Perry advocates debate and discussion, because "[t]he most excellent drill in argument is afforded by general informal class-room [*sic*] discussions upon which all are fitted . . . , and upon which there will naturally be some diversity of opinion" (35–36).[21] Perry's approach to argument also works against more agonistic, persuasion-oriented models. As Perry explains, "Too often the young orator and debater takes as an example for emulation the demagogue, the man who plays upon the ignorance and weakness and prejudice of his hearers and relies upon his skills in doing so to make his point" (27). Instead, Perry suggests students look to models from "the philosophers, the scientists, the statesmen, men who assume on the part of their readers and hearers an intelligence equal to their own" (27). In addition, several examples in the book are drawn from social issues such as immigration, corporal punishment, prison reform, temperance-related reform, and labor unions. While Perry's approach is progressive and shares many similarities with Buck's, her text does not seem to include examples related to women's suffrage, nor does she include as many examples related specifically to women's issues.

In *English Composition for College Women* (1914), Elizabeth Moore, Dora Gilbert Tompkins, and Mildred MacLean do include a chapter that prepares women for more active public roles. More frequently, however, the book, written fifteen years after Buck's, seems to emphasize educating women for more traditional domestic roles. For instance, although the authors do not specifically address argumentation, they do include a section on "The Persuasive Address," or "a talk prepared with the purpose of inducing such action on the part of the auditors as seems desirable to the speaker" (94). In this section, the authors declare, "Women who wish to make the most of themselves should elect courses in mathematics and argumentation. No drill in exactness is wasted time,—the leaders among the women of to-morrow must be able to think straight" (96). This section also includes an essay titled "The Woman Question," and it offers the following topics among a list of "Suggested Subjects": "There should be a law prohibiting women from working more than eight hours a day in factories and shops," "There should be state laws fixing a minimum wage for women," and "The better class of women should be willing to accept the suffrage." However, several chapters of the book focus on more traditional roles. For instance, there are chapters titled "Story-Telling for Children," "The Diary Theme," and "Letter Writing." The chapter "The Demonstration or Illustrated Talk" includes the following essays: "Setting and Serving the Table," "Suggestions for Artistic Dress," and "Color in Home Decorations." Buck's textbook, with its focus on suffrage, argumentation, and democracy seems quite significant when examined in relation to other turn-of-the century rhetoric and argumentation textbooks.

A Handbook of Argumentation and Debating

In 1906, Buck and Kristine Mann coauthored *A Handbook of Argumentation and Debating*.[22] Similar to her 1899 textbook on argumentation, Buck's handbook includes topics on suffrage and issues related to women. For instance, Buck and Mann ask students to "write a three-minute speech to persuade: [w]omen who believe in suffrage, that the suffrage would not be a good thing for women" (12). As Kathryn M. Conway points out, such activities not only allowed the anti-suffrage student to develop persuasive arguments but also helped the pro-suffrage student to better understand potential counterarguments and ways she could refute them (216).

In addition, examples are drawn from social issues concerning various disadvantaged and oppressed groups (Ricks 209). Buck and Mann ask students to write arguments on "The education of the negro should be liberal rather than industrial" and "The education of the negro should be industrial rather than liberal," for example (6). To prepare their arguments, students are encouraged to consult, for instance, *Education of the Negro*, *The Negro Problem*, and *Solving the Race Problem* by Booker T. Washington and *The Training of Black Men* by W. E. B. Du Bois (7). Some of the examples in the handbook, though, are negative and could be seen as reinscribing racial stereotypes. For example, students are asked to group a list of assertions into a few main headings "for the exclusion of Chinese laborers from the United States" (14). The list includes some of the following assertions: "Because they gamble"; "Because they carry on a secret system of slavery"; "Because they are barbarous" (14). However, these and the other examples could also be viewed as encouraging students to focus on broader social issues and patterns of oppression within society. The reference lists in the handbook also suggest that Vassar women would need to research carefully their position on either side of the issue. As Ricks asserts, the social concerns debated by students

> were not merely idle topics . . . but included problems that Vassar students were becoming involved in: settlement houses for the poor, schools for minorities, living conditions for immigrants, working conditions for laborers, humane treatment for the sick and incorrigible, and of course, equity for blacks and women. All these issues . . . challenged Vassar women's values, life-styles, and traditional images. (209)

These were the same issues that were attracting the attention of progressive education groups, women's organizations, and others concerned with social justice and inequity during the Progressive Era (Ricks 209). By having students debate and research these topics, Buck pushed students to reconsider some of their long-held values and assumptions, to investigate various social concerns, and to gain an awareness of the issues facing various oppressed and underprivileged groups.

As mentioned, several topics in the handbook deal with a variety of issues relating to women, including working women's concerns, and employment and education for women. For instance, one topic includes "[w]rit[ing] a three-minute speech to persuade". . . [t]he members of a working girls' club to read the newspaper every day" (12). Another asks students to prepare a formal debate on the following subject: "Resolved, That rich women should not enter any occupation where they will compete with those who must be self-supporting" (27). The handbook also asks students to organize arguments relating to the segregation of the sexes during the first two years of college. In a note, the authors point out that a Chicago University alumnae committee drafted the arguments when the coeducation question was being debated by the faculty (14).

In addition, suffrage was debated in the interclass debate teams, which included the *T. & M. House of Commons* (*Tempus et Mores*) for students in odd-year classes and *Qui Vive* for students in even-year classes (Ellis 25). In fact, as Conway points out, suffrage was "distinguished as the only topic out of more than fifty debated more than once in a ten-year period at Vassar, demonstrating both Buck's influence and the students' sustained interest" (216). The debating societies, moreover, were extremely active organizations, despite the college's original official stance that "[o]ratory and debate are not feminine accomplishments; and there will be nothing in the college arrangements to encourage the practice of them" (qtd. in Ellis 25). According to Mary Yost, a student of Buck who taught argumentation and debate, Vassar College "was the pioneer in debating for women" ("Intercollegiate" 129).

Involvement in debate was keen despite the fact that debate was an extracurricular activity that required much time and preparation. Students had to research their topics, develop persuasive arguments and refute potential opposition positions, write their arguments so that they resembled a forensic brief, and practice the oral presentation of their arguments (Conway 216). In correspondence to her parents, Helen D. Lockwood writes of her intense preparation for an upcoming debate:[23] "Only two more weeks before debate but those two weeks are going to be mighty strenuous. But after that you won't have to read so much about how we had a debate this afternoon and yesterday, etc. But when one is spending all her energy on that there really isn't room for anything else to happen so I guess you will have to put up with it" (5 Mar. 1911, 1).

According to the article "The History of Debating," published in the *Vassar Miscellany* special fiftieth anniversary number in 1915, interest in debating at Vassar reached a "climax" from 1897 to 1899 (West 149). Those years coincided with the period when Buck, along with other instructors, taught argumentation as a required course and when she alone taught advanced argumentation as an elective course from 1897–98 to 1898–99. During this time, Buck also wrote *A Course in Argumentative Writing*, which was published in 1899.

Moreover, during this period subject hours in argumentation were significantly increased. In 1894, argumentation became a required subject. Scheduled for the sophomore year, it originally was a two-semester course, meeting one hour a week. From 1898 to 1903, only one semester of argumentation was required. However, the class met three hours per week instead of just one, so that the total hours were increased by 50 percent. In 1903, argumentation became an elective rather than a required subject (West 149).

The growing interest in debate may also be traced to the fact that an innovative class in argumentation was introduced in 1898–99. Buck gave her Advanced Argumentation and Oral Debate course in connection with an economics course entitled "The Relation of the State to Monopolies," which Herbert E. Mills, professor of economics at Vassar, taught. Buck describes the course in Appendix C of *A Course in Argumentative Writing*. She explains that students first meet for introductory lectures from Buck and Mills, and then the "students themselves take charge of the course" (168). In the introduction, Buck contends that the study of argumentation is enhanced by debating. This is true not only for the advanced course but also for the required course in argumentation. Buck explains that one of the three meetings per week is devoted to a formal or impromptu debate in which the entire class participates: "These debates are not only regarded by the students as the most interesting feature of the course, but they seem fully to have justified their institution by the impetus they have given to the written work" (vii). The fact that argumentation was a required course for nine years is also significant (1894–1903). Students who may not have taken the course as an elective were able to have their interest in debate stimulated. Similarly, other students whose talent for debate might have remained undiscovered were encouraged through the course in argumentation.

The growth of debate and acceptance of women speaking in public at Vassar directly parallels the period when women's suffrage was being debated nationally. This interest in debate was not limited to Vassar. Mount Holyoke, Wellesley, Bernard, Bryn Mawr, Radcliffe, and Smith all participated in intercollegiate debate, "often with suffrage as the topic" (Mastrangelo, "Learning from the Past" 54). On 26 April 1902, Vassar and Wellesley held the first women's intercollegiate debate. Vassar was expected to send some sixty students and thirty alumnae from Boston with the college's debating team ("Wellesley-Vassar Debate" 1). The debate did not finish until about 10:00 P.M., and the results were then phoned in to Vassar (letter from Margaret M. Shipp to her mother, 26 Apr. 1902, 1). In a letter to her friend Gige, Mabel Stanwood (Vassar class of 1904) describes the excitement at the college over the news that Vassar won the debate:

> Everybody was crazy. We were all howling and running around, and in
> about one second all the stairs and hall were jammed with girls in all
> sorts of undress costumes, and everybody yelling and jumping with all
> her might. We quieted down once Miss C. [Cornwell] came out with the
> official message from Caroline Sperry, the President of Students [*sic*].' It
> said "Vassar won. It was an even debate." You never saw such wild girls.

We had to get out somewhere, so we started for the front door, starting up
"The Rose and Gray," and singing it as I suppose I'll never hear it again.
(letter to Gige, undated, 1)

Another student, Margaret M. Shipp (Vassar class of 1905), writes her friend
Mamie of the song sung by "eight hundred girls tonight as we marched
round the campus waving torch lights, and accompanied by drums, flutes,
tinpans, combs, everything you can think of to make a noise with":

> Ain't got no time to tarry but—
> Hurrah! Hurrah!
> We've won the big debate!
> Hurrah! Hurrah!
> Come out and celebrate.
> Committee and debaters too
> We'll carry round in state!
> Now we're marching through Vassar!
>
> (28 Apr. 1902, 1)

From the student letters, it is easy to get a sense of the excitement and
importance of debate to the young women of Vassar. In addition, these
letters, as well as illustrations in the student yearbook, the *Vassarion,*
reveal the competitive nature of the debates. For example, drawings
related to debate show fighting cocks, boxing maidens, and jousting female knights. Thus, although Buck's approach to argument emphasized
equality and cooperation, it is difficult to tell how these principles played
out in actual practice.

The significance of debate is also evident in the fact that it is interwoven
into scenes in "Vassar Milestones: A Play," composed by Vassar alumnae
and staged by "the Dramatic Committee of the New York Branch of Vassar
Alumnae" ("Vassar Milestones" 249). The play was performed during the
fiftieth anniversary of the opening of the college. The scene featuring debate, "In the Nineties," is set in the room of Dorothy Fairley and Jeannette
Niles, and their mothers, Vassar graduates, are visiting. The mothers and
daughters are interrupted by "Oshima San, a Japanese girl . . . distressed
because after she has read all the books which the honorable professor
has assigned, she has become a socialist 'by true religion'—and she is to
marry a prince" ("Vassar Milestones" 253):

"Chuck him," says Dorothy. "Educate him," says Jeannette, and the girls break into a mock argument, Jeannette jumping upon a table and haranguing quotations from a recent debate, "Does the higher education unfit man for matrimony?" "We maintain that it does," shouts Dorothy, and goes on quickly, "Will knowledge of Greek help him to understand the furnace? Will differential calculus pay the butcher? Or will philosophy convince the butcher that he is better off unpaid? No. He and the butcher will both remain dissatisfied." The hilarious fun shocks Mrs. Niles, and the outburst subsides. ("Vassar Milestones" 253–54)

In this scene, the more typical debate question, "Does the higher education unfit woman for matrimony?" is turned on its head, and the practical benefits of formal education are challenged. Similar to other student parodies, the cleverness of this scene demonstrates the students' familiarity with debate and their ability to have fun with its conventions.

The play eventually turns to the "modern period," which is titled "The New Springtime," and is set outdoors. Jeannette Niles has married Dorothy Fairley's brother Tom, and they have a daughter, Jean, who is now attending Vassar. Dorothy Fairley, who became an instructor, is now a warden.

An anti-suffrage parade marches across the stage, bearing signs which read: "Woman's place is in the home!" A socialist band follows, with Jean Fairley, a senior, haranguing the crowd. They pass on, and Mrs. Fairley [Jeannette] and her mother, Mrs. Niles, arrive, having caught sight of Jean in the distance making a stump speech. Mrs. Fairley is shocked; she thinks the whole proceeding improper and unwomanly; but her mother is reminded that she herself had been shocked when she found Mrs. Fairley—in the nineties—wearing gymnasium bloomers and shouting from a table in mock argument. "Unwomanly," adds Mrs. Niles speculatively. "That is what they called me too." ("Vassar Milestones" 255–56)

Jeannette Fairley, though, is not happy with the changes to the college; she "believes in a certain amount of freedom, but certainly not in 'ranting on street corners about the vote,' or in 'this absurd effort to compete with men in their own fields'" ("Vassar Milestones" 256). However, her friend Dorothy Fairley "insists that it is good for Jean and others like her to go out and see what society is made of, and that the new age will be one of co-operation rather than of competition" ("Vassar Milestones" 256). Dorothy's words reflect the optimism of the period. These scenes also suggest that education in debate in the 1890s was a precursor to Vassar women speaking out on issues in the public arena in the early decades of the twentieth century. In addition, the scenes capture the seemingly contradictory reaction women of earlier generations had to these changes and the realization by some that they, too, are part of this tradition of women gaining and using rhetorical power.

In this examination of Buck's approach to argumentation and debate at Vassar, I have shown how just as women were gaining more of a public voice in the national arena, Buck and other women were teaching their students to use that voice in women's colleges. Through debating activities, Buck helped to prepare Vassar women for a more vocal pubic role, one that encouraged them to break away from domestic concerns and to focus on community activism.[24] By emphasizing the social and public nature of Buck's work, I provide a counterexample to claims that with the entrance of women into higher education, the teaching of rhetoric became feminized and personalized in the latter part of the nineteenth century.

In addition, I have demonstrated how Buck's assertion that argument has traditionally focused narrowly on persuasion anticipates efforts by contemporary feminists to revise traditional approaches to argument. In particular, similarities between Buck's work and the efforts of contemporary feminists are evident in terms of the values that both promoted. Based on a transactional epistemology, Buck's pedagogy underscored the democratic principles of cooperation, freedom of inquiry, and equality, values characteristic of contemporary feminist pedagogy. These values were apparent in her emphasis on cooperation rather than subordination in her approach to argumentation. This focus was evident in Buck's use of the syllogistic brief, which encouraged students to view argumentation as a communal activity. These values were also revealed in her stress on free inquiry or the inductive method of argumentation so that young women could learn to think for themselves rather than to simply accept the ideas of others. The student's individual intellectual growth then was viewed in terms of gaining a deeper understanding of the interrelated or communal nature of life. Finally, these values were evident in her emphasis on equality, in which Buck tried to encourage communication on an equal basis. Buck's approach to argumentation was also based on a premise of psychological equality. Buck rejected the idea that women should be relegated to "a separate, inferior intellectual sphere" (Ricks 163). Instead, Buck believed that all individuals follow the same cognitive processes. Thus, men and women do not argue differently if argument is understood as a thinking process.

These democratic ideals were also central to the suffrage movement. For Buck and Wylie suffrage was necessary because it was democratic—it promoted equality and individual freedom. Moreover, these democratic ideals became central as suffrage became inextricably connected to issues of equality and freedom that emerged during President Taylor's administration. By contextualizing Buck's approach to argumentation within the debates concerning suffrage at Vassar, I have demonstrated how Buck's ideas, in significant ways, represented an indirect response to the suffrage question at Vassar and in society as a whole. It is easy to understand why establishing a more democratic approach to discourse was so important to Buck. Since Buck viewed language as a social act, a more democratic discourse meant a more democratic society at every level of social existence—something Buck and other women at Vassar wanted and were struggling to achieve. Thus, although Buck's ideas reflect contemporary practices, in significant ways they also seem deeply interconnected with the issues she and other women faced during this period.

5

THE LITTLE THEATER MOVEMENT AND BUCK'S DEMOCRATIZED VIEW OF DRAMA

The movement [Poughkeepsie Community Theatre] is experimental in character and differs from any other community theatre now in existence. It seems, however, to be adapted to the needs of Poughkeepsie and has already received enthusiastic support from all classes of towns-people. The possibilities of a really democratic participation in this movement and of genuine artistic achievement seem almost limitless.
—Laura Johnson Wylie, "Report of the Department of English," 1919–20

During the fiftieth anniversary of the opening of Vassar College in 1915, Vassar presented the *Pageant of Athena,* which "represented the weaving of a web of noble women by the maidens of Athena; each scene depicting an incident from the life of some typically great woman, and covering the period from the early days of Greece to the 16th century" ("Christening of the Outdoor Theater" 1). Women honored in the performance included Sappho, Hortensia, the Abbess Hilda of Whitby, Marie de France, Isabella d'Este, Lady Jane Grey, and Elena Lucrezia Cornaro (Rourke, *Fiftieth Anniversary* 223–46). The pageant involved a cast of more than four hundred Vassar students and was directed by Hazel MacKaye, a pageant maker who knew the political and propagandistic potential of theater (K. Taylor 4; Blair 139). MacKaye created several all-women's pageants, which served as persuasive tools in promoting suffrage and equal rights for women.[1]

The year that the *Pageant of Athena* was presented, Gertrude Buck became involved in the Little Theater movement through her participation in George Pierce Baker's innovative "47 Workshop" at Radcliffe College. The Little Theater movement eventually succeeded pageantry; however, from 1905 to 1925, the pageant, "a large and spectacular outdoor civic rite," was extremely popular, particularly among women (Blair 118, 143). Middle-class women's organizations endorsed pageantry because it supported their civic goals. Pageantry provided beneficial recreation, education, and aesthetic appreciation, while demonstrating "America's special democratic effort to involve all citizens in all its work" (Blair 121). However, as Karen J. Blair explains, "The massive effort required to produce pageants was simply too taxing to be sustained," and the Little Theater movement became its successor (143). The Little Theater movement provided a more manageable and less costly form of drama than pageantry, but it still achieved some of the same "recreative, moral, and cooperative goals as pageantry" (Blair 143).

Buck participated actively in the Little Theater movement in the early decades of the twentieth century and was one of Baker's first women students.[2] She not only pioneered the introduction of the new drama curriculum in women's colleges but also helped to organize the Poughkeepsie Community Theatre, creating an egalitarian connection between the town and the college. In significant ways, Buck's participation in this movement represented her attempt to improve understanding and relations between these two groups. Beyond healing divisions within her community, Buck's workshop had broader social significance. Buck's drama courses provided a space for her female students to explore themes that challenged traditional gender roles, to write and receive feedback from an all-female audience, and to work collaboratively and develop as writers. In *A Group of Their Own: College Writing Courses and American Women Writers, 1880–1940*, Katherine H. Adams asserts that through workshops like Buck's, college writing courses, literary magazines, college newspapers, and collaborative groups made possible through their college experience, "many women writers found their own voices and began to find their own futures" (97). One such woman was Edna St. Vincent Millay, among the first students of Buck's dramatic workshop courses. Ultimately, as Adams argues, the first generations of college-educated women used their collaborative groups to transform writing itself.

Buck joined many other women who participated in the Little Theater movement. The Progressive Era's climate of reform was also felt in the arts; and similar to several other reform efforts during this period, middle-class women played a central role. As Blair emphasizes, "From the start, women were the mainstay of the movement in every capacity from audience member to player, donor to seamstress, director to founder" (145). Women ran playhouses across the nation, and women's organizations were extremely active in supporting the Little Theater movement (Blair 145). In addition, according to Baker, who taught playwriting classes at Harvard and Radcliffe, the "most promising writers were women" (Kinne 154).[3] In fact, Baker's 47 Workshop was created through his efforts and through the planning and support of his former female graduates from Radcliffe and other women who raised five hundred dollars to start the workshop (Kinne 154–58; Fawson 15). In many ways, the Little Theater movement can be viewed as directly related to the new opportunities and freedoms for middle-class women and their participation in a variety of social reform efforts during the Progressive Era. The movement provided an acceptable outlet for many women to expand their sphere of influence and use drama to promote social reform.

Although middle-class women were the driving force behind the movement, virtually all facets of society were caught by the enthusiasm to create plays: "Young working people in Manhattan spent their two-week vacations at Catskill Mountain resorts, striving to replicate Broadway hits. Immigrants in settlement houses, workers in labor colleges, children on playgrounds, students from primary grades to university-level, all joined amateur bands of thespians" (Blair 143). The diversity of the movement is evident from the different theaters it created. Like Buck, many theater directors sought to transcend social and economic barriers by offering the public the latest in modern drama with little or no admission fee (Mackay 54).

The Little Theater Movement

Buck's involvement in the Little Theater movement was closely connected to her feminist ethics. To understand this connection, it is necessary to know more about how the Little Theater developed. The movement grew in opposition to the commercial theater, which primarily featured melodramas, romances, and musicals but seldom addressed the significant social and political issues facing industrial America (Heller and Rudnick 5). In the United States, the Little Theater movement went by various names—the Community Theater, the Community Players, and the Civic Theater. Middle-class women were active in the amateur theater movement because it fostered the democratic values that they supported (Blair 146). These ideals are evident in the words of Percy MacKaye, the older brother of Hazel MacKaye and an originator of the U.S. pageantry movement (Blair 136). MacKaye argues that the civic theatre "implies the conscious awakening of a people to self-government in the activities of its leisure" (15). For MacKaye, the little theater is the drama of democracy, emphasizing participation and self-expression:

> To this end, organization of the arts of the theatre, participation by the people in these arts (not mere spectatorship), a new resulting technique, leadership by means of a permanent staff of artists (not of merchants in art), elimination of private profit by endowment and public support, dedication in service to the whole community; these are chief among its essentials, and these imply a new and nobler scope for the art of the theatre itself.
>
> Involving, then, a new expression of democracy, the civic theatre—in the meaning here used—has never existed in the past, and has not been established in the present. (15)

Moreover, for MacKaye, the theatre is a vehicle for social transformation. MacKaye contends that the aim of traditional commercial theaters is to *"copy rather than counteract the civilization of the day"* (135, emphasis in original). But the new noncommercial Civic Theatre is not merely a mirror; it has another purpose: "[T]he theatre should guide the drama's reflection by a definite ethical policy calculated steadily to improve the impressionable souls of men who gaze in the mirror" (136). For critics like MacKaye, the theater was transformative—its aim was to better industrial society by making it more democratic.

Two well-known settlement house workers who utilized the reform potential of theater were Jane Addams and Ellen Gates Starr of Hull House, important pioneers in the Little Theater movement. The first settlement theater in the nation, Hull House Theatre, had a sociological emphasis. Many of the plays produced by the theater dealt with problems associated with adjusting to modern industrial life (Mackay 115). Hull House's Dramatic Section presented its first production in 1893, opened its own theater in 1899, and hired its first director, Laura Dainty

Pelham, in 1900 (Henderson 235). The acting was done by a troupe of amateurs, and the plays were priced at a quarter of the commercial rates (MacGowan 47). In significant ways, their theater challenged social and economic distinctions.

The workers' theater movement also understood the transformative potential of drama. One significant offshoot of this movement was the labor drama produced at the Bryn Mawr Summer School for Women Workers. Karyn L. Hollis contends that "of all the summer school's literacy practices, labor drama was likely the most transformative, by enabling the women to grow intellectually, politically, and aesthetically" ("Plays of Heteroglossia" 152).[4] As noted, the school had important connections to the Vassar English Department. Wylie, who worked with Buck to establish the Poughkeepsie Community Theatre, taught at the Bryn Mawr Summer School from 1924 to 1926 (Smith 295). Helen Drusilla Lockwood, a student of Buck and Wylie's who was keenly interested in workers and labor history, was connected to the Bryn Mawr School and its successors for some forty years. In addition, as Hollis points out, "the 'living newspaper,' or dramatized news story," popular in workers' theaters, was often produced at the Bryn Mawr School ("Plays of Heteroglossia" 155). The living newspaper was popularized in America by the Federal Theater Project, which was headed by Hallie Flanagan (Hollis, "Plays of Heteroglossia" 155). Also a student of Baker's and an innovator in theater, Flanagan was Buck's successor in drama production at Vassar.[5]

A view of knowledge as a communal activity that is tested through application was central to many drama and Little Theater efforts during the early decades of the twentieth century. Perhaps due to the growth of experimental psychology and the faith in science, laboratories became the place where new truths could be tested. They also became a new intellectual tool of universities. In a laboratory, knowledge is seen not as fixed or absolute but as a working hypothesis, something incomplete until tested and criticized through application. According to Katherine Camp Mayhew and Anna Camp Edwards, authors of *The Dewey School: The Laboratory School of the University of Chicago 1896–1903*, this view of knowledge was central to the laboratory school. Quoting Dewey and his summary of the original plan for the school, Mayhew and Edwards explain that knowledge represents a collective effort; members of a research team are familiar with past efforts but not "enslaved" by them and "are possessed of the best skills that have been worked out by the coöperative efforts of human beings" (7). The laboratory method assumes that participants are responsible and equally involved in the investigatory process. As noted, Buck's view of invention in argumentation was based on a similar approach. For Buck, the laboratory or experimental research method had broad application and was intertwined with the future of democracy.

An important practitioner of such an approach was Buck's teacher, Baker, who used a dramatic "laboratory" to teach students practical techniques in playwriting, acting, and stage design. A teacher of rhetoric who later switched to theater, Baker was an early catalyst in establishing theater arts in formal education (Fawson 1).[6] As mentioned, it was the planning and support of his former female graduates from Radcliffe that enabled Baker to start his workshop. In addition, in developing his courses, Baker usually tried them out first on the Radcliffe women, where classes were smaller. Baker started English 47, his course in playwriting, in 1904; however, it wasn't until the spring of 1906 that the course was available to the Harvard men. English 47A, his advanced course in playwriting, was given first in 1910–11 at Radcliffe and in 1915–16 at Harvard. The production side of these writing courses, the 47 Workshop, was established in 1912, with both men and women working collaboratively ("George Pierce Baker" 10). The purpose of the workshop was to test or "try out" plays written by students in English 47 through production of the plays (Dickinson 107). It was also a practical laboratory where students could gain knowledge of all facets of the theater (Fawson 17).

A significant aspect of the 47 Workshop was its emphasis on audience cooperation (Dickinson 108–9). According to Baker, "What is needed to round the play into final shape is just what the author it [sic] unable to get,—an opportunity to see the play adequately acted before an audience that is sympathetic yet genuinely critical" ("English 47 Workshop"). Baker conducted the dramatic process like a large-scale writer's workshop. Each of the four hundred audience members was selected and approved by a committee. Although no admission or fees were charged, each audience member was expected to send in his or her opinion of the entire production within a week of the performance. If an audience member failed to send in a critique, he or she was not asked to return the next season. The critiques were first read by Baker, the names were removed, and then they were given to the playwright, the student director, and the theater group.

After reviewing the critiques, the playwright consulted with the director about potential revisions. For Baker, the audience was an integral part of the production process (Dickinson 108–9; Fawson 17–18).

In reviewing the Little Theater movement, it is evident that, like other reform movements of the period, middle-class women played a significant role. In addition, a central aspect of the movement was an ethics, which seemed closely connected to Buck's feminist ethics. Aimed at breaking down traditional hierarchies, this ethics was based on viewing knowledge as a communal rather than an exclusionary construction. In practical terms, this meant that the theater was no longer under the control of the theater manager and dependent upon commercial success. In theaters modeled after Baker's workshop, the audience now helped to shape the productions. Most importantly, many of the theaters emphasized drama as a tool for social justice, a way of dealing with problematic issues associated with modern industrial life.

Buck, the Little Theater Movement, and the Vassar Context

As mentioned, Buck became involved in the Little Theater movement through her participation in Baker's workshop. She took a year's leave to study with him during the 1915–16 school year and started a similar workshop the following year at Vassar College. In 1920, Buck helped to organize the Poughkeepsie Community Theatre, uniting the "town and gown," or the people of Poughkeepsie and the college, in a cooperative artistic activity. Throughout much of her teaching career at Vassar, she worked to improve mutual understanding between the two groups. In many ways, Buck's participation in the Little Theater movement can be viewed as her response to the split between the "town and gown."

This split seems to have been an issue that not only Buck but also the broader college community was struggling to resolve. This conflict was particularly evident in after-dinner speeches given in October 1915 during the fiftieth anniversary celebration of the opening of Vassar.[7] Participants in the after-dinner event included representatives from various colleges including Wellesley, Yale, Cornell, and Bryn Mawr. Vassar alumnae, including Elisabeth Woodbridge Morris, who coauthored two textbooks with Buck, also were among the speakers at the dinner. According to reports, the topic for the speeches was "The College and the Community," with speakers sharply disagreeing over the nature of this relationship.

Some speakers underscored the importance of establishing relations between town and gown to promote democracy. For instance, Edward Bliss Reed, professor of English at Yale University, argues, "Town and gown must of course be united. America is the greatest experiment in the world to-day [*sic*]; and that experiment is not concluded. Our democracy is on trial; our very education is on trial, and we must prove its worth" (Rourke, *Fiftieth Anniversary* 270). Others, like Lucy Madeira, Vassar class of 1896 and principal of her own school, contend that college "should be the place set apart where learning is conserved . . . the place to which the community looks for guidance in things intellectual, the flame within the shrine to which the pilgrim returns" (282). Speakers like Madeira believed that a closer relationship could harm the academic community's intellectual pursuits.

Besides controversy surrounding the town and gown relations, the role of women in solving such dilemmas was of key interest at Vassar in the early decades of the twentieth century. In her speech, Dr. Mary Sherwood, Vassar class of 1883, argues that "we are now living in an era which will accord her [women] full rights as a citizen" (280). According to Sherwood, "With the increase of recognition has come an increase in responsibility; she must now take her active place in the community" (280). This emphasis on women needing a "'social mind'" and "accept[ing] their share of civic responsibility" similarly was urged by Alice Barrows Fernandez, Vassar class of 1900 (280). In order to gain more rights, women felt compelled to take a more active role in civic life. An emphasis on broader social responsibility in general and the need for women to participate more actively in social concerns more specifically also were apparent in other presentations at the anniversary celebration.

Although not listed among the speakers, Buck, like several of the presenters, believed there should be more interaction between the college and community to promote the socialization of learning and the elimination of class divisions. Buck's emphasis on furthering democracy by improving relations between the town and gown can be seen in two of her articles, "College Commencements To-Day and To-Morrow" (1915) and "The Commencement Opportunity" (1918).[8] Buck argues that typical commencement exercises are nonrepresentative, usually "presenting Jim or Susie upon the platform in the rôle of orator or essayist" ("College Commencements" 735). If the college did not invite a student speaker, it often featured a visiting speaker, who typically gave a presentation on a topic unrelated to the college or the audience. However, Buck contends that colleges and universities should view commencement as a chance to promote cooperative relations between the college and the community. Buck declares, "If education is to be democratized, public interest in it must assuredly be increased" ("Commencement Opportunity" 496). Buck argues that commencement provides the ideal opportunity because audience members already have "some interest" in the college ("Commencement Opportunity" 495). She adds that "since interest proverbially grows by what it feeds on, each college has only to satisfy this interest wherever and whenever it appears, to insure its increase . . . until new channels of information about this college and others are imperatively demanded" ("Commencement Opportunity" 496).

Of the commencement programs Buck collected and reviewed, she points out that "only five of the sixty institutions on our list attempt to give on commencement day any account of themselves to the public" ("College Commencements" 739). However, Buck argues that such an approach strengthens connections between colleges and the public by reemphasizing the college's accountability to the public. For Buck, the college is not an isolated entity but a broader social institution. The type of relation that exists between the college and the community enhances this social connection.

To foster public accountability, Buck advocates that colleges and universities use commencement to discuss such subjects as "[a]n annual authoritative statement of what the college has accomplished in various directions since the last report, of the problems which it is engaged in solving, of its plans for the immediate future . . ." ("College Commencements" 740). Commencement represents a significant opportunity for institutions to build relationships between the college and the community, thus furthering democracy: "The opportunity is, soberly speaking, immeasurable; and the colleges that take advantage of it are hastening not only for themselves but for us all that cooperation in thought and action between town and gown which alone can socialize education and educate society" ("College Commencements" 740). Buck concludes by emphasizing that some institutions already have moved from "the individual conception of commencement" to "the communal conception" (743). Her aim was to prevent colleges from acting in isolation, to make them aware of their broader social obligation, and, most significantly, to create "a more intelligent and effective cooperation" (743).

Buck's Social View of Literature

During the time Buck was calling for colleges to have a broader sense of social responsibility, she was developing her social view of literature. In 1916, she published *The Social Criticism of Literature*, which provides a theoretical framework for her approach to literature, including dramatic literature. Buck then applied her theory in the dramatic workshop courses she taught at Vassar. Traditionally, nineteenth-century critics had allowed "conventional morality and supposedly timeless standards [to] determine their judgments" (Rubin 11). In contrast, Buck argues against an elitist view of literature and instead supports her social approach, which she contends provides the critic with a "vitalized, democratic conception of literature" (*Social Criticism* 31). From this perspective, reading involves a transfer of the poet's "intensified consciousness" to the reader. Where this transfer occurs, "society is at that point leveled up to the poet," and the poet's "gain in perception or emotion has been socialized" (39). For Buck, a social view of literature symbolizes the progressive, democratic evolution of society. It emphasizes the principles of cooperation, equality, and freedom of thought. As JoAnn Campbell notes, Buck's text "may be the earliest treatise in the tradition of reader-response criticism, preceding Louise Rosenblatt's *Literature as Exploration* by twenty-two years" (*Toward* 56).

Buck specifically connects her social view of literature to her work in drama when she redefines the critic's role. Rather than enforcing his/her readings of the text on readers, the critic "shall then hold them as essentially tentative and personal, not only refusing steadfastly to impose them upon other readers, but giving no sanction to their use by any reader as a substitute for his own critical activity" (*Social Criticism* 51). From Buck's democratic perspective, the ability of individuals to develop their own critical reading and thinking skills rather than to rely on the authority of the critic is imperative. The social value of literature "depends primarily not on what is read, but on how it is read" (56). The primary characteristic of reading then "is found in no mere perfunctory turning of leaves, but in active participation, however limited it may be, in the experience which the writer would communicate" (20). Therefore, the main purpose of the critic is to promote in each individual this reading experience, which Buck calls "genuine reading" (52). In addition, the critic can help to make the reader "more acutely conscious of the defects in his own reading and of the means of remedying these defects, by presenting before him in the concrete form of critical essays a full, rich, personal experience with literature" (52). The presentation of such information "should serve to stimulate and clarify his reactions to literature, should help to make him a better reader" (53). If the critic is successful, "he makes literature count for more in the lives of individuals, hence for more in the social order" (54). In other words, the critic promotes the broader social value of literature.

According to Buck, the critic is not the only one who can promote a social view of literature and progress:

> This activity may be carried on in an English classroom or on a lecture-platform; its results may be published in a popular magazine or in a learned review; it may take the form of club-work at a social settlement or of a dramatic experiment such as Professor George P. Baker's "Workshop"; . . . but in all these and in many other guises, it seeks always the same end, namely, to further the activity of literature as an agent of social progress. (60)

In creating the Vassar Dramatic Workshop and Poughkeepsie Community Theatre, Buck herself would choose a role similar to Baker's. Ultimately, Buck's efforts in drama would allow her to promote a rhetorical view of literature, one that envisioned "literature as an agent of social progress."

In the preface of her book, Buck acknowledges her gratitude to Fred Newton Scott, Dewey, Wylie, and her Literary Criticism students. Buck writes that Scott's courses "more than twenty years ago, explicitly recognized the social significance of literature . . ." (vi). She asserts that Dewey's "philosophy of society has directed all of my thinking about literature" (iv). Buck's ideas reflected the Progressive Era belief that the goal of education is to further democracy. However, instead of education being the vehicle, literature is used to achieve these ideals (Rubin 12–13). As Buck emphasizes, literature has transformative potential because it "is not alone a creature but also a creator of the society it serves" (60).

Buck also acknowledges the influence of Wylie, "under whose leadership every course in English at Vassar College is animated by the social conception of literature" (iv). The same year that Buck published her book, Wylie published *Social Studies in English Literature* (1916), which explores literature from a social perspective.[9] Wylie applied this approach in her teaching at Vassar. For instance, Constance Rourke recalls how in Wylie's class, students "were struggling with a revolutionary idea—that poetry itself might be revolutionary. We were trying to discover what we had never supposed existed—social forces beneath rhyme and rhythm and metaphor" ("Vassar Classrooms" 72). Rourke later adds that what she learned from Wylie was "a method, the beginnings of a habit of critical synthesis" and "a greatly heightened sense of social values in literature" ("Vassar Classrooms" 74). Buck also thanks her Literary Criticism students, "who for many years, attacking its problems with me, have stimulated and clarified my understanding of them" (iv). Similar to her other textbooks, Buck's book grew out of her classroom efforts. Buck and Wylie's social view of literature was central to how the English Department approached the teaching of literature.

From this analysis of Buck's book, it is evident that in her English courses and in her dramatic workshop classes, she applied her social and rhetorical view of literature. In turning her efforts to the Poughkeepsie Community Theatre, Buck broadened her emphasis on "literature as an agent of social progress" by moving beyond her elite students at Vassar to the people of Poughkeepsie (60).

Buck's Involvement in Drama

The Social Criticism of Literature was published while Buck was on leave (her first in eighteen years) to study drama under Baker (letter to Baker, 8 Feb. 1915, 1). After returning to Vassar, she applied what she had learned from Baker and started a similar dramatic workshop in 1916. Just four years later, Buck helped to organize the Poughkeepsie Community Theatre, uniting the town and gown in a cooperative artistic activity. During the final years of her life, Buck seemed particularly concerned with critical intervention and practical action in her world. She actively sought to break down the scholastic, ivory-tower view of the academic world. By eliminating social and economic barriers, Buck's work in drama allowed her to achieve her goals.

In a memorial meeting a year after Buck's death, Baker described how she came to study with him, saying it was "very characteristic, as I grew to know her" ("Address by Professor" 10). Buck wrote Baker asking if she could observe his classes because she planned to offer similar courses at Vassar. Baker explained that he had to answer her request with his typical response, "that the work was intended only for people who are so mad that they think they want to be professional playwrights, and that I am obliged to exclude all other persons" ("Address by Professor" 10). Baker reiterated Buck's reply and his response:

> She then wrote, "I notice in the pamphlet you have sent me that if one submits a play that is satisfactory, one is admitted to the course. Is there any reason why, if I submit a satisfactory one-act play, I shouldn't be admitted?" Of course there was only one answer to that, and thereupon she presented an entirely satisfactory play, and became a regular member of the class. ("Address by Professor" 10–11)

This story reflects the determination and creativity Buck brought to her effort to become a member of Baker's class. After joining, Buck continued to impress Baker. He pointed out that it can be difficult for a veteran teacher like Buck to return to being a student, particularly since she was so much older and more experienced than her fellow students: "She did it with such admirable poise that you never would have suspected for a moment that she had behind her all those years of extremely successful teaching. She simply was there to learn; she was there to learn as the others were to learn. She spared herself nothing in the regular work" ("Address by Professor" 11).

After completing her training with Baker and returning to Vassar, Buck rapidly and successfully developed a similar workshop. During her first year back, Buck created the Vassar Dramatic Workshop and courses in dramatic production. In December 1916, the Vassar Dramatic Workshop presented its first production, a Christmas play written by two of its members ("Try Out Vassar's Plays"). Produced, staged, and acted entirely by women in the workshop, the play was adapted from *A Christmas Guest* by Selma Lagerlöf, the first woman to receive the Nobel Prize for literature (1909) and a supporter of women's suffrage (Campbell, *Toward* 187; Mral 168). Buck gleefully wrote Baker about her workshop's premier production (letter to Baker, 27 Dec. 1916):

> It seemed to me very successful in point of writing, and the audience was certainly spellbound throughout the performance. . . . Members of the class did literally everything that was done, before and behind the scenes— even

to the violin playing by Liljekrona himself off-stage! This last was, of course, merely a happy accident—Miss Thorpe being capable of playing <both> Liljekrona and the violin—but we plumed ourselves upon it as if it had been an excellent contrivance of our own! The costumes were a windfall, as Miss Thorp's parents had brought them from Sweden several years ago, so we were saved that expense. The scenery, also, was cleverly adapted to our purposes by members of the class, having first served a performance of the college dramatic society. You would hardly believe that the whole performance cost only about twenty-five dollars! (1)[10]

Here, the financial ingenuity Buck brought to the Vassar Dramatic Workshop is apparent. In addition, as Kevin James Koch points out, the passage shows how the production itself, which involved members of the class, the community, and the audience, represents invention as a social, communal activity (172).

Although modeled after the 47 Workshop, Buck's workshop soon achieved its own level of success. In 1919, the workshop presented three plays that were written and performed by undergraduates (Redding 19). In previous workshop productions, some of the plays presented were adaptations. By 1919, eight workshop plays had been presented outside of Vassar. Edna St. Vincent Millay had appeared in *Two Slatterns and a King,* which she wrote at Vassar and performed with the New York Players. In addition, she also wrote and starred in *The Princess Marries the Page* when she was at Vassar ("Literary Spotlight" 112). Through the creation of the Workshop Bureau of Plays, Buck edited and published a list of plays available for public performance (Redding 19). In addition, she received assistance from New York play producers. M. Jacque Copeau, director of the Theatre du Vieux Columbier, read and judged a "prize" play presented by the workshop in 1920; and Arthur Hopkins, the producer of plays including *The Poor Little Rich Girl* and *Redemption,* spoke in March 1919 on "Play Production" at the college (Buck, "Primer of the Vassar Dramatic Workshop"; "Workshop Up-To-Date" 156). Buck also was able to attract guests "of distinguished connection with the drama" to her productions. Dramatic critic Walter Prichard Eaton and actor-playwright C. Rann Kennedy and his wife Edith Wynne Mathison attended the opening of the 1919–20 season ("Noted Guests at Vassar Play").

Evert Sprinchorn, professor emeritus of drama at Vassar, emphasizes the significance of such efforts, explaining that "in academic circles the study of dramatic literature was considered one thing, and a good thing; and that playwriting was considered another sort of thing, and not so good; and that there was a third thing, play production, which was not to be considered at all, except as an extracurricular activity, like tennis or fencing" (21).[11] Buck's courses in play production, then, pushed against the grain of traditional perceptions concerning the role of drama in academic institutions. Fortunately for Buck, she had a very progressive department in which to try out her experiment.

Buck's dramatic workshop courses were offered through the English Department, and the performers in the dramatic workshop also received their training through the English Department—the English Speech division. According to Sprinchorn, after 1917, when the curriculum committee required every student to complete two years of study in vocal expression, the speech section grew rapidly during the next few years. Enrollment in speech courses swelled from under fifty students in June 1917 to more than four hundred by June 1921 (22). Among the courses available were classes on Interpretive Reading, Technique of Dramatic Expression, Dramatic Presentation, and Dramatic Production. As Sprinchorn points out, "The impression left on one is that the speech division was becoming a mini drama department" (22). The development of her workshop seemed to support this contention.

Initially, the best plays written in Buck's two-course sequence, The Technique of Drama, were produced by members of the class. Later, students in English Speech produced the plays; in 1918, students in English Speech, who had produced two sets of workshop plays that year, formed the Workshop Players to present the plays before the college. Membership in the Players was limited to thirty and included students "skilled in acting, stage-setting, scene-painting, costuming, lighting, or any of the arts of the theatre" ("Workshop Up-To-Date" 155). According to Buck, the Players "attempt to give the audience simply and sincerely what the play-wright meant, with no self-exploitation or meaningless stage conventions" ("Primer of the Vassar Dramatic Workshop").

In 1920, Buck achieved her goal of transforming the Vassar Dramatic Workshop into a "larger community enterprise" (Buck, "Poughkeepsie Community Theatre" 198). Friend and associate Katherine Warren discusses Buck's efforts to form a "true community activity":

> For years there had been growing in Miss Buck's mind the idea of the service possible through a community art centre, and this after a time defined itself clearly as a theatre;—not a charitable provision of entertainment of a worthy kind for those who had little pleasure, but a true community activity, in which the people of the town, regardless of those racial or occupational differences which ordinarily separate them, should coöperate to produce artistic drama. ("Miss Buck" 30–31)

In helping to organize the Poughkeepsie Community Theatre, Buck broke down the social and economic obstacles separating people by uniting them in a cooperative activity.

The community theater project began with a meeting at Buck and Wylie's house in January 1920 to organize the establishment of a democratically run community theater. The theater administration was organized similar to the "commission form of city government," and the officers included a director, secretary, and a treasurer (Warren, "Miss Buck" 31). According to Katherine Warren, "The entire control was given to an executive committee made up of the director, Miss Buck, and the heads of five committees having charge severally of membership and finance, choice of plays, securing of actors, staging and costuming, and seating and ushering" ("Miss Buck" 31). Buck served as the chair of the executive committee.

Members of the Advisory Board, comprised of thirty citizens interested in the movement, included Vassar President Henry Noble MacCracken and his wife; Wylie; Winifred Smith also of the English Department; and college alumnae ("Poughkeepsie Organizes" 1; "Vassar Girl Elected" 1). Warren adds that "the plan for membership was also simple, and as democratic as possible. Every person who gave either a minimum of one dollar or service of any kind, thereby became a member of the association, and was entitled, equally with the donor of three hundred dollars, to two tickets for every performance given during the season" ("Miss Buck" 31–32). In describing the new venture, Buck reveals her genteel, middle-class principles when she writes that the plays presented by the theater "will be 'popular' in the best sense but without the vulgarity of many a 'Broadway success.' Such clean and satisfying recreation as the War Camp Community Service gave our soldiers will thus be provided for the entire community" ("Poughkeepsie Community Theatre" 198). She adds that no admission will be charged "but all who support the enterprise in any way, either by money or by service may secure tickets for themselves and their friends" ("Poughkeepsie Community Theatre" 198). The plan was to present plays for children each Saturday afternoon and plays for adults each Saturday evening. The performances "were to be given not only for, but by the community" (Redding 19).

According to newspaper reports, the community theater was to be modeled after the Neighborhood Playhouse in New York. The project would be "carried out along democratic lines, with active co-operation from all groups of people in the city" ("Organize for New Community Theatre Here" 249). The Neighborhood Playhouse, like the Hull House Theatre in Chicago, represented "the Little Theater movement in its socio-logical aspect" (Mackay 54). With its lack of admission fee and emphasis on presenting plays with social concerns, the Poughkeepsie Community Theatre had a similar focus.

Vassar faculty and students played a significant role in the develop-ment of the community theater. However, as one newspaper article em-phasizes, the theater was not built only by Vassar faculty and graduates: "[M]erchants, professional men, factory emplyes [*sic*], college students and faculty have done it together, unselfishly and thoroughly" ("Community Theatre Aiming High" 30). Written in 1925, the article recognized Buck's efforts to establish the theater and traced its five-year history. Buck's ef-fectiveness in connecting with the city is evident in Poughkeepsie Mayor Frank B. Lovelace's "formal appreciation of the theatre's work":

> By the hardest kind of work the theatre has achieved a reputation for astute craftsmanship in management and acting that has grown with each performance. . . . Miss Buck's experiment of five years ago has been amply justified. We have a Community Theatre whose productions rank as high as any of the best being produced by the smaller theatres that are springing up throughout the country in the wake of the Little Theatre movement. The unending work that has built up the theatre is a story of which the city can be proud and of which it should never fail to be appreciative. ("Community Theatre Aiming High" 30).

The mayor's statement indicated the degree to which the theater had moved beyond the gates of Vassar to become a community endeavor.

Mayor Lovelace's description of the struggle to establish the theater seems accurate when examining the early beginnings of the theater. Buck's effort to create the Poughkeepsie theater was, in many ways, the "hardest kind of work." She had difficulty getting the college to recognize her time commitment to the project. In the 1920 English Department report, Wylie requests that the college release Buck from one-third of her teaching duties to further Buck's and the college's contribution to the community theater effort. In her request, Wylie underscores the importance of the community theater to Poughkeepsie. Wylie adds that the opening of the community theater has been significant for many groups interested in drama, and that "they appreciate the service of Vassar in leading the way for a coöperative community enterprise, in their eyes of the first importance" ("Report of the Department of English," 19 Apr. 1920, 2). According to Wylie, these groups assume that the college "has allowed Professor Buck time to carry out this enterprise" ("Report of the Department of English," 19 Apr. 1920, 2). Wylie requests that the college release Buck from one-third of her teaching duties.

Buck reiterates Wylie's request in her own letter to President Mac-Cracken in June 1920. She emphasizes that the community theater is "recognized by dramatic experts such as Professor Baker, Stuart Walker and the New York Drama League, as an educational experiment of notable significance to other communities and as an example of what all colleges should do for their communities" (letter to MacCracken, 3 June 1920, 1). To guarantee the success of the project, Buck asserts that she must devote considerable time to "making connections" with various educational organizations in town, and that, because of her knowledge of the community and drama, nobody but herself "can do this work successfully" (3 June 1920, 1). Buck continues with her request:

> The opportunity to render such a service as this does not occur more than once in a life-time [*sic*]. I feel that I must render it, at whatever sacrifice to me, personally. But my energies are not limitless. And I shall be able to serve the college and the community longer if I may be allowed to apply three hours of college time to this work, instead of adding it to a full-time schedule plus at least one-third of a full-time schedule given to the Workshop productions that must be continued for the first semester. I have during the past four years been heavily overworked, but this was by my

own choice and I do not grudge the strength and time given, <although it has made any work of my own quite impossible>. It does not, however, seem quite right to continue indefinitely a program so over-weighted.[12] (letter to MacCracken, 3 June 1920, 1)

Buck concludes by stressing that her request will not "serve as a precedent for other requests from the faculty, if it is clearly understood that this special service to the community is directly in line with my particular department of teaching" (3 June 1920, 1). Buck views her community theater work as "a direct extension" of her work in teaching drama at the college (3 June 1920, 2).

In his response, President MacCracken informs Buck that the Trustees' Committee on Faculty and Studies carefully considered her request, "but they did not feel that they could grant the request at this time" (letter to Buck, 8 June 1920, 1). MacCracken adds, "After long personal thought on the matter I coincided with their judgment, chiefly because of the precedent that would be established . . . it is possible that should similar requests arise in other fields the administration of our budget might become extremely difficult" (8 June 1920, 1). He concludes his letter, saying, "You have, as you know, my own interest in your plans, although it must be unofficial" (8 June 1920, 1). Although MacCracken did not approve Buck's request for time off, in the past he had unofficially supported her drama efforts and was a lover of theater. In 1918, MacCracken donated one thousand dollars for the establishment of a drama fund "for the purchase and care of books in Drama and allied themes" ("Gertrude Buck Drama").[13] MacCracken also served on the Advisory Board for the new Poughkeepsie Community Theatre. It is difficult to speculate why the Trustees' Committee on Faculty and Studies denied Buck's request. The 5 June 1920 minutes of the committee's meeting only indicate that "it was voted that the request for an allowance of part time to Professor Buck should be refused" (Trustees Minutes). However, based on Buck's letter and MacCracken's response, the question of setting a precedent and the potential economic ramifications seemed a major concern. Committee members probably felt that they would be opening up the college to future requests for release time by accepting Buck's proposal.

Nevertheless, Buck's efforts came with a personal sacrifice to her health. Less than two years after starting the community theater, Buck died in January 1922. After her death, Frank Stout and his wife, Helen, previously from the Neighborhood Playhouse in New York, took over as the director and art director of the theater (Warren, "Miss Buck" 34). As noted, Hallie Flanagan eventually filled Buck's position.

Drama, Rhetoric, and the Middle-Class Women's Movement

In examining Buck's participation in the Little Theater movement, important points of intersection in her efforts in drama, rhetoric, and the women's movement emerge. In Buck's work in drama and rhetoric, as in her work in pedagogy, she highlighted broader social consciousness in general. This emphasis coincided with Buck's feminist ethics and her dynamic, organic view of life. This organic, transactional view of the individual and society was central to Buck's view of democracy. Furthermore, as Lois Banner points out, a focus on "social justice for women and the disadvantaged" was central to the women's movement of this period (93). Although contradictions were part of this movement, as Banner points out, this "social feminism" developed out of the expanded rights and new opportunities for middle-class women and the social reform climate of the nation (93).[14] An emphasis on social justice and responsibility for women also was central to Buck's efforts in drama.

This focus becomes evident when examining Buck's dramatic activities. In significant ways, Buck's creation of the Vassar Dramatic Workshop and the Poughkeepsie Community Theatre can be viewed as closely connected to her feminism and to the women's movement of the period. Similar to several other Little Theaters, Buck's efforts were predominantly supported by women. For instance, in a 1918–19 list of supporters, Vassar President Henry Noble MacCracken is the only male on the list of thirty-six workshop supporters ("Supporters of the Workshop"). In addition, Vassar women wrote all the plays for the college's dramatic workshop. Buck's theater activities also seemed to reflect the call for women to have a "social mind" and to take more social responsibility since gaining broader rights in society. By starting the Poughkeepsie Community Theatre, Buck accepted and tried to further her social obligations by presenting her solution to the town and gown split. This emphasis on social obligations is evident in a description of the founding of the Poughkeepsie Community Theatre. The letter, written by a citizen of Poughkeepsie, was submitted to the college twelve years after Buck's death to clarify the founding of the theater:

The organization of the Vassar Community Theatre was undertaken by Professor Gertrude Buck not long after her year's leave-of-absence for study with Professor George Baker, of Harvard University. She had long carried on her plan of an association with the community by residence on Market Street and by participation in town life. She wished now to bring to Poughkeepsie the fine art of drama in connection with the little theatre movement. (Acker, letter to MacCracken, 24 May 1934, 1)[15]

This passage reveals how many of Buck's actions, from her choice of living in Poughkeepsie (rather than on campus) to starting the theater, reflect her feminist ethics. Buck, like many other middle-class women involved in little theaters and settlement theaters, emphasized social responsibility and used theater as a vehicle for promoting cooperation among different classes of people.

An emphasis on achieving social justice for women also was evident in the persuasive potential of the theater, which suffragists understood and used to their benefit. In December 1916, the Poughkeepsie Suffrage League, which was led by Wylie, presented two women's rights plays, *Sam's Surrender* and *The Salt Cellar*. In addition, an anti-suffrage monologue was delivered between acts. According to newspaper reports, in the first play the audience

> learned all about "Sam's Surrender" to a frail little woman who turned like the traditional woman, awoke from her twenty-five years of impassive submission to the iron rule of her husband, realized for the first time that she had a mind and certain rights of her own and as typical of millions of women in her position, showed plainly and clearly just why she is just as much entitled to the vote as her obstinate husband. ("Suffragists Give Play" 5)

By using the play to promote its cause, the Suffrage League hoped to persuade women to join its side "through the arguments embodied in the cleverly enacted farce" ("Suffragists Give Play" 5). The plays were presented the year Buck returned from her study of drama with Baker. Since Buck, like other suffragists, viewed language as moral action, she understood the transformative potential of the theater. In descriptions of her drama courses, Buck writes that such courses prepare students for "[t]he writing of pageants and masques for community and civic celebrations, propaganda purposes, etc.," ("English Course 111–112" 1). Similar to others involved in the Little Theater movement, Buck saw the theater as a persuasive tool that could be used to promote social reform.

In Buck's work in rhetoric, her feminism and reform ideals were evident in her view of writing as a social activity, fostering the values of cooperation, equality, and participation. These values were central to her approach to drama. For instance, Buck frequently highlighted the importance of cooperation in the dramatic workshop process. When discussing the workshop's first production, *A Christmas Guest,* Buck declares, "Every member of the class coöperated to give the play a fair chance of reaching its audience. In a very literal sense it may be said that the producer was the class, acting as a coöperative unit" ("Vassar Workshop" 181). This cooperation extended beyond the limits of the stage. According to Buck, "By the spontaneous reactions of the audience the writers were enabled to judge in how far they had actually conveyed what they meant to convey,—at just what points they had hit or missed their mark" ("Vassar Workshop" 181). The workshop itself was an activity that promoted social cooperation on multiple levels, a movement toward a more democratic theater.

Buck's approach to drama, like her efforts in argumentation and the women's movement, also underscored equality and active participation. For Buck, a play was created through the transaction of the dramatic workshop with the audience. The play was not merely the product of the stage manager. The audience's comments helped the playwright to revise her work. The audience took part in the play's construction and was not there purely for passive enjoyment. According to Buck, the success of the workshop "depends not alone on financial support, but on the active co-operation of a college audience which goes to see the Workshop plays not merely as another 'good show,' but as a dramatic experiment in which it has an active part" ("Coming—Workshop Plays" 3). At her productions, Buck, like Baker, required each member of the audience to provide written criticisms of the plays. Signatures were eliminated from the criticisms, and then they were turned over to the playwrights for use in revision ("Work-Shop Plays" 1). For Buck, the process was beneficial not only to the playwrights but also to the audience and ultimately to society: "Such education of audience is going on very fast these days in many different quarters; and every play which is, through presentation to a college audience, prepared for success before a wider public, contributes its bit to this great educational movement. It is a movement which affects not only the drama, but society itself" ("Two Minor Hall Plays"). The dramatic workshop had broad transformative possibilities in terms of educating the playwright, the audience, and ultimately society.

Finally, Buck's social emphasis and feminism are evident in her pragmatic belief that ideas are incomplete until tested for application in the real world. For Buck the dramatic workshop is the site where theory and practice merge. It is "a place where plays are actually made, or at least wrought out into their final form" ("Vassar Workshop" 182). The workshop is

> to serve as an experimental laboratory for the play-wrights of Vassar College. The most promising plays written are "tried out" by actual production. This gives them a practical test and furnishes a definite writing standard. Every member of the audience at a Workshop production is pledged to send in . . . criticism or comment on the plays. These criticisms are of real service to the writers in their task of revision, and incidentally serve to quicken the dramatic sense of the audience. (Buck, "Primer of the Vassar Dramatic Workshop")

Similar to her approach to argumentation, Buck used a "laboratory" technique to teach practical playwriting, which she saw as mutually beneficial to the workshop members and the audience. As Thomas H. Dickinson points out, universities traditionally had failed to apply laboratory methods to the arts because of a "temper that presumed that art is fixed and static, that it is worth while [sic] only after it is dead, while politics is vital and is subject to immediate judgment" (100). Dickinson contends that this temper has made the universities' efforts "simply a survey of past processes and has closed the door to any laboratory work in the living principles of the arts" (101). But for Buck, drama was a living art, not a static study of the past.

Buck's Plays and Adaptations

Buck's feminist ethics and social reform emphasis are also central to her own plays and adaptations. For instance, in her dramatic works, Buck's main characters are strong women who challenge feminine and class-based stereotypes. Buck's plays, like her efforts in drama, rhetoric, and the women's movement, also have a more general social reform dimension. The female heroines in her plays have a heightened sense of social conscious-

ness, and they strive to build relationship and to further social cooperation. In the actions and values of Buck's female protagonists, significant
parallels to the care ethics discussed by authors such as Carol Gilligan
and Nel Noddings are evident. As Gilligan emphasizes, "The psychology
of women that has consistently been described as distinctive in its greater
orientation toward relationships and interdependence implies a more
contextual mode of judgment and a different moral understanding"(22).[16]
With their emphasis on relationships and responsibilities, Buck's female
characters taught the audience the significance of a relational ethics by
embodying these ideals.

Buck wrote one of her plays, *Mother-Love,* while on leave at Radcliffe
College with Baker.[17] At a memorial service a year after Buck's death,
Baker admits that when he first read the play, it seemed a "dangerous
venture" and a "very disagreeable play":

> But as I read it more carefully, I began to feel that if properly played it
> would be something quite different. When I first read it aloud to the
> Workers, they did not like it. They said it was too intensely disagreeable.
> They did not believe we could save it. So I picked my actors very carefully;
> and when it was played, we found that Miss Buck had given to the actors
> in these two parts [the mentally disabled daughter and the selfish mother]
> such that when they handled it rightly the play became one of infinite
> pathos. . . . It touched the audience profoundly. ("Address" 11)

The play's heroine is Maggie Ross, an unmarried dressmaker who becomes "mother" to her fifty-year-old sister, Lura, who because of an early
illness remains like a child, and to her mother, Mrs. Ross, an extremely
self-centered woman (Ricks 214). Maggie's brother, Jim, has been away
for twenty-eight years, and, as Maggie tells us, "[I]t's sixteen years this
Christmas since we heard from him" (172). Valuing her son more than
her two daughters, Mrs. Ross fixates on Jim and hopes for his eventual
return. She saves every penny for Jim and keeps his room the same as when
he left, forcing Lura and Maggie to share a room. When Jim does return
home one evening near Christmas, he leaves that same night because he
cannot stand his mother's "pettin' and play-actin'" (181).

In the play, Buck challenges traditional social perceptions about what it
means to be a mother, a privileged son, and even a child. As Vickie Ricks
points out, the play "explores and redefines motherhood more through

one's selfless actions and caring attitude than as a biological event" (214). Buck revises typical notions of motherhood by contrasting Maggie's self-less love of her mentally disabled sister, Lura, with Mrs. Ross's selfish love for her son, Jim, who calls his mother "the old vampire" and cannot wait to escape her clutches. Buck also foregrounds the sharp difference between Maggie's unconditional love of Lura and Mrs. Ross's feelings of repulsion toward her daughter and belief that she should be "put in an institution" (178). Rather than viewing Lura as her own child, Mrs. Ross takes on the role of a selfish child and considers her competition for Maggie's love. Mrs. Ross complains, "Nobody cares about me. It's all Lura with you. . . . Anybody'd think she was your child, instead of mine" (169–70). Mrs. Ross's words and other scenes in the play cause the audience to question what it means to love and to be a mother. In a later scene, for instance, Maggie tells Jim how she can't be considered Lura's mother: "Mother says if you're not really a mother, you can't know how a mother feels" (174). Jim quickly counters these words, noting that he has seen women with many children "that was no more mothers than I am. An' some ole maids—Why Good Lord! They mothered everything in sight" (174). Jim's words challenge the idea that all biological mothers are necessarily good, loving mothers. They also emphasize that many unmarried women may have better mothering skills than some biological mothers.

Although Buck revises the traditional "mother" role, she similarly redefines relationships in terms of a broadened sense of family responsibility. In so doing, the play questions the social favoring of males, namely firstborn sons, through the character of Jim (Campbell, *Toward* 167). For instance, at one point in the play, Maggie tries to get Jim to be more responsible and, despite his feelings for his mother, to stay and take care of his sister Lura. Maggie tells Jim: "Oh, Jim dear, I know she didn't bring you up right. But can't you bring yourself up, now? Oh, do stay and help make things comfy for Lura. *Can't* you, Jim" (181, emphasis in original). Despite Maggie's entreaties for a broader sense of family duty, Jim still departs, leaving Maggie with full responsibility for her mother and Lura. However, Maggie does not hold this against Jim and accepts the responsibility for her family herself.

Similarly, Buck reconceptualizes relationships in terms of a selfless, unconditional love. Mrs. Ross blames her son's leaving on Maggie and Lura: "There's another attraction for our happy home! An idiot as well as a Pharisee! No wonder he didn't care to stay" (184). In response, Maggie eventually tells her mother, "You can do *anything* to me, but you mustn't hurt Lura. . . . I'll—I'll *kill* you, if you do" (184, emphasis in original). As JoAnn Campbell points out, Maggie's self-sacrificing attitude toward her sister "is likened to the mythical fierceness of a mother's love" ("Gertrude Buck" 168). Despite Mrs. Ross's harsh words, Maggie forgives her mother and vows to take care of her and Lura: "I'll take care of you both—my two children" (185). Through her play, Buck forces the audience to question society's assumptions about privileging sons over daughters and biological mothers over more caring individuals. The play also encourages the audience to reconsider what it means to love and to be a child. In addition, it highlights Buck's feminist ethics, underscoring the need to value human responsibilities and relationships. These ideals are embodied through Maggie's words and actions, presenting a compelling and persuasive counter to society's more typical emphasis on individualism and competition.

A stress on social justice for women and broader social consciousness in general also is evident in Buck's adaptation of *The Girl from Marsh Croft,* also written by Lagerlöf. The play challenges traditional views associated with the upper class through its lower-class heroine, Helga (Ricks 215). Like Maggie Ross, Helga has a strong social consciousness, which is shown through her actions toward others. For instance, in the opening scene, Helga brings suit against her former employer, Per Martensson, to force him to support their baby. However, when the judge asks Martensson to swear under oath that he is not the father of the child, Helga withdraws her suit to prevent Martensson from swearing falsely. Helga believes that by committing perjury, Martensson would "lose his soul" (191). Although Helga drops her case, her selfless actions win her the respect of the judge and many of the court spectators. One young farmer, Gudmund Erlandsson, is so moved by Helga's actions that he asks her to be a housekeeper for his mother, who is bound to a wheelchair. Gudmund tells Helga, "You have given us something that we may remember when there seems to be no goodness in the world" (192).

The central social and moral conflict of the play occurs when Gudmund is charged with stabbing a peddler to death the night before his wedding. When Hildur, his fiancée, finds out, she calls off the wedding because she does not want to "marry someone who has been in prison" (227). Helga, though, is able to bring forward evidence proving Gudmund's innocence. As Vickie Ricks points out, Helga further upholds her good character when she becomes part of a "love triangle" (215). Helga denies her own love and tries to bring Gudmund and Hildur together. Previously Hildur had believed "it is better to disappoint another than oneself" (206). However, near the end of the play Hildur has learned Helga's social sense of values, and instead of trying to rekindle her relationship with Gudmund, she helps Gudmund and Helga come together.

Although *The Girl from Marsh Croft* is an adaptation, the play reflects several significant aspects of Buck's feminist ethics. For instance, in this play, as in Buck's feminism and her approach to rhetoric, she highlights reform through her emphasis on a social rather than an individual consciousness and the need for broader social justice for women. As in *Mother-Love,* Buck uses strong female heroines to challenge traditional social values. The play also redefines typical values associated with class. Helga not only teaches Hildur what is right but also teaches the audience that moral values are not attached to class, and that individuals can learn from the actions of others. Each time Helga faces a moral dilemma, she places the values of others before those of her own. In important ways, Helga's ethics reflect Buck's feminist ethics. As mentioned, Kantian ethics "subordinated feeling to reason. He insisted that only acts done out of duty to carefully reasoned principle are morally worthy" (Noddings, *Educating* 14). This meant that morals typically were discussed without reference to human feelings, relationships, and experience. However, for Buck, ethical decisions involve the interplay between the individual's own desires and a broad critical analysis of the consequences in terms of human relationships. The audience sees Helga applying this method in her decisions and actions. Through her actions, Helga teaches the audience to act in terms of a broader social rather than an individual consciousness. Finally, Buck's plays are aimed at persuasion in terms of moral action; she views drama as a potentially reconstructive medium.

A focus on strong female characters and challenges to patriarchal authority and feminine stereotypes also is evident in several of the plays written by Vassar students. The influence of Buck's teaching is vividly illustrated in the work of one of her most famous students, Edna St. Vincent Millay. As Suzanne Clark asserts, "Millay criticized gender roles and sexuality explicitly, in defiant lines that made her notorious in 1923 and that once again delight feminist students today" ("Uncanny Millay" 3–4). Clark also notes other differences in Millay's writing that set her apart from prominent male modernist poets of her period, like Stevens or Eliot. In her essay "The Unwarranted Discourse: Sentimental Community, Modernist Women, and the Case of Millay," Clark examines what she calls a "cruel paradox" for modernist women writers in the early decades of the twentieth century: "[T]he more successfully they wrote, both to appeal to a feminized community of readers and to help readers feel part of the literary community, the less they could be considered serious writers. The more clearly they appealed to the shared feelings of a popular community, the more they risked being labeled 'sentimental' or merely popular" (248). This paradox existed for women writers because, as Clark explains, the modernist agenda for several prominent male poets of the period was to shift away from popular culture, "to establish a distance between literature and other forms of writing" (248). In her analysis, Clark demonstrates how Millay's poetry clashed with modernist poetics because it was sentimental as opposed to intellectual, and combined rhetoric and poetics instead of sharply separating the two. Thus, Clark asserts that "Modernist poetics excluded female poets at the level of theory" (248).

Although other factors obviously shaped Millay as a writer, the differences that Clark outlines are elements that were underscored in Buck's two-semester dramatic workshop sequence, Courses 111 and 112 Technique of the Drama, as well as in her approach to rhetoric and pedagogy. For instance, Buck joined rhetoric and literature, blended thought and feeling, stressed the role of audience, and emphasized the community-building potential of literature and discourse in general. While in Buck's drama courses, Millay revised her plays based on the feedback she received both from her female community at Vassar and the broader audiences who saw her plays. She developed her craft as a writer learning to negotiate the demands of both types of audiences. As noted, Buck's *Social Criticism of Literature* also highlighted a rhetorical approach to literature, one that stressed the persuasive potential of literature. In addition, her approach to rhetoric and drama underscored the need for speakers and writers to identify with their audiences, to further cooperation. During her four years at Vassar, Millay honed her craft as a writer, and as can be seen, she learned an approach that was quite distinct from the dominant male poets of her period. Although not all of Buck's students would become professional writers like Millay, Buck's course provided her female students with the opportunity to write for a female audience and explore women-centered issues, to work collaboratively, and to develop as writers.

Katherine H. Adams asserts that during this period, the dramatic growth of women working as professional writers was made possible because women were able to extend the collaborative methods they had learned in college to other realms. In so doing, they were able to move beyond the more traditional and limited career opportunities available to women: "Immediately after graduating, they began participating in clubs, workshops, political parties, and government agencies where they could continue working within groups as they had done in college" (xvii). Buck's workshop is significant because it also provided a method, a collaborative organizational model that her female students could draw upon and use in their diverse organizational and professional endeavors beyond their college experiences. Ultimately, as Adams argues, women like Buck, Millay, and the first generations of college-educated women used their collaborative groups to transform writing itself, so that "Writer could no longer be situated within the circle of Man . . ." (xvii–xviii). As Adams asserts, this transformation meant new styles of writing, redefined genres, and an expanded sense of what it meant to be a Writer (xviii).

This examination of Buck's social view of literature, her plays, and her work in the Little Theater movement deepens understanding of her efforts in drama, and it shows how her activities were closely interrelated to her other work and writing. The analysis contextualizes her efforts so that her work in drama can be viewed as a response to a problem during her time—namely the town and gown issue. Buck's goal was to socialize education, to promote a closer understanding between the college and community, ultimately to further democracy. As noted, she viewed literature and drama from a rhetorical perspective. Buck saw both as persuasive instruments that could be used in the movement toward a more democratic society.

In addition, the chapter highlights how social reform was central to Buck's feminism and her approach to drama and rhetoric. In her efforts in these areas, Buck advocated broader social justice and responsibility for women in particular and wider social consciousness in general. By examining these activities, I have shown how they wove together and mutually supported each other and Buck's approach to drama. These

THE LITTLE THEATER MOVEMENT

different ideas all came together in Buck's creation of the Poughkeepsie Community Theatre, her attempt to create a "true community activity" (Warren, "Miss Buck" 31). Buck's work in drama provided an acceptable outlet for her to expand her sphere of influence beyond the college and use drama to promote cooperation among the different classes of people in her community. More significantly, as Adams argues, it provided a collaborative method, a support network that her female students could draw upon in their professional endeavors beyond the college. These changes meant more women were taking on the title of author, which reconceptualized writing.

In her work in drama, Buck used this collaborative model to reconnect the college and the neighboring community of Poughkeepsie. She envisioned the college as an integral, not an isolated, aspect of the community. These social ideals were also central to Wylie's teaching and administration, and they were evident in the teachings and writings of two of their students, Mary Yost and Helen Drusilla Lockwood. The final chapter examines this significant tradition of teaching at Vassar.

6

SOCIALLY CONSCIOUS WOMEN
TEACHING WRITING

By the way I didn't tell you the subject did I [debate topic].
Resolved that the labor unions are justified in their demands
for the closed shop. Isn't that a splendid subject. I am getting so
interested in things like that that I shouldn't wonder if I should
want to be doubling in Economics next. This argumentation
has done wonders for me in that direction for the world around
has become full of interest. I just delight in studying out labor
problems.
 —Helen Drusilla Lockwood, letter to her family, 6 Feb. 1910

Gertrude Buck's work in argumentation and debate complicates claims
that with the entrance of women into higher education, the teaching of
rhetoric shifted from an oral, agonistic discipline to a "less contestive and
more interiorized, even personalized" field (Connors, *Composition-Rhetoric*
66). This argument can also be made more complex by examining the efforts of Mary Yost (1881–1954) and Helen Drusilla Lockwood (1891–1971),
two students of Buck and Wylie's. Yost, like Buck, developed an ethical
approach to argumentation that responded to the persuasive, agonistic
tradition and the Progressive Era insistence on democratic forms of education. Likewise, Lockwood's pedagogical approach stressed a social rather
than an interiorized perspective.

Buck, Wylie, and their students' efforts also underscore the need
to rethink conventional evaluative criteria for measuring influence. In
traditional histories of rhetoric, scholars' yardsticks often have measured
success in terms of the number of times a text has been published and

republished. These accounts typically do not consider the significant impact teachers can have on their students and how those individuals, in turn, may become influential teachers of the next generation. While texts that have been published and republished certainly merit investigation because of their often broad and continuous impact, it is important to consider other types of yardsticks based on more wide-ranging and inclusive criteria. Measuring Buck's success primarily in terms of her textbook editions is too narrow; Buck's clear influence on her students speaks more significantly. This chapter demonstrates that Buck's writing and her work with Laura Johnson Wylie at Vassar had a much more profound impact by documenting the intellectual progress and careers of Yost and Lockwood. The impact of Buck and Wylie lived on in the lives and teachings of their students. Both Yost and Lockwood carried on and extended Buck and Wylie's tradition of encouraging feminist teaching practices that fostered democratic communication, activism, and broader intellectual and social responsibility for women.

A 1904 graduate of Vassar, Yost taught in the English Department from 1907 to 1921, with the exception of a few years during which she pursued graduate work at the University of Michigan. Like Buck, Yost developed a feminist theory of argument quite separate from the agonistic, patriarchal approach that Robert Connors argues was displaced after women entered higher education but also different from the "irenic rhetoric" that he claims took its place (*Composition-Rhetoric* 24). Yost's theory challenged the traditional basis in logic and faculty psychology and instead stressed the social significance of argument in terms of communication and community building.

Described as a "Vassar College legend," Helen Lockwood received her bachelor's from Vassar in 1912 and went on to teach in the English Department from 1927 to 1956 (Heller 163). Like Wylie, Lockwood taught at the Bryn Mawr Summer School for Women Workers, where she served as a composition instructor and specialist in public speaking. At Vassar, Lockwood developed several innovative courses that pushed her students to challenge their basic assumptions, avoid unsupported generalizations, and think for themselves. In significant ways, Lockwood's courses were "transgressive," as bell hooks defines the term, "a movement against and beyond boundaries" (12).

Mary Yost

With the exception of Herman Cohen, scholars have not considered Yost's work in previous histories of the field.[1] Building on Cohen's work, I will focus on Yost's teaching of argumentation and debate at Vassar College; her 1917 dissertation, "The Functional Aspect of Argument as Seen in a Collection of Business Letters"; and her 1917 article, "Argument from the Point-of-View of Sociology," which draws on her dissertation research and was published in *The Quarterly Journal of Public Speaking*.[2] I also will explore her approach to administration because it was greatly influenced by her research in argumentation. I will demonstrate how Yost created a democratic method of argumentation and debate that included significant elements characteristic of modern feminist approaches to pedagogy and argument. More specifically, parallels to Sonja K. Foss and Cindy L. Griffin's invitational rhetoric are evident in Yost's focus on developing an ethical basis for rhetoric underscoring cooperation and group cohesion rather than persuasion and the domination of others. Although Yost resisted the persuasive, agonistic tradition, she did not view argument as interiorized or personalized. She developed a socially focused, ethical approach to argumentation that encouraged Vassar women to push beyond the domestic sphere and take a more active and public role in society.

To better understand Yost's approach to argumentation, it is helpful to know more about her. Yost, like Buck, came from a privileged background. Yost was born in Staunton, Virginia, and her father, Jacob Yost, served in the House of Representatives from 1887 to 1889 and from 1899 to 1901 (Howton 24, 34). Yost left Staunton to study at Vassar, where she served as senior class president (Howton 24). A student of Buck and Wylie's, Yost received her bachelor's degree in 1904, was a Graduate Scholar at Vassar from 1904 to 1905, and then served as an assistant in English at Wellesley for one year (1906–7). Yost returned to Vassar, where she was an English instructor from 1907 to 1913 and where she earned her master's degree in 1912 (Bacon, Farnsworth, and Winbigler 1). She became a fellow in rhetoric at the University of Michigan from 1913 to 1914, studying with Fred Newton Scott. Yost's work at Michigan aligned her with a significant group of women who obtained progressive education there.[3] Buck was instrumental in forging this link to Michigan by urging Vassar women to pursue graduate study there and by hiring top candidates from Michigan. Buck's influence is evident in the following letter to Scott, checking the progress of her two former Vassar graduates who went on to complete graduate work at Michigan: "I hope Miss Yost and Miss Hincks will do us credit in your work" (11 Oct. 1913, 1). The fact that Buck and Yost were educated in the same tradition helps to explain why they had similar pedagogical and administrative approaches later in their careers.

After completing her fellowship, Yost returned to Vassar and worked as an assistant professor of English from 1915 to 1921. In 1917, she received her Ph.D. in Rhetoric from the University of Michigan, becoming, most likely, the first person in the field of Speech Communication to earn her doctorate (Cohen 66). She served as a reader for the College Entrance Examination Board from 1912 to 1918 and was head reader and examiner from 1918 to 1921 (Bacon, Farnsworth, and Winbigler 1).

Like Buck and Wylie, Yost supported women's suffrage. In December 1912, Yost and Abby Leach, Vassar professor of Greek, were the speakers at a Poughkeepsie Equal Suffrage meeting at the Elks Club. According to newspaper reports, the meeting was "the first of its kind held in this city," and its purpose was to "awaken interest among [Equal Suffrage] club members in the object of the league" ("Suffrage Meeting" 5). The presentations were followed by questions from the audience. Yost was not only teaching argument and debate but also practicing these skills in her support of suffrage.

In her presentation, Yost emphasized that the suffrage movement was more than the latest trend:

> This desire for women's suffrage is bringing great changes in social and political conditions. If we take our ideas of woman's suffrage from the funny papers, of gay remarks, it appears to be a fad: and the woman in the home does not want it.[4] If we look back 70 years we find the same old jokes. The most important fact is state legislatures have embodied it in state constitutions. In England women have municipal suffrage, in New Zealand, and the state of Colorado, full suffrage. ("Suffrage Meeting" 5)

Yost continued, stressing that full suffrage for women had also been achieved in France and Canton, China, and that it soon would be approved in Peking. In the United States, Yost asserts that meaningful progress had been gained in the past seventy years. For instance, she explains that nine states had approved full suffrage for women and that "in all but 16 states women have some form of suffrage" ("Suffrage Meeting" 5). Yost concluded by underscoring the significance of the issue: "The question is, are we going to recognize the importance of the matter and help it. It needs the help of all to bring it more swiftly and to prepare us for what is coming" ("Suffrage Meeting" 5). Yost, like Buck and Wylie, embodied the social ideals that she taught in the classroom.

The year that Buck suffered her first stroke (1921), Yost left Vassar to become the dean of women and associate professor of English at Stanford University, a position she held until her retirement in 1946. During her first six years at Stanford, Yost lectured in composition and argumentation and debate; however, she soon had to devote all of her attention to her increasing administrative duties as the dean of women ("Eleven Faculty Members" 5). In addition to her administrative duties, Yost was active in regional and national organizations. In 1917, Yost served as the first vice president of the National Association of Academic Teachers of Public Speaking. In 1922, she served as the vice president of the Western Division of the Department of Deans of Women of the National Education Association. In addition, from 1933 to 1937, she was the first vice president of the national board of the American Association of University Women, and in 1923 she served as the vice president of the California section ("Doctor Mary Yost"). When Yost retired, she was awarded an honorary L.L.D. from Mills College "in recognition of her long service to women" ("L. L.D. to Dean Mary"). In 1954, Yost died of a heart attack at age seventy-two ("Doctor Mary Yost"). Always retaining her connection to Vassar, Yost was serving on a committee planning the fiftieth reunion of her 1904 Vassar class at the time of her death ("Editor at Bat" 4).[5]

Yost's Approach to Argumentation and Public Speaking

In addition to promoting debate at Vassar, Yost, like Buck, developed a feminist theory of argument that emphasized argument as a community-building endeavor, one that helped to create identification and understanding between the speaker and audience. A key idea underlying Yost's approach to argumentation and public speaking was her social view of language. Buck had similar ideas that were based on an organic concept of society. Although Yost and Buck both advocated a more cooperative and democratic approach to argumentation than the traditional male-biased approach, their methods differed in terms of focus. Buck highlighted the connection between the logical structure of argumentation and its substructure based in psychology. In her pedagogy, Buck encouraged Vassar women to critically evaluate their own thought processes so that they, in turn, could better understand the thought processes of others. Yost, in contrast, pushed for a more outward analysis than Buck. She asserted that argumentation should be studied from the perspective of social groups rather than the traditional emphasis on logic. Yost's approach contrasted with traditional argument's emphasis on the individual speaker and his abilities to use agonistic rhetoric to persuade others to his perspective. Because she viewed argument as the glue of human relationships, Yost stressed that it needed to address both logic and emotion to connect individuals. It wasn't simply about logic, persuasion, and winning as more traditional approaches suggest. In addition, Yost highlighted the public and rhetorical nature of argumentation. She encouraged Vassar women to become effective speakers on Progressive Era concerns aimed at fostering social justice.

During her twelve years at Vassar, Yost frequently taught a two-semester elective course on argumentation, which emphasized writing, criticism, and oral debate. According to the 1911 English Department Report, the textbooks used in the course included Gertrude Buck's *A Course in Argumentative Writing* (1899), Buck and Kristine Mann's *A Handbook of Argumentation and Debating* (1906), William Trufant Foster's *Argumentation and Debating* (1908), George Pierce Baker's *Specimens of Argumentation* (1893), and the Lincoln-Douglas Debates. In addition, students drew on daily newspapers and periodicals for reference and "illustration work."

As part of the course requirements, students wrote ten papers each semester, which included everything from short arguments to lengthier briefs. The course also featured informal and formal debates, with topics drawn from college and broader social issues. Here is a sampling of subjects: "That the membership in debating societies should be voluntary"; "That men and women should have equal suffrage"; "That the election of the Republican ticket will further the best interests of New York State"; and "That the present immigration laws be amended by the addition of an educational test" (Wylie, "Report of the Department of English," 1911, 5). In examining the course requirements and debate topics, it is evident that argumentation and debate were, in fact, a significant part of a "woman's course." In addition, Vassar's approach to argumentation encouraged women to become effective speakers on issues of civic concern, more specifically, Progressive Era concerns related to furthering social justice.

This public emphasis, as well as Yost's focus on the significance of the rhetorical situation, is also evident in her article "Training Four Minute Men at Vassar" (1919), which discusses a public speaking program at Vassar aimed at raising funds and interest in World War One-related activities. Working in cooperation with the National Four Minute Men's Association, Vassar's program began with the development of a Speakers' Bureau to train students in public speaking. Following the national program, Yost explains that Vassar students "worked on the Fourth Liberty Loan . . . [and] joined in the campaign for Red Cross membership both in the college and in the schools of the neighborhood" (248). Vassar women, Yost notes, were asked to give their Fourth Liberty Loan campaign speeches "in the dining halls and also from soap boxes on the campus at the noon recess and as the students were on their way to the evening chapel for service" (251). According-ing to Yost, speaking from a soap box introduced the students to "their first shifting, moving audience" (251): "This experience . . . emphasized as no amount of class lecturing could do, the fact that the occasion has much to do with determining the audience's attitude toward the ideas of the speaker. Also it brought out most clearly that a speech has no one form suitable for all occasions, but that the form is determined by the audience, the occasion and the purpose of the speaker" (251). The passage demonstrates how important the rhetorical situation was to Yost's view of public speaking. After gaining this understanding, the students then took their speeches beyond Vassar's gates. As noted, speeches were developed for the Red Cross and presented at local schools. In addition, Vassar women gave presentations on health education for the Dutchess County Health Association. Yost declares that this work "has been a good advertisement for us, and now we are called upon for all kinds of services from telling stories to the school children . . . to showing the students of the Montclair High School why a girl should go to college and what Vassar offers her" (251). Because of the positive response to the women speakers, Yost notes that the Speakers' Bureau was permanently incorporated into the debating society and the speaker-training program was continued beyond the war. The Four Minute "Men" program was significant because it provided an acceptable outlet for Vassar women to broaden their sphere of influence and to develop their public speaking skills.

Emphasizing Group Interaction and Audience

The public and rhetorical nature of Yost's work is particularly evident in her dissertation and her 1917 article, in which she contends that argument should be viewed from the perspective of sociology. (Both texts are discussed together since the article is based on her dissertation research.) In a 1924 University of Michigan Alumnae Survey, Yost acknowledges her intellectual debt to Michigan: "The stimulus to independent thinking and to gaining an organic philosophy was given me richly by Professor Scott, Professor Cooley, and Professor Shepard, the three men under whom I did most of my work."[6]

In her project, Yost inductively examined a group of letters selected from more than one hundred complete business letters printed in three volumes of *Business Correspondence* (1911) ("Functional Aspect" 4). In all, Yost examined fifty separate letters and three sets written on the same subject to the same audience (two sets of four letters and one set of nine) (6). Yost explains that these letters were selected for four reasons: (1) they were not written for academic purposes "but to sell goods, adjust complaints and collect bills . . . simply and directly media of communication in real situations" (4); (2) the letters also represent "arguments," which Yost defines broadly to include both conviction and persuasion, which "is found also in popular usage, and is the way in which *argument* is used in this study" (145, emphasis in original); (3) their briefness allows Yost to compare many letters; and (4) "the problem of determining the means by which they gained their end was simpler than it is when a speech is examined" (5). In her research, Yost borrowed the term *prospect* from *Business Correspondence* to refer to the audience: "My justification of this borrowing is that *prospect* makes more vivid the relation between the writer and the person to whom the letter is sent than does either of the conventional terms, audience or reader" ("Functional Aspect" 22, emphasis in original). From her discussion of methodology and her use of the term *prospect,* Yost's emphasis on argument as a communicative process is evident.

Yost undertook her study because although beneficial work in argumentation had been completed to improve its practice and theory, she contends contemporary ideas are still "unsatisfactory whether we ask from them a consistent and inclusive theory of argument or practical guidance to effective writing and speaking" ("Functional Aspect" 136). Improvements in theory have resulted in some authors questioning the value of the traditional approach to argument. The generally accepted theory was based on faculty psychology, which Yost contends does not reflect how the mind actually works. One obvious example is the distinction many textbooks typically made between the terms *conviction* and *persuasion*. (Some textbooks today still emphasize this distinction.) Yost explains that "conviction" is typically defined as "an *appeal to the reason, persuasion, an appeal to the emotions*" ("Argument from the Point-of-View" 110, emphasis in original). The two terms are defined as if they are completely distinct and separate concepts. Yost contends that these definitions were developed "when the belief held sway that the mind was divided into three compartments, the reason, the emotions, the will—roughly the assumptions of the old faculty psychology" ("Argument from the Point-of-View" 111). However, she argues that contemporary developments in psychology have called this model into question and replaced it with a view of the mind "as an organic unit performing a particular function—reasoning, feeling, willing—as may be demanded by the situation the individual is meeting . . ." ("Argument from the Point-of-View" 111). For Yost, reason and emotions are not discreet entities but inextricably connected in the communicative process.

According to Yost, those authors challenging the traditional approach to argumentation include James Albert Winans and Gertrude Buck. She claims that Winans's *Public Speaking* (1915) questions the faculty psychology on which contemporary theories of persuasion are based and instead approaches persuasion from the perspective of functional psychology and attention. Buck's *A Course in Argumentative Writing* (1899) approaches argumentation inductively from experience and practice rather than deductively from principles of formal logic. Yost asserts that Buck's approach "puts new life into the part logic plays in argument" ("Argument from the Point-of-View" 111). Beyond argumentation textbooks, Yost contends that Alfred Sidgwick, in *The Process of Argument: A Contribution to Logic* (1893) and *The Use of Words in Reasoning* (1901), has completed the most significant work. Yost explains that Sidgwick "aims to clarify and reinterpret the old ideas concerning argument where they are consistent with modern views of logic and psychology, and to discard those which rest on a false or inadequate interpretation of the mental life" (112). However, Yost contends that all three authors still consider only limited aspects of argument and not the entire field itself: "It is the process of reasoning rather than the process of communication which is dwelt upon" ("Argument from the Point-of-View" 112).

In her research, Yost moves beyond the scope of these authors to reconsider the whole field of argument. As noted, contemporary textbooks tended to discuss argumentation in terms of logic. According to Yost, this perspective is to be expected, "since the principles of argument were first given scientific expression by Aristotle in terms of logic, and the Aristotelian tradition in all rhetorical matters has been little questioned by modern rhetoricians" ("Argument from the Point-of-View"112). In her dissertation, Yost underscores the limits of this tradition: "The old formulae based on Aristotelian logic have proved deadening rather than stimulating to the student in his effort to argue effectively, and today in most of the text books, [*sic*] it seems that these formulae are retained more for the traditional dignity they lend than for their practical usefulness" ("Functional Aspect" 1).[7] In contrast, Yost contends that "[a]rgument as we read and hear and use it every day is directly and fundamentally communication between members of a social group, a *society* in the sociological meaning of the term" ("Argument from the Point-of-View" 113, emphasis in original). Yost asserts that argument should be viewed from the perspective of "social psychology." In her dissertation, Yost explains that social psychology, as defined by foremost sociologists of the time, considers "[t]he entire psychological aspect of the process of association"; Yost adds that this interpretation includes "reasoned, purposed action as well as imitation and suggestion" ("Functional Aspect" 146).

Thus, an emphasis of Yost's research is to explore argument as a "social product" ("Functional Aspect" 136). Such an approach involves "three problems" or questions that need to be considered ("Argument from the Point-of-View" 113). First, Yost explains that argumentation should be studied in terms of the characteristics of the social group from which it emerges. Second, the effects argumentation has on both speaker and audience should be explored. And third, argument needs to be examined in terms of the "characteristic stages" by which the effects are produced ("Argument from the Point-of-View" 113). In viewing argument as a "social product," Yost explains that "the attention [is] focused on the social group, the inter-relation between the writer and audience, rather than on the individual, whether writer or audience. The three questions of the genesis, function and method of argument in the social group were the three points considered" ("Functional Aspect" 137). Such an approach would not negate a logical analysis. Instead, Yost contends that it would lead to a "fuller, more organic theory of argument than is current now" ("Argument from the Point-of-View" 113). In addition, such an approach would mean that terms like *conviction* and *persuasion,* which are based on an outdated psychology, could be avoided.

Fostering Group Cohesion through Argumentation

A key reason Yost advocated approaching argumentation from sociology was to provide a communal justification for ethical behavior. As do Buck and Fred Newton Scott, Yost contends that a significant development in rhetorical history in the last twenty years "has been the reappearance of Plato's idea of discourse and its warm advocacy by the best modern rhetoricians" ("Argument from the Point-of-View"120).[8] Prior to this development, Yost argues that a sophistic approach had dominated and "to it may be traced much of the artificiality and insincerity of 'oratory'" ("Argument from the Point-of-View" 120). Yost and Buck's rhetorical approach, with its emphasis on ethical behavior, seemed to be a direct response to more agonistic, persuasion-oriented rhetoric. Such an approach was antithetical to the democratic values that both women supported.

Like Buck, Yost argues that one problem with the Platonic approach is that it has no grounding, except "what may be called the moral one" ("Argument from the Point-of-View" 120). However, Yost argues that this grounding can be found in a basic assumption underlying social organizations, which she says is "now advanced by many if not all of the leading sociologists" ("Argument from the Point-of-View" 121).[9] This basis, according to Yost, "is that the organization of the group when it is functioning normally is based on the principle of cooperation between the members for the mutual furthering of individual and therefore group interests" ("Argument from the Point-of-View" 120). In her dissertation, Yost quotes Louis D. Brandeis to show how this principle has developed in the business sector: "The old idea of a good bargain was a transaction in which one man got the better of another. The new idea of a good contract is a transaction which is good for both parties in it" ("Functional Aspect" 32). Yost agrees that this development "is not necessarily consciously ethical but the effect is, nevertheless, socially beneficial" ("Functional Aspect" 34). The business sector follows the principle, whether intentional or not.

Arguments may arise among members of a social group when "the expression of this principle [cooperation] in a given direction may be checked or blocked by lack of harmonious correspondence between the view of the group's needs and possibilities held respectively by the two members of the group [the speaker and the audience]" ("Functional Aspect" 137). Argument functions socially to reduce or change the differences between the speaker and the hearer and reestablish the cooperation that exists among group members, furthering group cohesion.

According to Yost, the characteristic feature of such conflicts is not in its reasoning process or structure but in the offering of a "genuine" option or choice to the audience or prospect. In other words, the audience has the option of choosing between the speaker's view of the group's need and the audience's perspective ("Argument from the Point-of View" 117). Yost explains that the concept of a "genuine option" is borrowed from William James's *Will to Believe*. James defines the term in the following manner:

> "Let us give the name of hypothesis," he says, "to anything that may be proposed to our belief; and just as the electrician speaks of live or dead wires, let us speak of my hypothesis as either *live* or *dead*. A live hypothesis is one which appeals as a real possibility to him to whom it is proposed. . . . Next let us call the decision between two hypotheses an option. Options may be of several kinds. They may be (1) living or dead; (2) forced or avoidable; (3) momentous or trivial; and for our purposes we may call an option a genuine option when it is of the forced, living, and momentous kind." (qtd. in Yost 117, emphasis in original)

In presenting an option, the speaker does not primarily focus audience members' attention on their differences. Instead, the speaker tries "to make the audience aware of the connections between them which make possible the normal functioning of the group" (117–18).

According to Yost, argument affects both writer and audience; both "gain a change in experience and a heightened realization of themselves in connection with the other" ("Functional Aspect" 134). More specifically, the audience's experience is "enlarged by new ideas, by the recall of old ones in a new light and by some modification of the emotional content of the mind" ("Argument from the Point-of-View" 115). However, the key aspect of this change is the reevaluation of ideas held at the start of the argument and the "disappearance of feelings of distrust and antagonism . . ." ("Argument from the Point-of-View" 115). The speaker, in contrast, has gained "a fuller realization of his audience"; however, the most dramatic aspect of the change "is that the ideas and emotions with which he started the communication have been clarified and intensified" ("Argument from the Point-of-View" 116). The writer's beliefs are stronger than they were at the beginning of the argument. Thus, the reevaluation that the audience goes through is not part of the speaker's experience. In addition, "there is a change also in the sense-of-self speaker and audience are feeling" ("Argument from the Point-of-View" 116).

> On the part of the audience there seems to be a more active awareness-of-self than is found as the result of every act of discourse, but the awareness is less tense at the end of the argument than it was at the beginning. On the other hand, the speaker's sense-of-self is not only greater in degree than the audience's, both at the beginning and at the end of an argument, but also the tenseness and aggressiveness have increased, not decreased. The combination of these effects on speaker and audience produces a social situation where the two can think, feel, and act in harmony with one another. ("Argument from the Point-of-View" 116)

As Herman Cohen points out, this "harmony" or identification between the speaker and the audience that Yost describes occurs when the speaker addresses the audience's interests (68). As Yost explains:

> The winning side of the contest is determined by which set of associations is the more vividly and closely connected with the interests and experience of the prospect. There is, however, no special nor characteristic way in which the writer translates his topic in terms of the prospect's interests and experiences. . . . On the whole, moreover, as we have seen, the conclusions at which the writer wishes the prospect to arrive are not presented necessarily, even frequently, as the logical outcome of an explicit line of reasoning. What we may call the formalities of reasoning are very little in evidence. From such a point of view *conviction* and *persuasion* as two means of effecting a change in belief become meaningless. ("Functional Aspects" 114–16, emphasis in original)

SOCIALLY CONSCIOUS WOMEN TEACHING WRITING

This identification process is not typically the result of an isolated logic or reasoning process, as Yost explains. Instead, identification is the result of a communicative process that interconnects reason and emotions.

Implications for Teaching Argumentation

Yost believed that such an approach had two important implications concerning the teaching of argumentation. First, it stressed the functional significance of argumentation, which often was ignored in theories of argument based on logic. However, when argumentation is viewed primarily as communication, the formal aspects seem less significant and rigid than the logical approach suggests. Yost's method means that form will follow function. As Yost points out, the student will find out that "he is sometimes using narrative to accomplish his purpose, sometimes description, sometimes explanation" ("Argument from the Point-of-View" 123). Yost's statement is innovative when considered within its context. From 1895 through the mid-1930s, the modes of discourse, which typically classified writing into narration, description, exposition, and argument, were the dominant pedagogical approach in writing courses (Connors, *Composition-Rhetoric* 210, 226). Teachers and students often approached writing in terms of formal requirements instead of communication. In addition, since the form of an argument is not typically an expression of logical principles, "the question of the presence or absence of so-called logical fallacies is not relevant" ("Functional Aspect" 141). For Yost, an argument was effective when it promoted cooperation and the mutual interests of the group.

However, the most significant implication for teaching was in terms of audience. Yost explains that in contemporary textbooks, audience often is not discussed "until we reach a short chapter near the end with the caption *Persuasion*" (121). Yost's statement describes, for example, George Pierce Baker's *The Principles of Argumentation* (1895). In addition to creating the 47 Workshop at Radcliffe and Harvard, Baker was a key theorist in argumentation in the early part of the twentieth century, and his book was highly influential. Baker's chapter on "Persuasion" is the penultimate chapter in the book, and it is here where he specifically discusses audience. Yost contends that audience should be introduced from the beginning of a course in argumentation:

The student must be trained to see that every argument arises from the need of some social situation in which there are two active participants, the speaker and the audience. Therefore, instead of studying the phrasing of propositions first, the student should be set to analyzing his everyday experience, then short newspaper controversies, in order to discover under what conditions *argument,* as he had understood the term, arises. The active part the audience plays in this situation is impressed upon him and through experience he learns that the more clearly he can enter into the thought and feeling of his audience, the more clearly defined become the real points at issue. ("Argument from the Point-of-View" 121, emphasis in original)

Yost contends that students typically approach argumentation in terms of phrasing propositions and outlining briefs. Consequently, the role of the audience often is pushed to the background. Yost asserts, though, that the analysis and study of the topic should be viewed as "a preparation for the argument, not as a step in its process" ("Argument from the Point-of-View" 122). Only by clarifying their ideas and studying the topic will students be able to communicate effectively with the audience. This focus on audience is also important in terms of drafting briefs. Yost views brief drawing as a heuristic process that allows students to test out their ideas, not just to outline their arguments.

More significantly, Yost contends that an emphasis on audience will make students aware of the ethical implications of their arguments. This awareness happens because students see that the "normal action of the social group is coöperation, and this cannot be furthered when the speaker or writer communicates false ideas either through ignorance or intent to deceive" (123). Yost's ideas were similar to those of Buck, who believed that the interests of both the speaker and hearer were "equally furthered by legitimate discourse" ("Present Status" 171). The goal of Buck and Yost's approach to argument was ultimately political: it democratized the communicative process, giving not just the speaker but also the audience a legitimate role.

Connections to Contemporary Feminists' Approaches to Argumentation

As noted, Yost's approach to argument includes significant elements that parallel contemporary feminists' revisioning of argumentation. In particular, connections to Sonja K. Foss and Cindy L Griffin's invitational rhetoric are evident. Foss and Griffin, like Sally Miller Gearhart, assert that rhetoric has traditionally been defined as persuasion; thus, they contend that rhetoric is "characterized by efforts to change others and thus to gain control over them, self-worth derived from and measured by the power exerted over others, and a devaluation of the life worlds of others" (3–4). Foss and Griffin provide an alternative to traditional conceptions of argument based on three feminist principles: (1) the development of equality in relationships and "the elimination of the dominance and elitism that characterize most human relationships" (4); (2) the recognition of the "immanent value of all living beings"; and (3) the fostering of "self-determination," which allows individuals choices in their decisions and lives (4). Foss and Griffin assert that their approach "suggests the need for a new schema of ethics to fit interactional goals other than the inducement of others to adherence to the rhetor's own beliefs" (16). In addition, the authors contend that an invitational rhetoric provides an alternative for women and marginalized groups "to use in their efforts to transform systems of domination and oppression" (16).

These feminist principles were also central to Yost's conception of argument. As noted, Yost believed that the "principle of cooperation" was central to normal group interactions and that arguments occurred when social cooperation was disrupted. Drawing on examples from business to illustrate this principle, Yost asserted that the goal was no longer to take advantage of another in a transaction but to benefit both parties. Built into this view was an emphasis on equality, and closely connected to this principle was the focus Yost placed on audience. As Foss and Griffin highlight, by emphasizing the power of the speaker to change others, traditional rhetoric "also devalues the lives and perspectives of those others" (3). However, Yost stressed the role of audience because she believed argument was integral in fostering broader social cooperation. In addition, Yost's approach to argument underscored the importance of freedom of choice. The audience must be presented with a "genuine" option or choice. In so doing, Yost recognized and respected the authority of audience members in making decisions about their own lives. Finally, Yost saw the need for "a new schema of ethics" in argument, one that built social cooperation and provided an alternative for women and marginalized groups not addressed in traditional approaches to argument (Foss and Griffin 16).

By highlighting the public and social nature of Yost's approach to argument, I have attempted to complicate the binary and essentialist conceptions of gender that are central to the feminization hypothesis. Instead of viewing this transformation as the loss of argumentation and debate, I have demonstrated how it represents the rise of a more ethical approach to argumentation. Yost's sociological perspective, with its stress on ethical behavior, provided a useful alternative to more agonistic, persuasion-oriented rhetoric. In reflecting male cultural practices, this agonistic approach ignored women's experiences and was antithetical to the democratic values that Yost and several other Progressive Era rhetoricians supported.

In her article, Yost notes that she has tried to teach her new approach to argumentation for the past year and a half. With this pedagogy, Yost underscored that arguments emerge not out of textbook examples but out of specific social situations, namely those marked by conflict. Thus, she had her students consider disagreements in their daily lives and then controversies in the newspapers. In so doing, Vassar women learned the significant and integral role the audience played in these various interactions, and they gained a broader civic perspective. They learned how powerful argumentation can be in building community and furthering social cohesion. In addition, Yost's focus on cooperation as the normal functioning of the group encouraged the speaker to have a broader social consciousness. The speaker must respond to the larger needs of the group, not just to his or her individual interests. Yost urged Vassar women to develop a keener sense of social responsibility so that they could communicate in a way that promoted equality, respect, and cooperation. Helen Lockwood exemplified Yost's success in fostering these qualities in her students, as will be shown later in the chapter.

Yost and "The Need of the Community-Mind"

Like Buck and Wylie, Yost's beliefs in a social perspective and cooperation went beyond her classroom to the administrative realm. In particular, her work in argument was helpful to her as the dean of women at Stanford: "[W]hile at the University my systematic work on my special problem—the functional aspect of argument, has been of inestimable value in helping me formulate a theory of my work as dean" (1924 Alumnae). The connection between her work in argument and administration is evident in the article "The Need of the Community-Mind," in which Yost responded to the following questions: "What is the significance of student government and the importance of organized student activities? What are the advantages and dangers of the shift from faculty to student control . . . ? Is the undergraduate learning the lessons to fit him for the place he should take in the larger community?" (131). Yost's article appeared in the alumni publication, the *Stanford Illustrated Review,* three months after she took over the position of dean of women.

In the article, Yost acknowledges that student government and activities provide students with "a civic laboratory where something of the constitution of society, something of the successful and unsuccessful methods of leadership, something of the realization of group responsibility and group loyalty could be developed" (131). However, more significantly, Yost emphasizes that both students and faculty need to recognize that they are part of the same community "and therefore have common problems and the necessity of working together to solve them" (133). Like many contemporary feminists, Yost believed that the process of working through decisions was more important than the decisions themselves. Thus, Yost highlighted process or, more specifically, the type of relationships that needed to be fostered through an ethical process. Yost's focus on the importance of human relationships and ethical processes also resembles Buck's feminist ethics. Both Yost and Buck believed that human interactions needed to build democratic relationships.

Yost writes that in society, the typical social group is more heterogeneous than in the college setting. Her relational ethics is particularly evident in the following passage:

> [T]he good citizen is he who sees not only how to advance his own interests and those of his class, but how to see his own interests in the group interests and to advance these even at what may seem at the time to be a sacrifice of his personal ones. This he does by studying the whole situation, seeing the relation of his community to others, getting light on the present problems from past experiences, and taking thought not only for the immediate present but for the future. (132)

However, college groups tend to be more homogeneous and so focused on their own interests that the broader interests of the community often are ignored. Consequently, student governance tends toward a narrow view of the community, and its perspective of the college is often limited to the present. According to Yost, "We have not only a world which is primarily of the present, but one which is very apt to be both local and personal. It is proverbial throughout the country how little even the college senior knows of what is going on beyond the campus" (132).

In reviewing Yost's work, it is evident that she rejected the idea that the faculty should reassert control over student government and reduce student activities. Such a move would eliminate the gains of such organizations and would "create an atmosphere of distrust and antagonism in the universities" (133). Instead, she argues that both students and faculty need to recognize that they belong to the same community, have common problems, and should work together to solve them. The most important issue, though, is not what is decided but "the spirit in which the decisions are made. There must be a thorough working together of all elements in the community, and this can not be gained without sincere respect of each for the others and a willingness to learn, each from the others" (133). She closes by noting an increase in efforts at achieving student-faculty coordination, pointing to the Bryn Mawr Summer School for Women Workers as a positive example. As in her approach to argumentation, Yost's administrative philosophy emphasized an ethical process in which both sides learn from the other.

In this chapter, I have demonstrated how Yost developed a feminist theory of argument that diverged from agonistic, patriarchal rhetoric. Yost's theory provided an ethical element that was missing from the traditional persuasion-oriented method, and it met the Progressive Era goal of promoting democracy at all levels, even at the level of communication. Her approach to argumentation challenged the traditional emphasis on logic and faculty psychology and instead focused on communication and community building. In so doing, Yost questioned the view of argument as simply persuasion or a reasoning process emphasizing logic and instead saw it as a communicative process that must involve both emotions and reason in order to foster relationships. With her social approach to argumentation, Yost helped to prepare Vassar women for a more public role, one that encouraged them to break away from the traditional family realm and to focus on the larger community and social responsibility.

Helen Drusilla Lockwood

Helen Drusilla Lockwood followed and extended the feminist teaching practices of Buck, Wylie, and Yost. Lockwood "had a lively sense of a tradition of great teaching at Vassar: a tradition of pioneering and originality. . . . She believed, then, that there was a tradition to perpetuate here, and she perpetuated it in her own way" (Gleason, Mace, and Turner 1). In fact, Lockwood even garners a brief mention in *The Group*, Mary McCarthy's autobiographical novel about eight members of her class (Vassar class of 1933) (Heller 163). One character's main interests in college had been journalism, and "her favorite course had been Miss Lockwood's Contemporary Press" (McCarthy 122).

Not all students, though, appreciated Lockwood and her approach to teaching. In the early 1950s, during the McCarthy period, Nancy Jane Fellers, a student in Lockwood's Contemporary Press course, accused Vassar, and Lockwood in particular, of denying Fellers's academic freedom. The case, which generated newspaper articles, even attracted the attention of the House of Representatives, where Rep. B. Carroll Reece of Tennessee presented Fellers's side of the issue, making his statements part of the *Congressional Record*. According to Barbara Swain, her colleague in the Department of English, Lockwood and Vassar were charged with "atheism, liberalism, collectivism, socialism, and communism—all at once!" (6)[10]

Lockwood was steeped in the college and its traditions even before she entered the gates of Vassar. Both her mother and aunt were members of the Vassar class of 1890, "and tales of their college experiences were household stories" (Simpson 5). Lockwood received her bachelor's in 1912 from Vassar and her master's in Intellectual History in 1913 from Columbia University (Swain 15).[11] At Vassar, Lockwood was a serious student, who, in addition to her studies, participated actively in debate and tutored in Latin and English. After graduating from Vassar, Lockwood taught for a brief time at a New Jersey public school, next worked two years at a Massachusetts girls' school, and then taught for six years at the Baldwin School in Byrn Mawr. Lockwood taught two semesters in Bryn Mawr's newly created Summer School for Women Workers in Industry, later serving as the director of English studies and as a representative on the Board of Directors (Swain 17). As Rita Rubinstein Heller points out, "[E]xtant Lockwood syllabi provide a striking illustration of the tough-minded liberal empowering workers through explicit skill development" (213). In her dissertation "The Women of Summer: The Bryn Mawr Summer School for Women Workers: 1921–1938," Heller places Lockwood among those teachers who had the "greatest impact" on the school during its first period (1921–27).[12]

In 1922, Lockwood returned to graduate school for three years, studying first at the Sorbonne in Paris and then completing her doctorate in Comparative Literature at Columbia University (Simpson 24). Lockwood's interest in workers and labor history carried over into her graduate work at Columbia. According to Swain, Lockwood later told her that she found her teaching experience at the Bryn Mawr Summer School to be "'devastating.'" As Swain explains, Lockwood "felt she had not known how to speak to the workers, what language would carry across the gap in experience" (19). In her dissertation, Lockwood examined the writing of workers in England and France from 1820 to 1850. Her dissertation, *Tools and the Man,* was published by Columbia in 1927. In her study, Lockwood "included some account of English worker-poets, but gave detailed accounts of French workers, those who wrote both poetry and articles during those years" (Swain 20). According to Swain, Lockwood's study reassured her that "'the people'—the workers—*could* find profit in the art of the middle class, and they had demonstrated their power to find their own voices . . ." (21, emphasis in original). Lockwood continued her connection to the Bryn Mawr School and its successors for some forty years by either serving on the board, planning and supervising the English program, or taking part in the Arts Workshop (Swain 21).

After completing her dissertation, Lockwood taught composition in the English Department at Wellesley College for two years. She then returned to Vassar in 1927 as an assistant professor of English and remained until her retirement in 1956, chairing the English Department from 1950 to 1956. In 1969 and 1970, she made "substantial gifts" to Vassar's Center for Black Studies (Gleason, Mace, and Turner 1). She died in 1971, leaving an estate of six million dollars to Vassar (Simpson 1). Lockwood left this unrestricted estate to the college "with the hope that my interest in the quality of teaching and my concern with pioneering in the reinterpretation and deepening of a liberal education will be remembered" (qtd. in Simpson 1). One tangible outcome of this gift is the Helen Drusilla Lockwood wing of the library, which "now stands as a memorial to the formidable 'HDL'" (Heller 163). Another legacy is Lockwood's college letters. Lockwood's typical Sunday letters to her family—"Dear people"—for instance, were "seldom less than fourteen pages and occasionally as many as twenty-four" (Simpson 2). These letters offer an inside glimpse of her life at Vassar: "how she is getting on in her courses, what she thinks of her teachers, her calls on the faculty, her attendance at chapels, lectures and concerts, her work in debate, her friendships and roommate troubles, and all the fun and games and tears that came her way . . ." (Simpson 2). The letters provide a detailed and fascinating record of the growth of Lockwood's intellectual powers, her self-awareness, and her interest in social issues. In particular, they document quite explicitly the profound influence that her participation in college debating had on her development and her subsequent career and life choices.

Lockwood's Intellectual Development and Debate

During her college years at Vassar, Lockwood participated strenuously and successfully in debate. This participation came through her sophomore argumentation course, taught by Mary Yost, and the college's two debating societies, *T. & M.* (odd-year classes) and *Qui Vive* (even-year classes). Lockwood had debated in high school, and her mother had given Helen her *Qui Vive* pin when she entered Vassar. In a 1953 article, Lockwood stressed the popularity and broader political significance of these early debating societies: "So long had it been taken for granted that Vassar women would be spokesmen in their communities. Everyone belonged" ("Past was Real" 6). The debating societies were important to students because Vassar faculty often assumed that their students would be leaders in their communities. In her first year, Lockwood already was looking forward to Yost's sophomore-level course in argumentation, which was closely connected with debate (Simpson 12). In the 1912 *Vassarion,* the following motto was set against her name: "In arguing, the simple heat / Scorched both the slippers off his feet" (89; qtd. in Simpson 53). As Alan Simpson points out, debate played a significant role in her intellectual development:[13] "She [Lockwood] made her mark as a debater in her sophomore year, was the power behind the speaker in her junior year, and then speaker herself. It is almost impossible to exaggerate what this activity did to sharpen her most characteristic intellectual powers, the capacity for close analysis, for rapid organization, for clear-cut exposition, and for relentless criticism" (12).

One exciting memory for Lockwood occurred when Yost told her that she had recommended Lockwood to the *Qui Vive* chair as a candidate for the "big debate" committee (Letter to her parents, 6 Feb. 1910, 1). These committees participated in the intersociety debate between *Qui Vive* and *T. & M.*: "[S]he asked me if I would like to serve. As if there could be any doubt! Well I was so thrilled I could hardly work" (6 Feb. 1910, 1). Lockwood also learned that she had been considered for a part in one of the hall plays. Unfortunately, she could not do both because rehearsals and committee meetings coincided. However, Lockwood chose debate over acting: "Isn't it maddening when you do get a chance to be in a play not to be able to? But I would rather be on the debate committee for I enjoy that sort of work, and it will count toward my arg. [course in argumentation] and it is one of the biggest honors in college. I guess you would think so if you saw the way everyone fusses over me. It is quite fun" (6 Feb. 1910, 4). In 1912, Lockwood served as the chair of the *Qui Vive* "big debate" committee. In the 1911 debate, the societies argued the following resolution: "That our present immigration laws be amended by the passage of the Gardner Bill, advocating the literacy test." The debate had three judges: "President Garfield of Williams College, son of the twentieth President of the United States; Miss Kristine Mann . . . she had been an instructor in English at Vassar and was now at the Cornell Medical School; and Professor D. W. Redmond, from City College" (Simpson 35). (Mann co-authored with Buck *A Handbook of Argumentation and Debating*, 1906.) Although Lockwood's team did not win, she was undaunted by the loss and already making plans for next year's "big debate":

> The great event is over and though the decision was given in favor of 1911 we are all very happy for they had a hard fight to win. . . . Miss Yost said that we far surpassed T and M's Junior debating. She added that if we improved next year as much as T and M had since last year, nothing could defeat us. So you see that we are all feeling that work well done is victory and are already making plans for next year. (The blot above is not due to tears but I spilled some water in fixing my flowers.) (qtd. in Simpson 40)[14]

According to Swain, the qualities that Lockwood later stressed in her own teaching were "[l]ogic, inductive reasoning, and structure . . ." (15). These were the skills that she had learned in Yost's argumentation class and debating activities at Vassar.

Lockwood's fascination with debate and argumentation and the influence of Yost led Lockwood to become interested in English. In one of her letters, she writes of a lengthy conference discussion she had with Yost concerning her future: "Oh yes and she [Yost] said if I had any thoughts of teaching English I certainly must take Miss Wylie's Senior English course and Miss Buck's course in critical writing. As Miss Buck is one of *the* personalities of the college I shouldn't object at all" (Letter to her parents, 10 Apr. 1910, emphasis in original, 4). Lockwood, who eventually wanted to teach English, already had taken K English, nineteenth-century prose, from Wylie in the fall, and she went on to take Buck's course in Literary Criticism in her senior year.

Lockwood's choice of English was made despite the recruiting efforts of the Latin and Greek faculty to convince Lockwood that she should join them. However, debate had enhanced Lockwood's ability to see multiple sides of an issue, and this skill led her to want more breadth in her studies (Simpson 12), as she explains: "We had a splendid discussion in Argumentation today finally culminating in the decision to debate on the subject, Resolved that the moving shows are a hindrance to the development of legitimate drama. So you see we get sociology, political economy and a lot else mixed up in this course. Miss Yost herself is so broad that her course cannot help being so" (qtd. in Simpson 13).[15] However, Lockwood's Greek teacher, Abby Leach, did not agree that Lockwood needed such breadth. Near the end of her sophomore year, Lockwood describes a conversation she had with "Miss Leach," whom she ran into after her argumentation class. Leach immediately asks Lockwood whether she plans to continue her Greek, and Lockwood then tells Leach about her plans to gain greater breadth:

> Whereupon she raked me over in great style. "Do you see what you are doing? You will go on this broadening plan of yours and when you get through there won't be a single thing you can teach." I explained that I would have English and then she went on to say how much help my Greek would be to English! Sometime I should like to pin her down and make her tell just how more advanced Greek is necessary for English. Well then I said [*sic* no quotation marks] But I must have some science (Miss Yost has just told me that I ought to take biology for English which Miss Leach flatly contradicted.) Well to my science argument she said "But you

are having your science now aren't you?" I said yes and before I could say another word she popped out "and you ~~didn't~~ don't like it either do you!" which I must say rather amazed me. . . . Well fortunately just then the bell rang and she had to go in for which I was more than thankful. Her last words were "Well you think it over. I want you for a graduate scholar in Greek and you could take your English too." I suppose I will have to have a real time with her before I get through. (Letter to her parents, 17 Apr. 1910, 1–2)[16]

Clearly, Leach's keen desire to recruit Lockwood as a graduate student was no match for Lockwood's even firmer resolve to make her own decisions. The passage also shows how influential Yost and debate had become in Lockwood's life.

Lockwood and the Feminist Teaching Tradition at Vassar

In addition to Yost, other mentors at Vassar were influential during Lockwood's formative years. According to Alan Simpson, the two teachers who made the greatest impact were Laura Johnson Wylie in English and Lucy Maynard Salmon in History: "They were inspiring teachers and they formed her ambition to be an inspiring teacher. She studied them, called on them in their Poughkeepsie homes, and took no important step without consulting them" (19). During her visits to Wylie's home in Poughkeepsie, Lockwood also frequently talked with Gertrude Buck, as is evident from the following letter: "Thursday I took Cordelia [her sister, then a first-year student] down to Miss Wylie's. While I was there I had such a nice talk with Miss Buck. Almost always when I go down there I do talk with her and I think it is quite as pleasant as talking with Miss Wylie for she doesn't pop out at you so" (Letter to her parents, 10 Dec. 1911, 2). Not only did the two women serve as mentors during Lockwood's undergraduate studies, but Buck and Wylie also appear to have been influential in encouraging Lockwood to pursue graduate studies at Michigan. In one of her letters, Lockwood writes of the strong connection between Vassar and Michigan:

I have given up Michigan for I think we have gone crazy over it here for several of our English instructors are from there. And Professor Scott is quoted on all occasions so that I really feel that I wouldn't be getting such a very new point of view if I were studying with him for Miss Buck and

Miss Wylie are both devotées of his work, methods and ideas so I guess I would rather go to Columbia. (Letter to her parents, 25 Feb. 1912, 18)

Although Lockwood chose Columbia instead of Michigan, it is apparent that Buck and Wylie encouraged their students to pursue graduate studies and that they then hired instructors with the same progressive education ideas as their own. Not only Wylie but also Buck played a significant role in mentoring Lockwood.

Buck and Wylie emphasized an experiential, publicly focused pedagogy that intellectually challenged students; Salmon's approach was similar. According to Elizabeth Daniels, Salmon "sent her students to primary sources to learn history, including places outside the Vassar campus: she rarely used textbooks and believed that personal observation and experience were as important as conventional authorities in print. Her classroom was informal and unconventional, but rigorous—a seminar to which each student was forced to make a contribution" (*Bridges to the World* 59). Lockwood continued this tradition, sending her students out into the community of Poughkeepsie "to find out what was there, who the people were, and what they wanted" (Daniels, *Bridges to the World* 176).

In Wylie's K English, Nineteenth-Century Prose, Lockwood writes that the course is intellectually demanding, requiring her full concentration: " . . . Miss W [Wylie] evidently is still trying to keep us in the air. I am wondering if she ever comes down to Earth or even near it so we can get within hailing distance" (Letter to her parents, 19 Nov. 1910, 13). In a letter written the following year, Lockwood describes a conference she had with Wylie in which Wylie encouraged Lockwood to talk more in class:

> She [Wylie] said "The strange part is you have the talking face, you respond instantly to an idea and look as though you were going to talk and then you don't talk. Now you are strong enough to force the class back if they get off the track, or if they pass by an idea quickly hold them back." And so she went on. I started out by saying that I had the feeling that I wasn't getting hold of things the way I ought to and she fairly pounced on me for saying so, "Why is that possible Miss Lockwood? Do you know I hadn't felt that way at all [*sic* no question mark]. I consider you one of my best girls and if you would only do that one thing, talk more in class!" It was an encouraging interview anyway although I am sure she gives me credit for a great many more ideas than I really have. (Letter to her parents, 19 Feb. 1911, 10)

Lockwood's comments suggest that she benefited from the individualized attention of the conference. The advice given by Wylie also encouraged a more confident, assertive young woman, different from the passive and quiet traditional role. An emphasis on independent thinking was also central to Wylie's approach to teaching. Young women in Wylie's classes "were not only stimulated to think for themselves, they were constrained to continue instant in so doing, and to make their thinking fundamental, honest, and clear" (Warren, "Retrospect" 90).

The English Department's stress on self-reliance and critical thinking is evident in Lockwood's reflections on her Vassar experience. In a draft letter written to Wylie nine years after leaving Vassar, Lockwood notes that

> I find that my work in English stands out above all my other academic work at Vassar as an intellectual and spiritual influence. This is due to several factors: the personalities with whom I worked, the fact that the courses were not cluttered with aspects of the subject that seem unessential to an undergraduate's mind . . . ; the fact that the truth was not given to me *ex cathedr*, but that I was expected to think independently and fearlessly. (1 June 1921, 1)[17]

Lockwood's reflections show that she is deeply aware of the impact that the department and its teachers had on her intellectual and professional development. In her draft letter, she discusses how the department continues to shape her current teaching practices: "Again and again my own natural experimental tendencies have been encouraged by yours at Vassar . . ." (1). This influence is evident in the fact that Lockwood also became known as a teacher who pushed her students to "think independently and fearlessly" (1).

As noted, during her undergraduate years, Lockwood frequently consulted with Wylie, Buck, and Salmon and visited them at their Poughkeepsie homes. Although these women were influential, Lockwood did not unquestioningly accept all of their ideas. For example, Wylie, Buck, and Salmon were active supporters of suffrage; however, Lockwood remained unconvinced by the pro-suffrage platform: "I don't go galloping off after wild ideas. Miss Salmon has just come back from New York where she marched in the suffragette parade. She says how inspiring it was to walk to music. If she had ever skated to music she wouldn't have to bother with the suffrage movement to get the feeling" (qtd. in Simpson 16).[18]

A product of her mentors' training, during her college years Lockwood expanded her ability to develop her own perspective.

However, in other ways, particularly in teaching, she continued the feminist tradition of Wylie, Buck, Yost, and Salmon. Lockwood's classes, like her mentors,' were socially focused and intellectually demanding. Lockwood's teaching has been characterized as "stunningly innovative" and "challenging," and she is described as someone who "did not suffer fools gladly" (Daniels, *Bridges to the World* 175; Swain 1; Gaines 14). As Rita Rubinstein Heller points out, Lockwood "was respected, but feared, by almost two generations of Vassar women, as well as her Bryn Mawr blue collar women" (163). In describing Lockwood's approach to life and teaching, colleague Barbara Swain writes that "[t]he challenge to know what you really think and are, to find your 'basic assumptions' and discover what has molded you, characterized her approach to everyone. This was the knife-point with which she probed all the minds, young and old, sluggish or lively, with which she worked" (1). Lockwood believed that such self-awareness would benefit students both intellectually and personally. This emphasis on forcing students to examine their "basic assumptions" also is evident in the following passage from economist Caroline Ware, who, like Lockwood, attended Vassar and later taught at Vassar and at the Bryn Mawr Summer School for Women Workers: "She was a great teacher by any dimension. . . . She was very unique—one of the very best. She had a way of posing the relevant questions which took the person outside the bounds of expectation. . . . At Vassar she was legendary for coming into a class of freshmen, looking around and saying, 'I suppose there are some of you here who still believe in God'" (qtd. in Heller 165). Lockwood's transgressive pedagogy is evident in this passage. Like Buck, Lockwood pushed her students to question commonly accepted knowledge. In significant ways, Lockwood's approach can be viewed as a reaction against patriarchal and conservative approaches. She wanted her students to think for themselves, to examine rather than simply reproduce traditional assumptions. By pushing students to examine and potentially move against their unexamined beliefs, Lockwood, like hooks, made "education the practice of freedom" (12).

Lockwood's Contemporary Press and Public Discussion Classes

Lockwood taught first-year composition, critical writing, American Literature, and English Romantic poetry. She also developed two courses that enacted her socially conscious pedagogy: The Contemporary Press and Public Discussion. The 1928–29 *Vassar College Catalogue* describes The Contemporary Press course as the "[s]tudy of the presentation of contemporary artistic and social problems in selected periodicals and newspapers of America and Europe. Each student will work on a chosen subject throughout the year and present her material in a series of articles" (*Vassar College Catalogue* 93). Lockwood's Public Discussion course focused on observing and discussing current public issues, activities, and debates. According to Lockwood, "This course aims at defining democratic processes of discussion and effective communication of matters of public concern" ("Outline" 4). The 1933–34 *Vassar College Catalogue* states that the course stresses "oral and written exposition of social and literary questions of public interest. Speaking to different audiences, discussion in conferences, cross questioning, working toward a consensus of opinion. Practice in finding issues, defining terms, and marshaling evidence" (*Vassar College Catalogue* 79). According to a 1933 article in the *Vassar Quarterly,* the course developed the English Department's "tradition of social criticism and debate," more specifically the department's previous courses in argumentation ("New Courses" 266).

Lockwood's emphasis on critical thinking and a broader social consciousness is evident in undated course notes on English 312, The Contemporary Press. Lockwood clarifies that she uses the term *Contemporary Press* "generally to apply to problems of present day communication rather than to newspapers alone, for they are all interrelated" ("Contemporary Press" 4). In the course, her female students critically analyzed magazines and newspapers; investigated strategies for appealing to different audiences (i.e., "mass," "scholarly," "liberal"); discussed "the history of freedom of the press, its meaning in terms of possible controls and possible alternatives for the survival of any magazine or paper at all . . ." ("Outline" 2); analyzed the "development of meaning in 'stereotypes'" (*Contemporary Press* 4); and practiced writing articles for magazines and reporting news for the college's weekly radio program. Students also completed surveys in Poughkeepsie or at the college and then reported the results in news stories and features. In addition, students were to examine "the way life works" ("Outline" 2). According to Lockwood:

> As a basis for this and indeed for other parts of the course, each student writes at the beginning of the year and checks again at the end of the

year a statement of her own values and a statement of those of some man or woman whom she knows very well, values concerning God and the universe, the state, earning a living, family, education, recreation, people different from her family group. This exercise presupposes that the students cannot get far with reporting or analysis without knowing their own presuppositions. They usually find this a surprising and important exercise. ("Outline" 2–3)

In writing their reflections, students applied critical analysis to their own values to become aware of the different social norms and assumptions that shaped their lives and their own thinking processes. The assignment implied that the course might cause students to change or rethink some of their long-held beliefs.

In addition, students in The Contemporary Press completed interdepartmental group exhibits on topics such as *Problems with Veterans* or *Activities of Organizations in the Dutchess County Social Planning Council* or *Constructive Forces to Measure up the Atomic Bomb*" ("Outline," emphasis in original, 3). In these group projects, Contemporary Press students developed the texts for the exhibit, while students in other departments such as painting, sculpting, and photography created accompanying visuals. The student exhibits were then displayed in Vassar's Social Museum or sometimes sent to different community organizations. One of Lockwood's early interdisciplinary projects, the Social Museum was created in 1936 and designed for student exhibits on subjects related to Dutchess County ("Social Museum" 11; Swain 11).

In their papers, Lockwood's students demonstrate the course's emphasis on strengthening their understanding of national and international issues and their analytical abilities. For example, in a 1945 paper titled "Poughkeepsie's Post-war World," Harriet Harvey completed brief and longer news articles for the *Poughkeepsie New Yorker* based on a public opinion survey on postwar policy questions conducted in the community. For the survey, Harvey explains that "[p]airs of girls were assigned to two representative blocks apiece where they went from door to door until each pair had collected twelve interviews. When they returned to college, they pooled their results which made a ninety-four interview total" (1). Students asked Poughkeepsie residents the following questions: "Should the United

States join a world organization after the war? Should the United States maintain a large military establishment in the post-war world? Should the United States have a year of compulsory military training in peace-time for 1) men, 2) women? What should we do with Germany after the war? What should we do with Japan after the war? and What are we fighting for?" (3–5). This assignment demonstrates Lockwood's interest in having her students involved in their community and thinking about broader social issues.

Similar pedagogical goals were evident in Lockwood's Public Discussion course. In her "Notes on English 218, Public Discussion," written 21 June 1956 at the time of her retirement, Lockwood presents the key principles of the course, asserting,

> Public Discussion is an alternative to war and to conformity without consent.
>
> It involves the full participation of every member of a group in his full capacity. It involves both his logic and his emotions.
>
> It involves his use of voice and his whole body; his written outlines and his oral presentation.
>
> ("Notes on English 218" 1)

Like many contemporary rhetoricians, Lockwood viewed public discussion as significant because it provided an alternative to violence; and like Buck and Yost, she emphasized the need for a democratic process, one that blended reason and emotions.

Lockwood explains that students are slow to embrace these principles; however, their acceptance of them "is crucial if there is to be the mutual respect based on recognized need of each other without which the processes of democracy are impossible" (1). (The references in the following discussion draw from Lockwood's "Notes on English 218.") Other significant course principles include students' participation in selecting the class topics. For example, at the beginning of the course, Lockwood asked students to outline the subjects they would like to discuss, present their ideas to the class, and then reach a consensus, as a class, on the topics they wanted to cover. As she explains, "The students always have as much responsibility as the teacher for making the program. The program is constructed by the group as it moves along" (2).

A significant element of the course was the brief form, which reflected Lockwood's training in argumentation and debate. There were seven main elements of the brief: (1) to define the problem, which requires defining key terms; (2) a two-part *"statement of the situation,"* which covers the present and the history of the issue; (3) *"admitted facts";* (4) *"clash of opinion";* (5) *"the issue, put in the form of questions";* (6) *"the proof of the argument";* and (7) *"the conclusion and summary"* (4–6, emphasis in original).

The "clash of opinion" was to be written in dialogic form in two adjacent columns, with each claim "answering the corresponding one in the opposite column" (5); however, she acknowledges that sometimes issues have more than two sides. According to Lockwood, the "clash of opinion is more than a rhetorical form. It is the explicit acceptance of differences, understanding of them, respecting them" (5–6). In acknowledging others' opinions, Vassar women were learning a sense of fairness in discussion, and, in so doing, they were broadening their own perspectives. In traditional argument and debate pedagogy, learning others' opinions typically was used to help students refute those opinions, not to deepen their understanding of others' views. The next important step was to reword the issue into a question. According to Lockwood, this step represents a "psychological attitude, a stage of suspended judgment explicitly recognized" (6). Students were learning a sense of openness in argumentation; they were learning to ask questions about the issue rather than to argue for a prefigured conclusion.

Although Lockwood's brief includes aspects of the traditional academic debate brief, it is a more dynamic, inquiry and audience-centered structure. As Lockwood explains, "Most classes the students go to, provide them with a fixed structure neatly made out by the teacher. Adult public discussion does not work this way" (4). Differences in Lockwood's approach are evident when examining Gordon Thomas and A. Westley Rowland's discussions of briefs in *Argumentation and Debate: Principles and Practices* (1954). Thomas and Rowland begin their discussion by describing the brief as a "'map,' a symbolic representation of all the evidence and arguments that are available" and a "blueprint of the ground to be covered" (462). However, after using these more open metaphors, they soon inform students that "[b]ased upon legal procedures and debate custom, a series of rules has been adopted which must be adhered to in drawing a brief" (462). The authors emphasis on "rules" that "must be adhered to" seems to reflect Lockwood's criticism of traditional briefs as fixed and neatly ordered structures. Thomas and Rowland then introduce a conventional three-part model for briefs: introduction, discussion, and conclusion. According to the authors, the introduction provides all the information necessary to understand the issue; the discussion or proof "should contain all available evidence and argument to be used on a given side of a proposition . . ." (464); and the conclusion should summarize the key discussion points. The traditional brief focuses on one side of the question, proving a position; in contrast, Lockwood's seven-step brief teaches students to consider thoughtfully perspectives different from their own and to suspend their judgments before determining their positions. It emphasizes a more democratic approach, but it still recognizes that individuals will disagree and have different positions.

Connections to Deborah Tannen's *The Argument Culture: Moving from Debate to Dialogue* are evident in Lockwood's seven-part brief. In her book, Tannen writes about "a pervasive warlike atmosphere that makes us approach public dialogue, and just about anything we need to accomplish, as if it were a fight" (3). Although Tannen doesn't believe this model of argument should be completely eliminated, she suggests that "we need to rethink whether this is the *only* way, or *always* the best way, to carry out our affairs" (26, emphasis in original). In addition, she suggests that "our notion of 'debate' [be expanded] to include more dialogue" (26). In examining Lockwood's approach to the brief, it is evident that she was trying to reconceptualize traditional approaches to argument, to move away from an emphasis on winning toward a more dialogic, inquiry-based process.

Other key aspects of Lockwood's course are the "Elements of persuasion" and "continuity." For Lockwood, the most important aspects of persuasion are "clarity and thoroughness" ("Notes on English 218" 6). As she explains, "The emotions need to be uncovered and the analysis carried through. The students should speak simply and carry their audience by their respect for the opinions of others and the soundness of their own reasoning" (6). Lockwood's ideas were similar to Buck's and Yost's, who believed that the interests of both the speaker and hearer were equally advanced by "legitimate discourse" (Buck, "Present Status").

At the beginning of each class, Lockwood encouraged continuity by having selected students present oral summaries of the previous class.

She explains that the summaries reveal "1) how much they have in their notebooks [and] 2) how much they have actually absorbed in usable form" ("Notes on English 218" 7). Thus, the summaries show students' abilities to listen and synthesize the information. Lockwood explains that summaries are often important components of public meetings: "Students need to be told dramatically that in many public meetings a recorder is appointed who rises at the end and summarizes the main points because otherwise people go away with vague impressions and an over-personalized emphasis" ("Notes on English 218" 8).

The course's political dimensions and emphasis on group problem-solving skills are evident in Lockwood's discussion of elements that have been part of previous year's courses. Near the end of the term, for example, students typically studied parliamentary procedure, and the class would follow *Robert's Rules of Order* for at least one week. Some years, students presented "some very interesting and lively" panel discussions over the local radio stations ("Notes on English 218" 24). As noted, when the Vassar Social Museum was in operation, students typically participated in an interdepartmental exhibit, "such as the one on *Man Can Live in Harmony with Nature,* an explanation of problems of population and land in terms of TVA [Tennessee Valley Authority], the Great Plains (Missouri Valley Authority), and similar efforts in China and the Andes" (24). According to Lockwood, the benefit of such a project was "seeing a big problem beyond any of them alone, become integrated and understandable by the use of all these groups of people and all of these disciplines in subjects" (24–25). In addition, students spoke at various county meetings, helped with elections, and assisted in planning a weekend conference. In diverse ways, Lockwood's course prepared Vassar women for participation in political organizations; it prepared them to be agents of change in their communities.

The following student description of Lockwood's Public Discussion course shows how she challenged students to explore their unexamined assumptions and unsupported generalizations and pushed them to think for themselves. According to Billie Davis Gaines (Vassar class of 1958), Lockwood's Public Discussion course was "dedicated to this proposition": "Identify the thorniest, most complex problems that face the world's societies, especially American society, and bring to bear on those problems all you can read, all you can learn, the sharpest analytical skills you can muster, the deepest compassion you can summon. Bring all of this to literate, civilized, public discussion, and those problems can be solved"(13). In the course, which was limited to about eighteen students, Gaines writes that "silence was not exactly an option. No matter. That course remains the most challenging I ever had, the breakthrough intellectual experience that shaped for the rest of my life the way I use resources to understand the nature of a problem and the manner in which I work with people to try to find solutions for them" (14). Lockwood's emphasis on full participation resembles the transgressive pedagogy that hooks advocates: "There must be an ongoing recognition that everyone influences the classroom dynamic, that everyone contributes" (8). This emphasis on full participation was also central to the pedagogy of Lockwood's mentors. In addition, Gaines's description demonstrates how, similar to her predecessors, Lockwood focused on civic discourse and encouraged Vassar women to think and speak for themselves.

In *Vote and Voice: Women's Organizations and Political Literacy, 1915–1930,* Wendy B. Sharer discusses how the League of Women Voters (LWV) also promoted rhetorical education to increase women's political influence. Sharer notes that the LWV "attempted to situate education for citizenship in locales familiar to women" (136), such as women's colleges, normal schools, and junior colleges. Several of Lockwood's teaching practices, including instruction in public speaking, parliamentary procedure, interviewing and surveying, and radio forums, parallel the rhetorical curriculum promoted by League instructors. Like many League teachers, Lockwood was training her female students to be politically active. In her analysis, Sharer asserts, though, that many of these practices favored those who had access to such methods. For instance, Sharer contends that while training in parliamentary procedure "was a familiar element in the tradition of middle-class women's organizations," women who were unable to gain access to these organizations, or to take League classes that taught such strategies, "did not possess the specialized vocabulary necessary for full participation in this form of deliberative procedure" (155). These limitations also apply to Lockwood's classes at Vassar; her teaching strategies primarily benefited those students privileged enough to attend Vassar.

However, it is important to note that many of these strategies, including parliamentary procedures, public speaking, and a focus on group problem solving, were part of the curriculum of the labor schools at which she was associated. This focus, for example, is evident in information on the 1946 silver anniversary of the Hudson Shore Labor School, for which Lockwood served as the chair of the school's Board of Directors. The description of the English curriculum indicates that the aim is to help students "to express themselves better, orally and in writing. This includes writing for the purposes of record-keeping, publicity, and correspondence. Here, too, is included work in parliamentary procedure" ("Hudson Shore Labor School" 2). In addition, students also participate in a "workshop—in which students work on individual problems of immediate concern. Usually the findings of research done on such problems are interpreted in some visual form . . . a chart, poster, or even poetry, a play, or dance choreography" (2). Lockwood's belief that the labor schools upheld equal access and democracy is apparent in an article she wrote on the Bryn Mawr Summer School: "To any believer in democracy, the Bryn Mawr Summer School for Women Workers in Industry is one of the most revealing and encouraging experiments in the United States" ("Bryn Mawr" 161). In Lockwood's work at the Hudson Shore and Bryn Mawr labor schools, it is evident that she was trying to cut across class and race lines to provide her students with skills so that they, too, could increase their political influence.

A significant aspect of Lockwood's curriculum at Vassar and at the labor schools at which she was affiliated was a stress on the connection between what happens in the classroom and broader society. This belief was evident as early as her college days: "I want thinking to be followed by doing. Emerson says that character is more important than brains, that a 'great soul will be strong to live as well as strong to think.' Doesn't that sum up culture?" (qtd. in Simpson 16). This focus also can be found in an unpublished pamphlet Lockwood wrote in 1967, detailing the students' experiences at Vassar under President Henry Noble MacCracken:[19]

 . . . Students at Vassar shared in the development of participation in the community. The vision of social responsibility and pubic service whether volunteer or paid, has pervaded the climate of the college.

From the time a student entered to her graduation, she heard it expressed by the leaders of the college, she saw them often acting it themselves in Poughkeepsie or the nation, and she found it assumed in her courses. She volunteered

in the social centers in Poughkeepsie and helped them [through fund drives]
financially. She expected to take part in making the college community. . . .
(qtd. in Daniels, *Bridges to the World* 175, emphasis in original)

This quotation captures a fundamental aspect of Lockwood's approach
to life and pedagogy, a focus on social responsibility, civic participation,
service, and activism. These ideals were also central to Lockwood's mentors at Vassar: Laura Johnson Wylie, Gertrude Buck, Lucy Maynard
Salmon, and Mary Yost.

Throughout this analysis, I have demonstrated how Buck's approach
to rhetoric, pedagogy, administration, and drama was inextricably connected to her feminism, women's activism, and Progressive Era reform.
Buck's reform efforts included her participation in progressive education,
women's suffrage, and the Little Theater movement. A recurring theme in
Buck's career was her attempt to foster equity by eliminating dualisms and
hierarchies, including class divisions, and insuring a transfer of knowledge so
that society was "leveled up" (Buck, *Social Criticism* 39). This emphasis was
particularly evident in her efforts to reconceptualize traditional approaches
to argument, pedagogy, and administration. It was also apparent in her work
in the community theater and literary criticism. Although Buck's achievements weren't without contradictions and limitations, it is evident that
her goal was to create egalitarian and cooperative relationships in order to
build a more democratic society. Buck's efforts remind individuals that their
communities and their individual relationships profoundly influence them
and that they need to ensure that these relationships are democratic.

Buck's work was linked to the important contributions of women such
as Laura Johnson Wylie, Mary Yost, and Helen Drusilla Lockwood. This
project recovers their efforts and voices, contributing to the scholarly
project of writing women into the history of rhetoric. The description of
their achievements is meant only as a beginning; much more could be
written about these women. The accomplishments of Buck, Wylie, Yost,
and Lockwood demonstrate a vibrant tradition of women theorizing ethical approaches to teaching and argumentation that encouraged women to
consider various social issues, to gain a broader civic perspective.

It is obvious that Buck played a significant role in influencing her
students and their education. One way she did so was by introducing
them to progressive education and the feminist ethics that was integral

to her pedagogy and rhetoric. Buck's work highlighted a student-centered approach and a view of education as inherently political, rather than a value-free skill. Her ideas reflected the Progressive Era belief that the goal of education was to further democracy. In addition, Buck shaped the lives of her students through mentoring and encouraging them to pursue graduate education. This mentoring influence was evident in Lockwood's letter specifically noting how Buck and Wylie encouraged students to pursue graduate studies at Michigan with Fred Newton Scott. This connection was also evident in Buck's letters to Scott, in which she distinctly asked about the progress of her former Vassar students or about potential candidates that could be hired as teachers at Vassar.

Yet another way Buck's influence was played out was in hiring her former students as Vassar teachers. As noted, Yost and Lockwood returned to teach at Vassar after gaining their graduate degrees. In exploring Yost's work at Vassar, it is evident that Buck influenced her graduate studies and her ideas in argumentation. Yost carried on this tradition by theorizing a new approach to argumentation and by introducing her students, such as Lockwood, to these ideas. And Lockwood, in turn, was influenced enough by this tradition to know that she was perpetuating it and that it came from teachers like Buck, Wylie, and Yost. Buck and Wylie were among a group of women administrators at the Seven Sisters colleges who helped their graduates secure jobs. As Barbara L'Eplattenier and Lisa Mastrangelo emphasize, viewing women like Buck and Wylie as "administrators and as part of a network refutes the notion that these women. . . were individual actors, toiling, in isolation, with little or no support from those around them" (118). Both within and outside of Vassar, these networks were in place.

Most central was Buck's work in argumentation and debate. This tradition created a significant line of Vassar women involved in practicing and theorizing argumentation, a tradition that has been overlooked and mislabeled. It has been overlooked because of generalizations such as "[a]rgument and debate could not be major parts of a women's course," which have discouraged scholars from exploring women's contributions to argument during this period (Connors, *Composition-Rhetoric* 54). Likewise, it has been mislabeled because descriptions of women and men have tended to uphold binary and essentialist conceptions of gender. However, Vassar's tradition included women interested in approaches to argument that focused on issues of social concern and that reconfigured dominant practices. Similarly, Buck's textbooks and debating activities at the college helped to prepare Vassar women for a more vocal and public role, one that encouraged them to look beyond domestic concerns to focus on community activism. In a time when women were denied the vote and suppressed, Buck was teaching her students an approach to argumentation and pedagogy that underscored their full participation and equality, that assumed their intervention in the public realm. Buck completed her work in argumentation and debate despite the fact the college administration often worked to maintain a more traditional view of gender and women's role in society. Women like Buck and Wylie were focused on Progressive Era concerns, particularly social justice for women. Their goal was to achieve the Progressive ideal, which Buck defines as "the widest and deepest living possible at any given moment. Or it is the most highly developed interrelation of life—on the one hand the life of the individual, on the other that of the social organism" (Buck and Scott, *Organic Education* 16). Progressive education, rhetoric, drama, and argumentation not only are the products of social conditions; they have the power to transform society into the ideal. This spirit of progressive reform was at the heart of Buck's life and work.

Notes
Works Cited
Index

NOTES

Introduction

1. John Gage teaches this course at the University of Oregon.

2. Although this is the first book-length study of Gertrude Buck's work, JoAnn Campbell has published an excellent overview of Buck's work and life, and a collection of her writings in *Toward a Feminist Rhetoric: The Writing of Gertrude Buck* (1996). Several dissertations also have focused on Buck's work. See JoAnn Campbell's "Gertrude Buck and the Celebration of Community: A History of Writing Instruction at Vassar College, 1898–1922" (1989); Vickie Ricks's "Revisioning Traditions Through Rhetoric: Studies in Gertrude Buck's Social Theory of Discourse" (1989); Kevin James Koch's "Gertrude Buck and the Emergence of a Transactional Theory of Language" (1992); Suzanne Bordelon's "Gertrude Buck's Democratic Theory of Discourse and Pedagogy: A Cultural History" (1998); Barbara E. L'Eplattenier's "Investigating Institutional Power: Women Administrators During the Progressive Era 1890–1920" (1999); and Carol S. Chalk's "Gertrude Buck in the Writing Center: A Tutor Training Model to Challenge Nineteenth-Century Trends" (2004). In addition, Dana Hood Morgan wrote her master's thesis on Buck, "Gertrude Buck's Rhetoric: The Living Expression of Thought" (1995), as did Cheryl Carithers Tanner, "An Analysis of Gertrude Buck's Originality: Do Her Textbooks Reflect a Pedagogical and Rhetorical Theory Similar to Adams Sherman Hill's?" (1999).

3. Here, I draw upon John D. Buenker and Edward R. Kantowicz's definition of the era: "For our purposes, the Progressive Era is defined as a broad-gauged response by Americans from many backgrounds and walks of life to the emergence of the United States as a modern, urban, industrial, multicultural world power between 1890 and 1920" (xiii).

4. Robert Connors makes this argument in *Composition-Rhetoric,* pages 23–68.

5. See reviews of *Composition-Rhetoric* by Sharon Crowley in *Rhetoric Review* and Roxanne Mountford in the *Journal of Advanced Composition*. (See also Mountford's reply to Connors.) See Lisa Mastrangelo's "Learning from the Past: Rhetoric, Composition, and Debate at Mount Holyoke College" (1999) and Lisa Reed Ricker's "'*Ars* Stripped of Praxis': Robert J. Connors on Coeducation and the Demise of Agonistic Rhetoric" (2004).

6. In her article, "Questioning Our Methodological Metaphors," Barbara E. L'Eplattenier points out several limitations with the "map" metaphor. I appreciate L'Eplattenier's perceptive critique. However, even given the limitations with the map metaphor, I find it relevant because it has been and still remains the primary metaphor used by feminist revisionary scholars. In addition, as L'Eplattenier points out, virtually every metaphor that is used will have limitations.

7. Some of these collections include Andrea Lunsford's *Reclaiming Rhetorica: Women in the Rhetorical Tradition* (1995); Catherine Hobbs's *Nineteenth-Century Women Learn to Write* (1995); Molly Meijer Wertheimer's *Listening to Their Voices: The Rhetorical Activities of Historical Women* (1997); and Christine Mason Sutherland and Rebecca Sutcliffe's *The Changing Tradition: Women in the History of Rhetoric* (1999). In addition, the effort to write women into the history of rhetoric can be seen in recent anthologies that publish and/or republish primary texts. See, for example, Carol Mattingly's *Water Drops from Women Writers: A Temperance Reader* (2001); Joy Ritchie and Kate Ronald's *Available Means: An Anthology of Women's Rhetoric(s)* (2001); and Jane Donawerth's *Rhetorical Theory by Women Before 1900: An Anthology* (2002).

A selection of scholarly studies includes Cheryl Glenn's *Rhetoric Retold: Regendering the Tradition from Antiquity through the Renaissance* (1997); Carol Mattingly's *Well-Tempered Women: Nineteenth-Century Temperance Rhetoric* (1998) and *Appropriate[ing] Dress: Women's Rhetorical Style in Nineteenth-Century America* (2002); Shirley Wilson Logan's *"We Are Coming": The Persuasive Discourse of Nineteenth-Century Black Women* (1999); Jacqueline Jones Royster's *Traces of a Stream: Literacy and Social Change among African American Women* (2000); Jacqueline Bacon's *The Humblest May Stand Forth: Rhetoric, Empowerment, and Abolition* (2002); and Nan Johnson's *Gender and Rhetorical Space in American Life, 1866–1910* (2002).

8. Elizabeth McHenry's *Forgotten Readers: Recovering the Lost Histories of African American Literary Societies* (2002) examines another area that has been previously neglected: writing instruction of African Americans in nonacademic settings.

9. Carol Mattingly's *Appropriate[ing] Dress: Women's Rhetorical Style in Nineteenth-Century America* (2002) also raises new questions and expands the remapping effort. In her analysis, Mattingly demonstrates how effective women

speakers "understood the importance of clothing in negotiating the rigid power structure that permitted them little access to public attention" (5). As Mattingly points out, rhetorical ability has been traditionally defined according to masculine standards and qualities; thus, "the importance of clothing has been largely ignored, thereby diminishing our ability to recognize an essential component in the complex and often powerful rhetorical acumen on the part of women" (4). The feminist project of writing women into the history of rhetoric has tended to focus on recovering women speakers and their achievements. Mattingly broadens the scope of this project by redefining the "standards" of rhetorical effectiveness.

10. See Campbell's "Consciousness-Raising: Linking Theory, Criticism, and Practice" (2002).

11. L'Eplattenier presented these arguments in "Revising the Ideological Stance: Rethinking Methodologies of Archival Research" at the Conference on College Composition and Communication on 25 March 2006, in Chicago.

12. JoAnn Campbell, Jane Donawerth, and Barbara E. L'Eplattenier are among those scholars who have taken a contextual approach similar to mine. Campbell and Donawerth have focused on Buck's work within communities of women. L'Eplattenier has focused on Buck and Wylie's work as writing program administrators during the Progressive Era.

In her dissertation, Campbell explores Buck's work within the community of women she worked with at Vassar. In "Textbooks for New Audiences: Women's Revisions of Rhetorical Theory at the Turn of the Century," Donawerth challenges characterizations of Buck as the "exceptional woman" and shows how she was among a group of women "who responded to the challenges of teaching new students with new kinds of textbooks and, consequently, new theories of rhetoric" (338). Donawerth demonstrates how, at the turn of the twentieth century, Buck, Hallie Quinn Brown of Wilberforce College, and Mary Augusta Jordan of Smith College wrote textbooks that differed from their male counterparts. According to Donawerth, they "offer alternatives accommodating women's experiences, most frequently by using conversation rather than public discourse as a model" (337). In her dissertation, L'Eplattenier examines how Buck and Wylie "negotiated and garnered fiscal and political power within their university and for their department" (x).

13. This reference is to Heller's online abstract from her dissertation.

1. Buck's "Social" View of Ethics and Rhetoric

1. Katherine Pandora contends that the contributions of what she calls the "Vassar School of Social Critique" have been largely overlooked. Comprised of Wylie and Buck in English, Salmon in History, and Herbert E. Mills in Eco-

nomics, this circle of intellectuals, according to Pandora, "trained a number of women who would forge relativist cultural critiques during the 1930s, among them [Ruth] Benedict . . . ; Constance Rourke, a founder of American Studies; Caroline Ware, who took a leading role in promoting the study of American cultural history; and Lois Barclay Murphy," an influential figure in American psychology (161). Pandora argues that it is apparent "this cohort of students absorbed lessons in egalitarian politics along with critical theory" (162).

2. Rubin writes that Gertrude Buck's book, *The Social Criticism of Literature*, had a "lasting impact on her [Constance Rourke's] convictions and on the direction of her professional life" (10). More specifically, Rubin contends that Buck's book "legitimized the examination of such forms of popular expressions as folktales and frontier theatricals—materials to which Rourke would eventually turn" (11–12). For further details on Rourke, see Rubin's *Constance Rourke and American Culture* (1980).

3. For an interesting discussion of how John Dewey participated in this movement, see Lewis S. Feuer, "John Dewey and the Back to the People Movement in American Thought" (1959).

4. Constance Rourke, a former student of both Gertrude Buck and Laura Johnson Wylie, "arranged" for Wald, Lathrop, and Putnam to speak at the fiftieth-anniversary celebration (Rubin 25). Buck also served on the "Committee on Speakers" for the celebration (Rourke, *Fiftieth Anniversary* 331).

5. For a detailed discussion of Fred Newton Scott's achievements, see Donald C. Stewart and Patricia L. Stewart, *The Life and Legacy of Fred Newton Scott* (1997).

6. Rubin is quoting from Lawrence A. Cremin's *The Transformation of the School: Progressivism in American Education, 1876–1957* (1961), pages 118, 121, 123.

7. Buck's specific role in the collaborative effort is difficult to determine, as is the degree to which the ideas in the book are Buck's. The table of contents states that the book is "by" Harriet M. Scott and "assisted by" Gertrude Buck. In Fred Newton Scott's biography of his sister, Scott writes that "[t]he system of education which Miss Scott developed and put in practice in the school, is clearly set forth in her *Organic Education,* which was published in 1897" (3). Buck's work with Harriet Scott is explored more fully in chapter 2.

8. Dewey was at Michigan when Buck was completing her bachelor's degree. He left Michigan in 1894, when he became the chair of the department of psychology, philosophy, and education at the University of Chicago. At some point in 1894–95, Buck joined Dewey when she became a fellow in English at the University of Chicago (Ricks 4). While at Chicago, she attended a portion of a yearlong course on ethics that Dewey regularly taught. I was unable to find out exactly what courses Buck may have taken from John Dewey at Michigan. However, in the 30 January 1915 Department Report, Laura Johnson Wylie writes

that Buck studied under Dewey and Fred Newton Scott and that she "brought to Vassar not only a strong professional spirit, but a wide acquaintance with the most progressive educational theory" (2). Throughout her life, Buck appears to have maintained her relationship with Dewey. Buck and Fred Newton Scott's *A Brief English Grammar* was used in the Dewey School, which became known as the Laboratory School of the University of Chicago (Buck, letter to Manny, 16 May 1905, 1). In addition in 1918, Dewey gave a special lecture on the "New Social Psychology" at Vassar (MacCracken, "Report of the President" 8). The reference to Dewey's course on ethics comes from footnote 1, page 260, published in Buck's "The Sentence-Diagram."

Dewey's social view of ethics was central to his developing pragmatism. His ethics eliminated the traditional duality between feeling and reason by arguing that both were necessary for moral action. In addition, moral values for Dewey were not wholly absolute and objective, nor were they completely relative and subjective. Instead, value judgment involved the interplay between the individual's own desires and a broad critical analysis of the consequences. Dewey's ethics provided a method, a way of achieving cooperation among competing demands (Pappas 81). It assumed that all individuals were responsible and should be involved in the making of knowledge. This method was aimed at healing the deepening divisions within society by fostering democratic relationships among individuals.

9. The development of current-traditional rhetoric is related to changing cultural factors in the 1870s, including a shift in the student population and an emphasis on professional goals for a college education. These changes meant "rhetorical instruction was forced to move away from the abstract educational ideal of 'mental discipline' and toward more immediate instructional goals" (Connors, "Mechanical Correctness" 65).

10. See Buck's "The Present Status of Rhetorical Theory" (1900); Scott's "Rhetoric Rediviva," (originally delivered as a presentation at the Modern Language Association meeting in December 1909) (See Stewart's note on page 419 of the article.); and Mary Yost's "Argument from the Point-of-View of Sociology" (1917).

11. It is important to note that today composition scholars would probably disagree with Buck's analysis. For example, in "On Distinctions between Classical and Modern Rhetoric," Andrea A. Lunsford and Lisa S. Ede challenge the assumption that the goal of classical rhetoric is persuasion. Drawing upon the work of William M. A. Grimaldi, Lunsford and Ede argue that the aim of rhetoric for Aristotle "is an interactive means of discovering meaning through language" (44).

12. Buck and Laura Johnson Wylie's former home is now occupied by Hudson River Sloop Clearwater, Inc., a nonprofit environmental organization founded by folk singer Pete Seeger.

13. As Lillian Faderman points out, during this time "Mount Holyoke's president from 1901 to 1937, Mary Woolley, lived during all that time with her 'devoted companion,' Jeannette Marks, head of the English Department. Bryn Mawr's first woman president, M. Carey Thomas, lived on campus with another English professor, Mamie Gwinn. . . . Their lives as faculty couples were openly played out on campus. Love between women in the early decades of the women's college was a noble tradition" (xiii). See Anne MacKay, ed., *Wolf Girls of Vassar: Lesbian and Gay Experiences 1930–1938* (1992), foreword. See also Carroll Smith-Rosenberg, "The Female World of Love and Ritual: Relationships between Women in Nineteenth-Century America" (1975) and *Disorderly Conduct: Visions of Gender in Victorian America* (1980).

14. For further information on the Bryn Mawr Summer School for Women Workers, see Rita Rubinstein Heller's "The Women of Summer: The Bryn Mawr Summer School for Women Workers, 1921–1938" (1986). (This reference is from Heller's dissertation.) In addition, see Karyn L. Hollis's *Liberating Voices: Writing at the Bryn Mawr Summer School for Women Workers* (2004).

15. See Hollis's *Liberating Voices: Writing at the Bryn Mawr Summer School for Women Workers* (2004) for a detailed analysis of how labor drama was used to foster transformative education.

16. For a list of Yale graduates' positions and locations within drama, see Diane Fawson, Appendix II. As Fawson points out, "the list graphically depicts the vast number of Baker students who taught drama after leaving Yale." The list was originally published July 1933 in *Theatre Arts Monthly Magazine*.

17. For further information on Baker and his "47 Workshop," see Wisner Payne Kinne, *George Pierce Baker and the American Theatre* (1954).

18. This requirement remained in place through 1921–22, which is as far as I researched.

19. The influence of Buck and Woodbridge's textbook outside of Vassar is difficult to determine. In John Michael Wozniak's 1978 study of textbook use by thirty-seven eastern colleges from 1850 to 1940, he found that *A Course in Expository Writing* was used only by Wesleyan College for one year (277). However, in Wozniak's study, Mount Holyoke is the only women's college listed. In examining the on-line library catalogues of the Seven Sisters colleges, I found that the textbook was listed at Smith, Wellesley, Columbia-Barnard, and Harvard-Radcliffe colleges. Robert J. Connors says that three editions of the book were published ("Rhetoric of Explanation" 60). However, as will be discussed in chapter 6, textbooks can be very limited in revealing actual practices and influence.

20. For an interesting discussion of the nontraditional role of women in *A Course in Expository Writing*, see JoAnn Campbell, "Gertrude Buck and the Celebration of Community: A History of Writing Instruction at Vassar College,

1897–1922" 153–56, and Vickie Ricks, "Revisioning Traditions through Rhetoric: Studies in Gertrude Buck's Social Theory of Discourse" 147–48.

21. This belief that ideas or perception develop from a whole by successive differentiations also is a key concept in William James's approach to psychology. For James, perception begins with homogeneous sensations that, through continual discriminations, become perceptual knowledge. See James's *The Principles of Psychology* (1890) and *Psychology Briefer Course* (1892).

22. Like Buck, Wylie, and Lucy Maynard Salmon, Clark herself was part of this teaching tradition at Vassar through her work in the History Department. Clark, who died 17 June 2001 at age ninety-eight, "was part of the Vassar tradition of pioneering women historians who were at the forefront of their profession" ("Memorial Minute").

23. The year that Clark took Buck's course, Clark said that Buck "was probably not at her best" because she frequently was ill; thus, Laura Johnson Wylie often taught the course. Clark said that students "had the impression all of the time that she [Buck] was really just struggling to keep going" (20 Mar. 1999). That summer (August 1921) Buck suffered a stroke and died in January after suffering a second stroke (Reed, "In Memoriam" 128).

24. In a 1908 letter to Vassar President James Monroe Taylor, Laura Johnson Wylie writes that the department has tried "to meet the necessity of more individual work with the students" through "group interviews," or "group conferences." Wylie adds that the idea for group conferences came from the Princeton tutorial system, and that "so far appears to be giving us the opportunity for more stimulating, varied, and effective teaching" (3).

2. Progressive Education, Feminism, and the Detroit Normal Training School

1. Scholars have contributed to this move to examine alternate sites of formal education by exploring composition at normal schools. See Kenneth Lindblom and Patricia A. Dunn, "Cooperative Writing 'Program' Administration at Illinois State Normal University: The Committee on English of 1904–05 and the Influence of Professor J. Rose Colby" (2004); Beth Ann Rothermel, "A Sphere of Noble Action: Gender, Rhetoric, and Influence at a Nineteenth-Century Massachusetts State Normal School" (2003); Kathryn Fitzgerald, "A Rediscovered Tradition: European Pedagogy and Composition Studies" (2001); and Sandra D. Harmon, "'The Voice, Pen, and Influence of Our Women Are Abroad in the Land': Women and the Illinois State Normal University, 1857–1899" (1995).

2. Lawrence A. Cremin declines to forward any "capsule definition of progressive education," contending that such a definition is nonexistent. Instead, he argues that "throughout its history progressive education meant different things

to different people, and these differences were only compounded by the remarkable diversity of American education" (*Transformation of the School* x).

3. The articles were first published in nine consecutive issues from October 1892 to June 1893. They were republished in *The Public School System in the United States* (1893), which was the source quoted.

4. For a discussion of these movements and Dewey's reactions to all of them except the Kindergarten Movement, see Melvin C. Baker, *Foundations of John Dewey's Educational Theory* (1955), chapter 6. For further information on the Kindergarten Movement, see Nina C. Vandewalker, *The Kindergarten in American Education* (1908).

5. Dewey wrote the article in 1896 for the Herbart Yearbook, but he later revised and reprinted it in 1899. See note EW 5: 113.

6. For additional information on the American Herbartians and Johann Friedrich Herbart, see Harold B. Dunkel, *Herbart and Education* (1969).

7. I'm not clear of the exact date of her graduation. Lynch writes that Harriet Scott graduated from Indiana State Normal School in 1872. In his biography of his sister, Scott notes that she graduated in 1874.

8. Fredrickson specifically mentions Franklin H. Giddings, Charles H. Cooley, and Edward Alsworth Ross (312). Although I am unsure if Buck took classes from Cooley, he was teaching at Michigan when she was working toward her master's and Ph.D. Mary Yost, who is discussed in chapter 6, completed graduate work with Cooley.

9. For an interesting discussion of the discourse of civilization and racial dominance during this period, see Bederman's *Manliness and Civilization: A Cultural History of Gender and Race in the United States, 1880–1917* (1995), which investigates perceptions of manhood and masculinity during the Progressive Era.

10. The angle brackets indicate handwritten words that Buck inserted into her typed letter to MacCracken.

11. For information on the effects of industrialization and disputes between capital and labor, see Steven J. Diner, *A Very Different Age: Americans of the Progressive Era* (1998); and Nell Irvin Painter, *Standing at Armageddon: The United States 1877–1919* (1987).

12. Buck's work in drama is discussed more fully in chapter 5.

13. Buck's belief that the mind begins with a vague impression that develops into a more complex consciousness is also discussed by Vickie Ricks, "Revisioning Traditions through Rhetoric: Studies in Gertrude Buck's Social Theory of Discourse" (1989) 25; and by Dana Hood Morgan, "Gertrude Buck's Rhetoric: The Living Expression of Thought" (1995) 2 and throughout her thesis.

14. As noted, this approach, for instance, is evident in Adams Sherman Hill's

Foundations of Rhetoric (1892), which begins with words, then moves to sentences, and then to paragraphs.

3. The "Advance" toward Democratic Administration

1. For example, in the 1921 *Vassarion* list of English Department faculty and instructors, only two of the fifteen listed are men. They are Burges Johnson and President MacCracken.

2. In so doing, this study extends the work of Barbara E. L'Eplattenier, who, in her 1999 dissertation, examines how Wylie and Buck "negotiated and garnered fiscal and political power within their university and for their department" ("Investigating Institutional Power" x).

3. See Gunner's "Decentering the WPA."

4. According to Elisabeth Woodbridge Morris, the ministers called themselves "Covenanters" "[to harken] back with pride to those stern and militant documents drawn up in Scotland a century and more earlier, in which the Scottish clergy covenanted with each other to stand together against Rome and all her works" ("Laura Johnson Wylie" 1–2).

5. Information on the Bryn Mawr Summer School for 1921–27 indicates that Wylie served as an instructor during the years 1924, 1925, and 1926. See Hilda Worthington Smith's *Women Workers at the Bryn Mawr Summer School* 295.

6. Citations in this chapter are drawn from *Miss Wylie of Vassar*.

7. This movement, though, was not as seamless as Wylie depicts. For example, in December 1912 there was a major clash between Taylor and the faculty when the board of trustees voted on a resolution that some faculty members thought denied them any participation in the college's administration and educational policies. In response, Wylie, Herbert E. Mills, and Amy L. Reed drafted a "statement" or petition calling for a more democratic college administration (Reed, letter to Taylor, 15 Mar. 1913). Wylie and Buck were among the twelve who signed the petition ("Statement to President"). The petition apparently was not circulated.

8. Angle brackets are used to indicate handwritten words inserted by Wylie in the typed report.

9. In "The Costs of Caring: 'Feminism' and Contingent Women Workers in Composition Studies," Eileen E. Schell also emphasizes the limitations of the ethic of care in terms of feminist pedagogy.

4. The Suffrage Movement and Buck's Approach to Argument and Debate

1. The college Board of Trustees during James Monroe Taylor's time was similarly conservative, and it was predominantly male. Vassar President Mac-Cracken points out that the "men far outnumbered the women on the Board,"

with thirty men and three women serving (28). According to MacCracken, "Throughout Taylor's term Vassar was a college for women developed by men" (29). See MacCracken, *The Hickory Limb* (1950).

2. For an interesting discussion of how the women's suffrage movement provoked institutional reform at Vassar, see Elizabeth A. Daniels, "Suffrage as a Lever for Change at Vassar College" (1983) and *Bridges to the World: Henry Noble MacCracken and Vassar College* (1994), chapter 3. See also Dale Mezzacappa's "Vassar College and the Suffrage Movement" (1973).

3. If Taylor is unable to serve, Thomas asks if the committee can invite Lucy Maynard Salmon, who was the head of the History Department and in 1911 became a vice president of the National College Equal Suffrage League.

4. Angle brackets are used to indicate handwritten words Taylor inserted in his typed letter to Thomas.

5. See reports in the *New York Herald* 10 June 1908 ("To Punish Vassar Girl Suffragists") and the *New York Sun* 9 June 1908 ("Vassar Meets in Graveyard"). For other accounts of the 1908 and 1909 incidents at Vassar, see Margaret M. Caffrey, *Ruth Benedict: Stranger in this Land* (1989), 48–50; JoAnn Campbell, ed., introduction, *Toward a Feminist Rhetoric: The Writing of Gertrude Buck* (1996), xxiii–xxvii; Elizabeth A. Daniels, "Suffrage as a Lever for Change at Vassar College," (1983), 32–36, and *Bridges to the World: Henry Noble MacCracken and Vassar College* (1995), chapter 3; Elaine Kendall, *"Peculiar Institutions": An Informal History of the Seven Sisters Colleges* (1975), 145–46; and Louise Fargo Brown, *Apostle of Democracy: The Life of Lucy Maynard Salmon* (1943), 212.

6. According to Tamara Plakins Thornton, a "mania for masculine vigor and activity" characterized the 1890s (69). Penmanship was part of this mania, and an "athletic education" even included training in handwriting. The Palmer Method was in vogue, and it "represented the skill of penmanship as a form of athleticism" (69). Handwriting in the business world had traditionally been defined as a male skill. However, during this time, the New Woman began entering the office, replacing the male cuspidors. According to Thornton, "The Palmer method reasserted the masculinity of penmanship, even as male and female arms alike pushed and pulled and ovalled in its name" (70). See Thornton, *Handwriting in America: A Cultural History* (1996).

7. For instance, the first semester Department Report for the 1900–01 academic year indicates that Buck taught four sections of argumentation (a total of ninety-four students), two sections of description (a total of fifty-seven students), and one section of the development of rhetorical theory (a total of nine students). The first semester report for the 1905–06 academic year indicates she taught three sections of description (a total of ninety-one students) and one section of nineteenth-century prose (a total of seventeen students). In the 1900

Department Report, Laura Johnson Wylie writes that "Miss Buck has not only done a very large part of the shaping work of the last three years but has carried senior and graduate courses and represented the college ably by her writing" (qtd in Campbell, *Toward* 261). Although these statistics are not for the 1911–12 academic year, they do give an indication of Buck's teaching load.

8. For details concerning the adoption of a child, see "The Book Boat," column by Montgomery Cooper, Vassar class of 1909, in the *Memphis Commercial Appeal,* 29 May 1932. For Buck's membership in the Socialist Party, see John William Leonard, ed., *Woman's Who's Who of America* (1914).

9. For a discussion of how Lucy Maynard Salmon battled with President Taylor over the right of women faculty to live off campus, see Helen Lefkowitz Horowitz, *Alma Mater: Design and Experience in the Women's Colleges from Their Nineteenth-Century Beginnings to the 1930s,* 186–87.

10. In *Vote and Voice: Women's Organizations and Political Literacy, 1915–1930,* Wendy Sharer discusses how the League of Women Voters also "officially opposed" the reelection of Wadsworth (117).

11. The original poem spells Chantecleer with an "e."

12. Although Buck's feminist ethics may not be exactly the same as Wylie's, there does seem to be significant overlap. Thus, it is important to examine Wylie's speech.

13. Buck was not the only teacher at Vassar advocating such methods. In the English Department report for 1906–07, Laura Johnson Wylie asks for a building or room to serve as a "laboratory" for the English Department. Wylie writes, "The English teaching, as I have several times said, is practically laboratory teaching, and consequently needs a certain material equipment for effective work. The lack of it means incalculable loss to both teachers and students, and through them to the college (3)." Lucy Maynard Salmon also encouraged students to examine primary sources, sift through the material and develop their own conclusions instead of relying on traditional opinion. See Elizabeth Daniels, "Suffrage as a Lever for Change at Vassar College" (32); and Agnes Rogers, *Vassar Women: An Informal Study,* (55–56).

14. I am borrowing this definition of "knowledge" from John T. Gage. See "An Adequate Epistemology for Composition: Classical and Modern Perspectives" (1984), 156.

15. It is important to note that today composition scholars would probably disagree with Buck's analysis. As mentioned, scholars have challenged the assumption that the goal of classical rhetoric is persuasion. Similarly, in *The Formation of College English* (1997), Thomas P. Miller contends that Campbell extends the boundaries of rhetoric beyond persuasion "to define it in more modern terms as 'that art or talent by which the discourse is adapted to its end'" (218).

16. For a detailed discussion of the dreams and experiences of Vassar women in college and in society, see Debra Herman, "College and After: The Vassar Experiment in Women's Education, 1861–1924" (1979).

17. JoAnn Campbell and Kathryn M. Conway have explored the influence of suffrage issues on Buck's work, as I will do. In Campbell's 1996 introduction to a collection of Buck's writing and in her 1989 dissertation, she examines the suffrage debates to underscore differences in administrative philosophies between the college and the English Department. Campbell contrasts the patriarchal administrative style of President Taylor and the board of trustees with the cooperative and democratic approach of the English Department led by Laura Johnson Wylie and Buck (*Toward* xxiii; "Gertrude Buck" 100).

Conway's analysis focuses on connections between suffrage and rhetoric at the Seven Sisters colleges from 1865 to 1919. In her essay "Woman Suffrage and the History of Rhetoric at the Seven Sisters Colleges, 1865–1919," Conway briefly discusses Buck's use of suffrage issues in *A Handbook on Argumentation and Debating* (1906), which she coauthored with Kristine Mann. Conway details how suffrage issues were discussed in Buck's textbook and how suffrage was a topic of interest to the "debate societies" at Vassar. She concludes that rhetoric classes at the Seven Sisters colleges significantly added to the "intellectual growth" of suffrage (204) and that the societies provided women with "great confidence in their own ability to be effective public speakers and political leaders" (222).

18. For an interesting new perspective on Adams Sherman Hill, which challenges simplistic narratives that have tended to vilify him, see Charles Paine's *The Resistant Writer: Rhetoric as Immunity, 1850 to the Present* (1999).

19. Jordan received her undergraduate and master's degrees from Vassar. She served as a librarian and then an English instructor at Vassar until 1884 (Kates, "Subversive Feminism" 504). Kates also discusses Jordan in *Activist Rhetorics and American Higher Education 1885–1937* (2001), 27–52.

20. This statement is based on a search using FirstSearch's "WorldCat" database. It also is based on a review of Albert R. Kitzhaber's *A Bibliography of Rhetoric in American Colleges, 1850–1900* (1954).

21. See note 1 on the bottom of page 35.

22. An associate professor in the English Department from 1901 to 1905, Kristine Mann went on to study philosophy and psychology at Columbia University and medicine at Cornell University, where she received her medical degree in 1913. According to Beth Darlington, Mann and three of her Vassar students, who later earned medical degrees, "played major roles in the early history of analytical psychology" (20). See Darlington, "Vassar's Jung Folks" (1998).

23. A student of Lucy Maynard Salmon and Laura Johnson Wylie, Lockwood went on to become "a stunningly innovative" English professor, according to

Elizabeth A. Daniels (*Bridges to the World* 175). Lockwood, who graduated in 1912, taught at Vassar from 1927 to 1956 (Heller 163). She is discussed in greater detail in chapter 6.

24. Buck was not alone in her pedagogical approach. In her book *In Adamless Eden: The Community of Women Faculty at Wellesley,* Patricia Ann Palmieri argues that during the Progressive period, the all-female faculty at Wellesley similarly eroded the claims of the domestic sphere by emphasizing communal interests and activism. Like Buck, the women of Wellesley were linked to the intellectual currents of the time. Palmieri contends that "[t]his new vocabulary of the social self forged in society connects them with such intellectuals as Josiah Royce, Mary Follett, John Dewey, and Jane Addams, who saw education as a vehicle for creating a new organic culture" (150).

5. The Little Theater Movement and Buck's Democratized View of Drama

1. For instance, in 1913, MacKaye created the *Allegory* pageant, commissioned by the National American Women's Suffrage Party and presented in Washington, D.C. (Blair 137). The pageant was followed by a parade that included from "5,000 to 10,000" marching suffragists and several floats "portraying seventy-five years of suffrage struggle in America" (Blair 137).

2. JoAnn Campbell, Vickie Ricks, and Evert Sprinchorn are the main scholars who discuss aspects of Buck's efforts in drama. In her dissertation and collection of Buck's work, Campbell briefly discusses Buck's dramatic efforts. See "Gertrude Buck and the Celebration of Community: A History of Writing Instruction at Vassar College, 1897–1922" (1989), 112–14; and *Toward a Feminist Rhetoric: The Writing of Gertrude Buck* (1996), xiv, 253–57. In her dissertation, Ricks examines Buck's poems and plays. See "Revisioning Traditions through Rhetoric: Studies in Gertrude Buck's Social Theory of Discourse (1989), 201–37. And in "Stagestruck in Academe" (1991), Sprinchorn focuses briefly on Buck's efforts to bring drama to Vassar. My work extends theirs by discussing Buck's achievements in drama in greater depth and by contextualizing her efforts within the Little Theater movement and women's reform activities.

3. For more information on Baker and his workshop, see Wisner Payne Kinne, *George Pierce Baker and the American Theatre* (1954).

4. See Hollis's *Liberating Voices: Writing at the Bryn Mawr Summer School for Women Workers* (2004) for a detailed analysis of how labor drama was used to foster transformative education.

5. As Evert Sprinchorn points out, after directing innovative theater at Vassar for more than a decade, Flanagan in 1935 headed the Federal Theater Project, "the first and only people's theater that this country has ever had" (26). For

more information on Flanagan, see Joanne Bentley, *Hallie Flanagan: A Life in the American Theatre* (1988).

6. In 1888, Baker began his teaching career at Harvard as an instructor, assisting Adams Sherman Hill and Le Baron Russell Briggs in the first-year rhetoric courses and helping Josiah Royce with the junior- and senior-level forensics courses (Kinne 35). Baker continued teaching argumentation and debate until 1906, publishing *Principles of Argumentation* in 1895 and *Forms of Public Address* in 1904. As D. G. Myers points out, Baker takes a rhetorical approach to drama (69). According to Baker, "[T]he dramatist shapes his material more and more in relation to the public he wishes to address, for a dramatist is, after all, a sort of public speaker" (qtd. in Myers 69). In her work in theater, Buck also applies a rhetorical approach to drama.

7. The conflict seems representative of the times, particularly the change in leadership occurring at Vassar. The fiftieth celebration is significant because Henry Noble MacCracken was introduced as the new college president, and the faculty had experienced a year of self-government. It is a moment in Vassar's history when the status quo was questioned and when the faculty seemed to be reassessing both its role and that of the college.

8. Buck may have written the articles because of practical concerns. At Vassar, Buck was involved in commencement programming and argued for similar ideas. For instance, in a letter to MacCracken soon after he took over as president, Buck writes that commencement "constitutes a unique opportunity [for the President] to 'socialize' the ideas for which the college stands, not only for the audience gathered, but, by means of the newspapers, throughout the country" (22 Feb. 1915, 2).

9. Wylie and Buck were not the only English teachers to approach literature from a social perspective during this period. Vida Scudder of Wellesley also emphasized the social aspects of literature. See Garbus, "Service-Learning, 1902" (2002), for a discussion of Scudder's approach to literature and connections to service-learning.

10. Angle brackets are used to indicate handwritten words inserted by Buck in the typed letter.

11. For an interesting discussion of how theater became accepted as an accredited liberal arts program at Vassar College, see Sprinchorn, "Stagestruck in Academe: Acceptance of Theater as a Liberal Art Was No Overnight Success" (1991). Sprinchorn focuses on the efforts of Gertrude Buck, Winifred Smith, and Hallie Flanagan.

12. Angle brackets are used to indicate handwritten words Buck inserted in her typed letter to MacCracken.

13. After Buck's death in 1922, MacCracken's gift became the Gertrude Buck Drama Fund.

14. Lois W. Banner writes that the term "social feminist" refers "to women for whom social reforms take priority over strictly women's causes" (vi).

15. President MacCracken is writing back to Ernest R. Acker to inform him that "to clarify the lines on which the Community Theatre was founded, the following statement has been written into the Minutes of the Board of Trustees of Vassar College, and sent herewith for the records of the Theatre" (24 May 1934).

16. See Noddings's *Caring: A Feminine Approach to Ethics and Moral Education* (1984).

17. Quotations from *Mother-Love* and *The Girl From Marsh Croft* are taken from JoAnn Campbell's *Toward a Feminist Rhetoric: The Writing of Gertrude Buck.* Both plays are included in Buck's posthumously published *Poems and Plays.*

6. Socially Conscious Women Teaching Writing

1. In 1994, Herman Cohen called Yost's 1917 article on argumentation a "disturbingly modern essay," and he emphasized that Yost was one of the first to approach argument from contemporary sociology and psychology, breaking from "the traditional logic-based model of communication" (69). For a perceptive analysis of the significance of Yost's article, see Cohen, *The History of Speech Communication: The Emergence of a Discipline, 1914–1945,* 66–72. My analysis extends Cohen's work by exploring Yost's dissertation and her teaching of argumentation and debate at Vassar College.

2. For an interesting discussion of the response to Yost's article and the debates it spawned, see Cohen, *The History of Speech Communication,* 70–84.

3. See Lisa S. Mastrangelo's "Building a Dinosaur from the Bones: Fred Newton Scott and Women's Progressive Era Graduate Work at the University of Michigan" (2005) for a perceptive account of connections between the University of Michigan's graduate program in rhetoric and several women who taught composition and rhetoric at the Seven Sisters colleges during the Progressive Era.

4. The first two sentences of the article spell women's suffrage two different ways.

5. While at Stanford, Yost lived in an all-female household in which the women maintained close friendships that were similar in structure to those at Vassar and other Seven Sisters colleges in the late nineteenth century or to Hull House and other settlement houses during this period (Howton 10–11). After arriving at Stanford, Yost moved into a house at 534 Lasuen Street, which had previously been occupied by the former dean of women. English faculty members Edith Mirrielees, Elizabeth Buckingham, and Terri Russell soon joined Yost, as

did Nina Almond, "a librarian at the Hoover Library who became Yost's closest companion for the rest of her life" (Howton 26). From 1921 until 1946, when Yost retired, the women lived in three adjoining apartments in the house, sharing meals together. Yost and Almond lived in one apartment, Buckingham and Russell shared the second (until Russell's death in 1936), and Mirrielees occupied the third (Howton 57). After retiring, Yost and Almond lived in another house on campus until Yost's death in 1954 (Howton 26).

6. Yost's graduate transcript shows that all of her graduate courses were from these three men and that Scott was her thesis adviser (Transcript). As mentioned, Buck also worked with Fred Newton Scott at Michigan and had an organic view of society. A first-generation sociologist, Charles Horton Cooley, like Buck, was a graduate of Michigan and had studied under John Dewey. Similar to Dewey, Scott, and Buck, Cooley viewed society as an organism. Cooley's focus "on the organic link and the indissoluble connection between self and society is the theme of Cooley's writings and remains the crucial contribution he made to modern social psychology and sociology" (Ridener 2). According to the *University of Michigan Catalogue of Graduates, Non-Graduates, Officers, and Members of the Faculties, 1837–1921,* John Frederick Shepard was an associate professor in Psychology in 1917 (42). Yost's emphasis on the rhetorical situation is evident in the connections she made among rhetoric, sociology, and psychology in her dissertation and coursework.

7. See note 2 of Yost's dissertation.

8. See Buck's "The Present Status of Rhetorical Theory," 84–87.

9. In her article, Yost does not specifically mention which sociologists she is referring to. However, as noted, she did work with Charles Horton Cooley, a sociology professor at Michigan. In addition, her dissertation includes several references to sociology and psychology. For instance, her bibliography includes J. R. Angell, *The Relation of Structural and Functional Psychology to Philosophy* (1903); J. M. Baldwin, *The Individual and Society* (1911); C. H. Cooley, *Human Nature and Social Order* (1912) and *Social Organization: A Study of the Larger Mind* (1914); M. M. Davis Jr., *Psychological Interpretations of Society* (1909), J. Dewey, *How We Think* (1910) and *Studies in Logical Theory* (1903); C. A. Ellwood, *Sociology in Its Psychological Aspects* (1915); L. Gumplowicz, *The Outlines of Sociology* (1899); W. James, *The Principles of Psychology* (1893) and *The Will to Believe* (1897); G. T. Ladd and R. S. Woodworth, *Elements of Physiological Psychology* (1911); W. B. Pillsbury, *Attention* (1908), *Essentials of Psychology* (1911), and *Psychology of Reasoning* (1910); E. A. Ross, *Social Psychology* (1908); and W. I. Thomas, *Source Book for Social Origins* (1909).

10. Fellers wrote a letter rebutting a negative review of William F. Buckley Jr.'s *God and Man at Yale* in the student newspaper, the *Vassar Chronicle*. The

daughter of retired Brigadier General Bonner Frank Fellers, who had served on General Douglas MacArthur's staff, Nancy Fellers asserted that in a conference after the publication of her letter, Lockwood told her, "You do not hesitate to break into print with your dangerous ideas. If something is not done, your getting through Vassar will be imperiled (qtd. in United States 1)." Fellers asserted that Lockwood's negative reaction to the review may have been spurred by her earlier response to Lockwood's assignment asking students to "state their basic beliefs about God and the universe, the state, the family, money, culture, attitudes toward the grander, and education (qtd. in United States 2)." Lockwood typically had students repeat the assignment at the end of the school year and reflect on any changes in their beliefs. Fellers acknowledged that her first paragraph may have angered Lockwood: "I believe in God, human dignity, and the United States of America. Next June I shall believe in God, human dignity, and the United States of America (qtd. in United States 2)." Both the college and Lockwood denied Fellers's accusations, with Secretary John H. Holmes of Vassar affirming the college's principles "that education neither accepts nor indoctrinates but teaches a process of searching for truth ("Vassar Denies")."

11. At this time, Vassar students didn't declare majors; instead, they followed a prescribed curriculum, leading to the awarding of the bachelor's degree.

12. According to Heller, "For the School's first period, the 1921–1927 years, the economists Amy Hewes, Caroline Ware and Broadus Mitchell will be emphasized, as will the Professor of English Literature, Helen Drusilla Lockwood, and the scientist, Louise Brown" (159).

13. A former president of Vassar College, Simpson's essay was originally a convocation address delivered 1 Sept. 1976 for the dedication of the Helen D. Lockwood Library. His address was later published and included selected transcribed letters from Lockwood's college years.

14. This passage comes from a letter Lockwood wrote on 19 March 1911, which is reprinted in Simpson's article.

15. This particular passage includes no specific date.

16. The editing marks in this passage are Lockwood's.

17. Only the first page of her draft letter is included in her collection, so it is difficult to determine if she ever finished and sent the letter to Wylie.

18. Although Simpson's article includes reprinted letters from Lockwood, this particular passage includes no specific date.

19. The pamphlet was written in response to the potential "removal of Vassar College to New Haven Connecticut, to join with Yale University, at the time also a single-sex undergraduate college, in a coeducational enterprise" (Daniels, *Bridges to the World* 175). The move never took place.

WORKS CITED

Primary Sources

Acker, Ernest R. Letter to Henry Noble MacCracken. 24 May 1934, ts. (Box 65, Folder 70). Henry Noble MacCracken Papers. Courtesy of Archives and Special Collections, Vassar College Libraries.

Adams, Ruth. Letter to parents. Sept. 1900. Student Letters Collection, Jan. 1897–1901. (Transcribed letters). Courtesy of Archives and Special Collections, Vassar College Libraries.

Addams, Jane. *My Friend Julia Lathrop*. New York: Macmillan, 1935.

"An Address on Woman Suffrage: Before Mothers and Teachers' Association by Prof. Laura J. Wylie Tuesday Afternoon. At Cannon St. School." *Poughkeepsie Daily Eagle* 5 Feb. 1913: 5.

Bacon, Harold M., Paul R. Farnsworth, and H. Donald Winbigler. "Memorial Resolution Mary Yost 1881–1954." Mary Yost Biographical File. Courtesy of Stanford University Archives.

Baker, George Pierce. "Address by Professor George P. Baker, of Harvard University." *Gertrude Buck Professor of English 1897–1922*. Spec. [Gertrude Buck] issue of *Vassar Miscellany Monthly* Feb. 1923: 10–15.

———. *The Principles of Argumentation*. Boston: Ginn, 1895.

Buck, Gertrude. "Another Phase of the New Education." *Forum* 22 (1896): 376–84.

———. "Anti-Suffrage Sentiments." *The Masses* June 1913: 9.

———, ed. "Athletic Education for Women." *Inlander* April 1896: 291–301. Courtesy of Bentley Historical Library, University of Michigan.

———. "College Commencements To-Day and To-Morrow." *School and Society* 2 (1915): 734–43.

———. "Coming—Workshop Plays." *Vassar Miscellany News* 22 Feb. 1919: 3.

———. "The Commencement Opportunity." *Journal of the Association of Collegiate Alumnae* 11 (1918): 494–97.

———. "The Complaint of Youth." Buck, *Poems and Plays* 5.

———. *A Course in Argumentative Writing*. New York: Holt, 1899.

————. "English Course III–II2 Technique of the Drama" ts. Poughkeepsie, NY: Vassar College, n.d. Dramatic Workshop Notebook, 378.7V L799, page 1. Courtesy of Archives and Special Collections, Vassar College Libraries.

————. *Figures of Rhetoric: A Psychological Study*. Ed. Fred Newton Scott. Contributions to Rhetorical Theory 1. Ann Arbor: Inland, 1895.

————. *The Girl from Marsh Croft*. Buck, *Poems and Plays* 85–166.

————, ed. Introduction. *John Ruskin's Sesame and Lilies*. By John Ruskin. New York: Longmans, 1906. ix–lvii.

————. Introduction. *The Metaphor: A Study in the Psychology of Rhetoric*. Diss. U of Michigan. By Buck. Ed. Fred Newton Scott. Contributions to Rhetorical Theory 5. Ann Arbor: Inland, 1899. iii.

————. Letter to Frank A. Manny. 16 May 1905, ts. (Box 1, Jan.–May 1905). Frank A. Manny Collection. Michigan Historical Collections. Courtesy of the Bentley Historical Library, University of Michigan.

————. Letter to Fred Newton Scott. 11 Oct. 1913, ts. (Box 1, July–Dec. 1913). Fred Newton Scott Papers. Courtesy of the Bentley Historical Library, University of Michigan.

————. Letters to George Pierce Baker. 8 Feb. 1915, ts.; 27 Dec. 1916, ts. George Pierce Baker Archives. Courtesy of the Harvard Theatre Collection, Houghton Library.

————. Letters to Henry Noble MacCracken. 22 Feb. 1915, ts. (Box 20, Folder 104); 18 Nov. 1918 (Box 23, Folder 89); 27 Nov. 1918, ts. (Box 23, Folder 89); 2 Dec. 1918, ts. (Box 23, Folder 89); 3 June 1920, ts. (Box 23, Folder 89). Henry Noble MacCracken Papers. Courtesy of Archives and Special Collections, Vassar College Libraries.

————. *The Metaphor: A Study in the Psychology of Rhetoric*. Diss. U of Michigan. Ed. Fred Newton Scott. Contributions to Rhetorical Theory 5. Ann Arbor: Inland, 1899.

————. *Mother-Love*. Buck, *Poems and Plays* 55–84.

————. *Poems and Plays*. Ed. Laura Johnson Wylie. New York: Duffield, 1922.

————. "Poughkeepsie Community Theater." *Vassar Quarterly* May 1920: 198–99.

————. "The Present Status of Rhetorical Theory." *Modern Language Notes* 15.3 (1900): 167–74.

————. "A Primer of the Vassar Dramatic Workshop: How—, What—, Who—." Poughkeepsie, NY: Vassar College, n.d. Dramatic Workshop Notebook, 378.7V L799, page 28. Courtesy of Archives and Special Collections, Vassar College Libraries.

————. "Recent Tendencies in the Teaching of English Composition." *Educational Review* 22 (1901): 371–82.

————. "The Sentence-Diagram." *Educational Review* 13 (1897): 250–60.

————. *The Social Criticism of Literature*. New Haven: Yale UP, 1916.

————. "The Study of English." *Vassar Miscellany Weekly* 19 Jan. 1917: 6.

————. "Two Minor Hall Plays." *Vassar Miscellany News* 17 April 1917. N. pag. Dramatic Workshop Notebook, 378.7V L799, page 21. Courtesy of Archives and Special Collections, Vassar College Libraries.

————. "The Vassar Workshop." *Vassar Quarterly* May 1917: 181–83.

————. "What Does 'Rhetoric' Mean?" *Educational Review* 22 (1901): 197–200.

————. "The Work-Shop Plays." *Vassar Miscellany News* 1 May 1917: 1.

Buck, Gertrude, and Kristine Mann. *A Handbook of Argumentation and Debating.* Orange, NJ: Orange Chronicle, 1906.

Buck, Gertrude, and Fred Newton Scott. *A Brief English Grammar.* Chicago: Scott, 1905.

Buck, Gertrude, and Harriet M. Scott. *Organic Education: A Manual for Teachers in Primary and Grammar Grades.* 1897. Heath's Pedagogical Library 35. Boston: Heath, 1899.

Buck, Gertrude, and Elisabeth Woodbridge [Morris]. *A Course in Expository Writing.* New York: Holt, 1899.

Buck, Gertrude, and Elisabeth Woodbridge Morris. *A Course in Narrative Writing.* New York: Holt, 1906.

"Buck, Hon. George M." *American Biographical History of Eminent and Self-Made Men. Michigan Volume.* Cincinnati: Western Biographical Pub., 1878. N. pag. Clarence L. Miller Family Local History Room. Kalamazoo Public Library, Kalamazoo, Michigan.

Burk, Fredric. "Education by Dynamism." *Journal of the Association of Collegiate Alumnae* 11 (1917): 217–25.

"The Christening of the Outdoor Theater: The Pageant of Athena." *Vassar Miscellany Weekly* 22 Oct. 1915: 1–2.

Clark, Evalyn A. Personal interview 20 Mar. 1999.

"College Debating." [M.A.G., 1908] *Vassar Miscellany* Nov. 1907: 106.

"Community Theatre Aiming High with 'Enter Madame.'" *Sunday Courier* [Poughkeepsie] 8 Mar. 1925: 30.

"Condensed Report of the Executive Secretary of the Women's City and County Club Given at the Annual Meeting of the Club, May 24, 1920." Women's City and County Club. Poughkeepsie, NY: Dutchess County, NY: 1920–21. 5–10. [Call number 396.06 P86 (1920–21)] Courtesy of Archives and Special Collections, Vassar College Libraries.

Cooper, Montgomery. [Extract from] "The Book Boat." *Memphis Commercial Appeal* 29 May 1932. N. pag. Laura Johnson Wylie Biographical File (Box 4). Courtesy of Archives and Special Collections, Vassar College Libraries.

Dayton, Frank C. "George Machan Buck." *Kalamazoo Illustrated.* Kalamazoo: Ihling Bros. and Everard, 1892. 58. Clarence L. Miller Family Local History Room. Kalamazoo Public Library, Kalamazoo, Michigan.

"Death Call to Hon. G.M. Buck Very Sudden: Was for More Than Fifty Years a Member of the Kalamazoo County Bar." *Kalamazoo Gazette* 3 Feb. 1919.

N. pag. Clarence L. Miller Family Local History Room. Kalamazoo Public Library, Kalamazoo, Michigan.

Dewey, John. "Interest in Relation to Training of the Will." 1896. *John Dewey: The Early Works 1882–1898, Vol. 5: 1895–1898.* 5 vols. Ed. Jo Ann Boydston. Carbondale: Southern Illinois UP, 1972. 111–50.

———. *The School and Society: Being Three Lectures by John Dewey.* Chicago: U of Chicago P, 1900.

Dickinson, Thomas H. *The Insurgent Theatre.* New York: Huebsch, 1917.

"Doctor Mary Yost, Former Stanford Dean of Women, Is Claimed by Stroke." *Stanford Daily* 5 Mar. 1954. N. pag. Mary Yost Biographical File. Courtesy of Archives and Special Collections, Vassar College Libraries.

"Editor at Bat." *Daily Palo Alto Times* 9 Mar. 1954: 4. Mary Yost Biographical File. Courtesy of Stanford University Archives.

"Eleven Faculty Members Will Become Emeritus September 1, After Long Service on the Campus: Dean of Women, Department Head, and Six Professors among Those Slated to Join Retirement Ranks." *Stanford Alumni Review* May 1946: 5. Mary Yost Biographical File. Courtesy of Stanford University Archives.

"English 47 Workshop." *Harvard Alumni Bulletin* 29 Oct. 1913. N. pag. "Forty-Seven" Workshops, 1913–1930 (HUD 3403). Courtesy of Harvard University Archives, Pusey Library. [Title is handwritten on the article.]

"Equal Suffrage Meeting." *Poughkeepsie Courier.* 21 Nov. 1911, n. pag. Poughkeepsie Scrapbook, page 43/Laura Johnson Wylie Biographical File (Box 4). Courtesy of Archives and Special Collections, Vassar College Libraries.

"George Pierce Baker—and—His Magic '47." *Radcliffe Quarterly* Feb. 1961: 10–21. "Forty-Seven" Workshops, 1913–1930 (HUD 3403). Courtesy of Harvard University Archives, Pusey Library.

"Gertrude Buck Drama Fund." Gertrude Buck Biographical File. Courtesy of Archives and Special Collections, Vassar College Libraries.

Gleason, Josephine, Dean Mace, and Susan Turner. "Helen Drusilla Lockwood 1891–1971" ts. (Folder 1). [Read at Faculty Meeting 22 Sept. 1971.] Helen Drusilla Lockwood Biographical File. Courtesy of Archives and Special Collections, Vassar College Libraries.

Harvey, Harriet. "Poughkeepsie's Post-war World." [Student paper for English 312 Contemporary Press 1945] (Box 8, Folder 131). Helen Drusilla Lockwood Papers. Courtesy of Archives and Special Collections, Vassar College Libraries.

"The Higher Education Again." *Atlantic Monthly* Apr. 1917: 572-74.

Hill, Adams Sherman. *The Foundations of Rhetoric.* New York: American Book, 1892.

"Hudson Shore Labor School." [1946] (Box 17, Folder 256). Helen Drusilla Lockwood Papers. Courtesy of Archives and Special Collections, Vassar College Libraries.

James, William. *The Principles of Psychology.* 2 vols. New York: Holt, 1890.

————. *Psychology Briefer Course*. 1892. Cambridge: Harvard UP, 1984.

————. *The Will to Believe: And Other Essays in Popular Philosophy*. 1897. Cambridge: Harvard UP, 1979.

Johnson, Elizabeth Forrest. "A Great Teacher I." Woodbridge 100–06.

Jordan, Mary Augusta. "Spacious Days at Vassar." Rourke 47–69.

"Laura J. Wylie Dies Here at 76: Vassar Emeritus Professor Had Been on Its Faculty from 1897 to 1924." *Poughkeepsie Eagle News*. N.d. N. pag. (Apr. 1932). Laura Johnson Wylie Biographical File (Box 4). Courtesy of Archives and Special Collections, Vassar College Libraries.

Leonard, John William, ed. "Gertrude, Buck." *Woman's Who's Who of America: A Biographical Dictionary of Contemporary Women of the United States and Canada* [1914–1915]. New York: American Commonwealth, 1914. 141.

"L.L.D. to Dean Mary." *Stanford Alumni Review* June 1946: 7. Mary Yost Biographical File. Courtesy of Stanford University Archives.

Lockwood, Helen D. "The Bryn Mawr Summer School." *The Christian Register* 11 Mar. 1937: 161–63. (Box 4, Folder 5). Helen Drusilla Lockwood Papers. Courtesy of Archives and Special Collections, Vassar College Libraries.

————. "Contemporary Press." [Course description] (Box 8, Folder 135). N.d. Helen Drusilla Lockwood Papers. Courtesy of Archives and Special Collections, Vassar College Libraries.

————. Letter to Laura Johnson Wylie. 1 June 1921, ts. (Box 4, Folder 3). Helen Drusilla Lockwood Papers. Courtesy of Archives and Special Collections, Vassar College Libraries.

————. Letters to her parents. 27 Oct. 1908 (Box 1, Folder 13B); 6 Feb.1910 (Box 1, Folder 15B); 10 Apr. 1910 (Box 1, Folder 15B); 17 Apr. 1910 (Box 1, Folder 15B); 19 Nov. 1910 (Box 1, Folder 16A); 19 Feb. 1911 (Box 1, Folder 17A); 5 Mar. 1911 (Box 1, Folder 17A); 19 Mar. 1911 (Box 1, Folder 17A); 10 Dec. 1911 (Box 1, Folder 18A); 25 Feb. 1912 (Box 1, Folder 18B). Helen Drusilla Lockwood Papers. Courtesy of Archives and Special Collections, Vassar College Libraries.

————. "Notes on English 218, Public Discussion." 21 June 1956 (Box 7, Folder 119). Helen Drusilla Lockwood Papers. Courtesy of Archives and Special Collections, Vassar College Libraries.

————. "Outline of Work in English 312 (Contemporary Press), English 218 (Public Discussion), Interdepartment 301 and 302 (Problems of Communication through Documentary Films), also Today's Cities and a Note on Radio Writing." Spring 1946 (Box 8, Folder 135). Helen Drusilla Lockwood Papers. Courtesy of Archives and Special Collections, Vassar College Libraries.

————. "Past Was Real: It Was Earnest." *Vassar Miscellany News* 15 Apr. 1953: 1+.

"Lockwood, Helen Drusilla." [Biographical File] Courtesy of Archives and Special Collections, Vassar College Libraries.

MacCracken, Henry Noble. "Appreciations I." Woodbridge 149–51.

————. *The Hickory Limb*. New York: Scribner's, 1950.

———. Letters to Gertrude Buck, 9 Dec. 1918, ts. (Box 23, Folder 89); 8 June 1920, ts. (Box 23, Folder 87). Henry Noble MacCracken Papers. Courtesy of Archives and Special Collections, Vassar College Libraries.

———. "Report of the President to the Trustees." *Vassar College Bulletin*. 10 June 1918. 8. Poughkeepsie: Vassar College. [Call number 378.7V] Courtesy of Archives and Special Collections, Vassar College Libraries.

MacGowan, Kenneth. *Footlights across America: Towards a National Theater.* New York: Harcourt, 1929.

Mackay, Constance D'Arcy. *The Little Theatre in the United States.* New York: Holt, 1917.

MacKaye, Percy. *The Civic Theatre in Relation to the Redemption of Leisure: A Book of Suggestions.* New York: Kennerley, 1912.

Mayhew, Katherine Camp, and Anna Camp Edwards. *The Dewey School: The Laboratory School of the University of Chicago 1896–1903.* New York: Appleton-Century, 1936.

McCarthy, Mary. *The Group.* New York: Harcourt, 1963.

Mills, Herbert Elmer. "Appreciations II." Woodbridge 152–53.

———. *College Women and the Social Sciences: Essays by Herbert Elmer Mills and His Former Students.* New York: Day, 1934.

"Miss Wylie's Will Probated: Most of Estate Goes to Gertrude Buck Fund." *Sunday Courier* [Poughkeepsie] 17 Apr. 1932. N. pag. Laura Johnson Wylie Biographical File (Box 4). Courtesy of Archives and Special Collections, Vassar College Libraries.

Moore, Elizabeth, Dora Gilbert Tompkins, and Mildred MacLean. *English Composition for College Women.* New York: Macmillan, 1914.

"National College Equal Suffrage League." N.d. N. pag. Woman Suffrage Collection (Box 5, Folder 23). Courtesy of Archives and Special Collections, Vassar College Libraries.

"New Courses." *Vassar Quarterly* July 1933: 266.

"Noted Guests at Vassar Plays: See Production of Three by Workshop." *Poughkeepsie Star* 24 Nov. 1919. N. pag. Dramatic Workshop Notebook, 378.7V L799, page 30. Courtesy of Archives and Special Collections, Vassar College Libraries.

"Organize for New Community Theatre Here: Miss Buck Heads Committee; Commission Suggested." *Poughkeepsie Star* 24 Jan. 1920. N. pag. Vassar College Scrapbooks, Vol. 6, page 249. Courtesy of Archives and Special Collections, Vassar College Libraries.

Perry, Frances M. *An Introductory Course in Argumentation.* New York: American Book, 1906.

"Poughkeepsie Organizes Community Theatre: Vassar Workshop Furnishes Basis for New Departure. Students' Plays to be Presented." *Vassar Miscellany Monthly* 11 Feb. 1920: 1+.

Redding, B. F. "Poughkeepsie Community Theatre a Memorial to Miss Gertrude Buck." *Sunday Courier* [Poughkeepsie] 14 Jan. 1923: 9+.

Reed, Amy L. "In Memoriam: Gertrude Buck." *Vassar Miscellany News* 11 Jan. 1922: N. pag. Rpt. in *Vassar Quarterly* Feb. 1922: 128–29. Courtesy of Archives and Special Collections, Vassar College Libraries.

———. Letter to James Monroe Taylor. 15 Mar. 1913 (Box 17, Folder 74). James Monroe Taylor Papers. Courtesy of Archives and Special Collections, Vassar College Libraries.

———. "Report of the Department of English." 1921–22. Courtesy of Archives and Special Collections, Vassar College Libraries.

Rice, J. M. *The Public-School System of the United States*. New York: Century, 1893.

Rourke, Constance Mayfield, chronicler. *The Fiftieth Anniversary of the Opening of Vassar College: October 10 to 13, 1915: A Record*. Poughkeepsie, NY: Vassar College, 1916.

———. "Vassar Classrooms: 'English J' and 'Romanticism I.'" Woodbridge 72–76.

Salmon, Lucy M. "Progress in Education at Vassar College." *Vassar Quarterly* Nov. 1919: 1–10.

Scott, Fred Newton. "Address by Professor Fred Newton Scott of the University of Michigan." *Gertrude Buck Professor of English 1897–1922*. Spec. [Gertrude Buck] issue of *Vassar Miscellany Monthly* Feb. 1923: 3–7.

———. "Biography of Miss Harriet M. Scott" ts. Fred Newton Scott Papers (Box 2 [Articles]). Courtesy of the Bentley Historical Library, University of Michigan.

———. "Rhetoric Rediviva." Ed. Donald C. Stewart. *College Composition and Communication* 31 (1980): 413–19.

Scott, Fred Newton, and Joseph Villiers Denney. *Composition-Rhetoric: Designed for Use in Secondary Schools*. Boston: Allyn, 1897.

Shipp, Margaret M. Letter to Mamie. 28 Apr. 1902. Student Letters Collection, (Transcribed letters), (Folder 17). Courtesy of Archives and Special Collections, Vassar College Libraries.

———. Letter to Mother. 26 Apr. 1902. Student Letters Collection, (Transcribed letters), (Folder 17). Courtesy of Archives and Special Collections, Vassar College Libraries.

Smith, Hilda Worthington. *Women Workers at the Bryn Mawr Summer School*. New York: Affiliated Summer Schools for Women Workers in Industry and American Association for Adult Education, 1929.

Snell, Ada F. "History of English Studies in Mount Holyoke Seminary and College." Unpublished typescript, 1942. English Department Records. Mount Holyoke College Archives and Special Collections.

Snyder, Alice D. "The Philosophy of an English Teacher." Woodbridge 115–30.

"Snyder Describes Difficulties Here in Suffrage Years: Meetings Held in Cemetery or on Street Corners in Time of Pres. Taylor: Cause was Radical." *Vassar Miscellany News* 29 Feb. 1936: 4.

"The Social Museum: The College and the County Make Use of Each Other. *Vassar Alumnae Magazine* Dec. 1937: 11.

"Socialized Speech." *Vassar Miscellany* Mar. 1909: 335.

"Some Suggestive Subjects for A English." *Vassar Miscellany* Mar. 1905: 319.

Stanwood, Mabel. Letter to Gige. N.d. [Refers to Vassar-Wellesley debate 26 Apr. 1902.] Debate Subject File (Box 9, Folder 46). Courtesy of Archives and Special Collections, Vassar College Libraries.

"Statement to President Taylor and the Board of Trustees." 15 Mar. 1913 (Box 17, Folder 74). James Monroe Taylor Papers. Courtesy of Archives and Special Collections, Vassar College Libraries.

"The Study of English on Psychological Principles—the Required Work at Vassar College." N.p.: 24 Nov. 1898. N. pag. English Department Subject File (Box 10, Folder 41). Courtesy of Archives and Special Collections, Vassar College Libraries.

"Suffrage Meeting at the Elks Club: Miss Yost and Miss Leach of Vassar Make Addresses and Answer Number of Questions: Rev. Cadman Interested." *Poughkeepsie Daily Eagle* 14 Dec. 1912: 5–6.

"Suffragists Give Play Bearing on the Cause: 'Sam's Surrender' and 'The Salt Cellar' Delightfully Presented before a Large Audience—'Anti-Suffrage' Monologue Presented between Acts." *Poughkeepsie Eagle-News* 9 Dec. 1916: 5.

"Suffragists in Waiting for Sulzer. Bishop Doane Says the Pilgrims Are a Lot of Silly, Excited, Exaggerated Women." *Poughkeepsie Daily Eagle* 30 Dec. 1912: 1.

"The Suffragists Reach Rhinebeck. Left This City on Sunday Morning and Reached Rhinebeck Hotel Early in the Evening." *Poughkeepsie Daily Eagle* 23 Dec. 1912: 5.

"Supporters of the Workshop for 1918–19." Poughkeepsie NY: Vassar College, n.d. N. pag. Dramatic Workshop Notebook, 378.7V L799, page 17. Courtesy of Archives and Special Collections, Vassar College Libraries.

Taylor, James Monroe. "The 'Conservatism' of Vassar." N.p.: 1909. N. pag. (Box 16, Folder 67). James Monroe Taylor Papers. Courtesy of Archives and Special Collections, Vassar College Libraries.

———. Letter to M. Carey Thomas. 4 Nov. 1907, ts. (Box 16, Folder 62A). James Monroe Taylor Papers. Courtesy of Archives and Special Collections, Vassar College Libraries.

———. Report: In re Faculty discussion on freedom, etc., apropos of suffrage. [Transcribed notes from 19 Mar. 1909 faculty meeting] 3 Nov. 1911 (Box 16, Folder 64). James Monroe Taylor Papers. Courtesy of Archives and Special Collections, Vassar College Libraries.

Taylor, Katherine. "The Pageant's Permanent Value." *Vassar Miscellany Weekly* 22 Oct. 1915: 4.

Thomas, Gordon, and A. Westley Rowland. "The Brief." *Argumentation and Debate: Principles and Practices.* Ed. David Potter. New York: Holt, 1954. 461–74.

Thomas, M. Carey. Letter to James Monroe Taylor. 30 Oct. 1907, ts. (Box 16, Folder 62A). James Monroe Taylor Papers. Courtesy of Archives and Special Collections, Vassar College Libraries.

"To Punish Vassar Girl Suffragists: Forty Students, Led by English Woman, Leave College Campus for Cemetery Meeting." *New York Herald* 10 June 1908. N pag. (Box 16, Folder 66). James Monroe Taylor Papers. Courtesy of Archives and Special Collections, Vassar College Libraries.

Transcript of Grade Report. Mary Yost. The University of Michigan, Ph.D. 1917, Office of the Registrar, Ann Arbor, MI.

Trustee Minutes, 5 June 1920, as quoted in e-mail by Dean M. Rogers, Special Collections Assistant, Vassar College Library. E-mail to author. 4 Feb. 2004. Committee on Faculty and Studies, 1915–20 (Box 1, Folder 29). Henry Noble MacCracken Papers. Courtesy of Archives and Special Collections, Vassar College Libraries.

"Try Out Vassar's Plays on Vassar: Amateur Playwrights Have Students as Audience at Presentation of Dramas They Have Composed. First Effort Success." *Poughkeepsie Eagle-News* 18 Dec. 1916. N. pag. Dramatic Workshop Notebook, 378.7V L799, page 2. Courtesy of Archives and Special Collections, Vassar College Libraries.

United States. Cong. Rec. "Academic Freedom at Vassar? Extension of Remarks of Hon. B. Carroll Reece of Tennessee in the House of Representatives Thursday, March 12, 1953." [Proceedings and Debates of the 83rd Congress, First Session] (Box 2, Folder 3). Nancy Jane Fellers Papers. Courtesy of Archives and Special Collections, Vassar College Libraries.

University of Michigan Catalogue of Graduates, Non-Graduates, Officers, and Members of the Faculties, 1837–1921. Ann Arbor: U of Michigan P, 1923.

Vandewalker, Nina C. *The Kindergarten in American Education.* 1908. New York: Arno, *New York Times*, 1971.

Vassar College Catalogue. Poughkeepsie, NY: Vassar College, 1898–1904; 1928–29; 1933–34.

"Vassar Denies Student's Charges of Teachings Disparaging Religion." *Poughkeepsie New Yorker* 10 Nov. 1952: N. pag. (Box 2, Folder 5). Nancy Jane Fellers Papers. Courtesy of Archives and Special Collections, Vassar College Libraries.

"Vassar Girl Elected Director of Poughkeepsie Community Theatre." *Vassar Miscellany News* 21 Apr. 1920: 1+.

"Vassar Meets in Graveyard: College Girls Hold Suffrage Powwow." *New York Sun* 9 June 1908. N. pag. (Box 16, Folder 66). James Monroe Taylor Papers. Courtesy of Archives and Special Collections, Vassar College Libraries.

"Vassar Milestones: A Play." Rourke 249–57.

Vassarion. Poughkeepsie, NY: Vassar College, 1898, 1900, 1901, 1903, 1912, 1913, 1919, 1921.

Wald, Lillian D. "New Aspects of Old Social Responsibilities." Rourke 96–125.

Warren, Katherine. "In Remembrance of Gertrude Buck." *Vassar Quarterly* May 1922: 188–90. Rpt. in Spec. [Gertrude Buck] issue of *Vassar Miscellany Monthly* Feb. 1923: 17–20.

———. "Miss Buck and the Community Theater." *Gertrude Buck Professor of English 1897–1922.* Spec. [Gertrude Buck] issue of *Vassar Miscellany Monthly* Feb. 1923: 30–35.

———. "112 Market Street." Woodbridge 143–48.

———. "Retrospect, 1924." Woodbridge 81–93. Rpt. of "The Retirement of Miss Wylie." *Vassar Quarterly* Nov. 1924: 1–6.

"Wellesley-Vassar Debate." *Wellesley College News* 24 Apr. 1902: 1. Debate Subject File (Box 9, Folder 46). Courtesy of Archives and Special Collections, Vassar College Libraries.

West, Helen C. "The History of Debating." *Vassar Miscellany* Oct. 1915. Special Number Published by the Students' Committee on the Fiftieth Anniversary of the Opening of Vassar College: 144–61.

Whitney, M. P. "Town and Gown in the Suffrage Movement." *Vassar Quarterly* May 1916: 121–22.

Whitney, Mary W. Letter to Taylor. 7 Apr. 1909 (Box 16, Folder 64). James Monroe Taylor Papers. Courtesy of Archives and Special Collections, Vassar College Libraries.

"Women's City and County Club Soon to Close a Busy Season. Many Activities Mark Past Winter in This Organization. Miss Wylie Has Been the President since It Was Formed." *Poughkeepsie Star* 14 Apr. 1925: 2.

Woodbridge (Morris), Elisabeth. "Laura Johnson Wylie 1855–1932." Woodbridge 1–17.

———, ed. *Miss Wylie of Vassar.* New Haven: Yale UP, 1934.

———. "Pioneer and Humanist." Woodbridge 65–71.

"The Workshop Up-To-Date." *Vassarion* (1919). Vassar College: Poughkeepsie, NY, 1919: 155–57.

"Wylie, Laura Johnson." [Biographical File] Courtesy of Archives and Special Collections, Vassar College Libraries.

Wylie, Laura Johnson. Letters to Fanny Hart. 30 Apr. 1912; 9 May 1912; 18 Jan. 1913 (Letters all from Box 2 Correspondence, 1911–14; all ts.). Laura Johnson Wylie Biographical File. Courtesy of Archives and Special Collections, Vassar College Libraries.

———. Letters to President Taylor. 23 Nov. 1904, ts. (Box 2, Folder 29); 11 May 1908, ts. (Box 2, Folder 53). James Monroe Taylor Papers. Courtesy of Archives and Special Collections, Vassar College Libraries.

———, ed. Preface. *Poems and Plays.* By Gertrude Buck. New York: Duffield, 1922. N. pag.

———. "Report[s] of the Department of English." 1899–1922. (Box 2, Folder 47 to Box 2, Folder 56; after 1913–1914 reports housed in Henry Noble Mac-Cracken Papers Box 20, Folder 114 to Box 27, Folder 17). [Laura Johnson Wylie, chair 1899–1921; Amy Reed, chair 1921–22] English Department. Courtesy of Archives and Special Collections, Vassar College Libraries.

———. *Social Studies in English Literature*. Boston: Houghton, 1916.

———. Speaking on the Topic: "Education at Vassar, Its Ideals and Its Methods. Does the Present Undergraduate Training at Vassar Give the Student Sufficient Broad Participation for Her Future Activities?" (16 June 1921), ts. Quoted in "Stenographic Report," Fiftieth Anniversary, Associate Alumnae, Vassar College. 11–23. [Call number Q 378.7V T72] Courtesy of Archives and Special Collections, Vassar College Libraries.

———. *Studies in the Evolution of English Criticism*. Boston: Ginn, 1894.

———. "What Can Be Done about It?" *Vassar Quarterly* July 1918: n. pag. Rpt. in Woodbridge 131–42.

Yost, Mary. "Argument from the Point-of-View of Sociology." *Quarterly Journal of Public Speaking* 3 (1917): 109–24.

———. "The Functional Aspect of Argument as Seen in a Collection of Business Letters." Diss. U of Michigan, 1917.

———. "The Intercollegiate Debate." *Vassar Quarterly* May 1916: 128–29.

———. "The Need of the Community-Mind: In which the Dean of Women Says Some Things That Every Stanford Man and Women Should Think About." *Stanford Illustrated Review* Dec. 1921: 131–33. Courtesy of Stanford University Archives.

———. 1924 Alumnae Survey. University of Michigan Alumnae Association (Box 109, MF 418, Roll 9). Courtesy of the Bentley Historical Library, University of Michigan.

———. "Training Four Minute Men at Vassar." *Quarterly Journal of Speech Education* 5 (1919): 246–53.

Secondary Sources

Adams, Katherine H. *A Group of Their Own: College Writing Courses and American Women Writers, 1880–1940*. Albany: SUNY P, 2001.

———. *Progressive Politics and the Training of America's Persuaders*. Mahwah, NJ: Erlbaum, 1999.

Allen, Virginia. "Gertrude Buck and the Emergence of Composition in the United States." *Vitae Scholasticae* 5 (1986): 141–59.

Bacon, Jacqueline. *The Humblest May Stand Forth: Rhetoric, Empowerment, and Abolition*. Columbia: U of South Carolina P, 2002.

Baker, Melvin C. *Foundations of John Dewey's Educational Theory*. New York: Atherton, 1966.

Banner, Lois W. *Women in Modern America: A Brief History*. New York: Harcourt, 1974.

Beck, Robert Holmes. "American Progressive Education, 1875–1930." Diss. Yale U, 1942.

Bederman, Gail. *Manliness and Civilization: A Cultural History of Gender and Race in the United States, 1880–1917*. Chicago: U of Chicago P, 1995.

Bentley, Joanne. *Hallie Flanagan: A Life in the American Theatre*. New York: Knopf, 1988.

Bergon, Frank. "Teaching Writing: 'What Can Be Done about It?'" Evalyn A. Clark Annual Symposium on Excellence in Teaching. Vassar College, Poughkeepsie, 6 Apr. 1990.

Berlin, James A. *Rhetoric and Reality: Writing Instruction in American Colleges, 1900–1985*. Carbondale: Southern Illinois UP, 1987.

———. *Writing Instruction in Nineteenth-Century American Colleges*. Carbondale: Southern Illinois UP, 1984.

Blair, Karen J. *The Torchbearers: Women and Their Amateur Arts Associations in America, 1890–1930*. Bloomington: Indiana UP, 1994.

Bohan, Chara Haeussler. "Go to the Sources: Lucy Maynard Salmon and the Teaching of History." Diss. U of Texas at Austin, 1999.

———. "Lucy Maynard Salmon: Progressive Historian, Teacher, and Democrat." *"Bending the Future to Their Will": Civic Women, Social Education, and Democracy*. Ed. Margaret Smith Crocco and O. L. Davis, Jr. Lanham, MD: Rowman, 1999. 47–72.

Boice, Eva C. "Woman Suffrage, Vassar College, and Laura Johnson Wylie." *Hudson River Valley Review* 20.2 (2004): 37–49.

Bordelon, Suzanne. "Gertrude Buck's Democratic Theory of Discourse and Pedagogy: A Cultural History." Diss. U of Oregon, 1998.

Brown, Louise Fargo. *Apostle of Democracy: The Life of Lucy Maynard Salmon*. New York: Harper, 1943.

Buenker, John D., and Edward R. Kantowicz. Preface. *Historical Dictionary of the Progressive Era, 1890–1920*. Ed. Buenker and Kantowicz. New York: Greenwood, 1988. xii–ix.

Burke, Rebecca J. "Gertrude Buck's Rhetorical Theory." *Occasional Papers in Composition History and Theory*. Ed. Donald C. Stewart. Kansas State U, 1978: 1–26.

Caffrey, Margaret M. *Ruth Benedict: Stranger in This Land*. Austin: U of Texas P, 1989.

Campbell, JoAnn, [Louise]. "Gertrude Buck and the Celebration of Community: A History of Writing Instruction at Vassar College, 1897–1922." Diss. U of Texas at Austin, 1989.

———, ed. Introduction. Campbell, *Toward* ix–xliii.

———, ed. *Toward a Feminist Rhetoric: The Writing of Gertrude Buck*. U of Pittsburgh P, 1996.

Campbell, Karlyn Kohrs. "Biesecker Cannot Speak for Her Either." *Philosophy and Rhetoric* 26 (1993): 153–59.

———. "Consciousness-Raising: Linking Theory, Criticism, and Practice." *Rhetoric Society Quarterly* 32.1 (2002): 45–64.

———. *Man Cannot Speak for Her: A Critical Study of Early Feminist Rhetoric.* Vol. 1. 2 vols. New York: Greenwood, 1989.

Carr, Jean Ferguson, Stephen L. Carr, and Lucille M. Schultz. *Archives of Instruction: Nineteenth-Century Rhetorics, Readers, and Composition Books in the United States.* Carbondale: Southern Illinois UP, 2005.

Chalk, Carol S. "Gertrude Buck in the Writing Center: A Tutor Training Model to Challenge Nineteenth-Century Trends." Diss. Ball State U., 2004.

Clark, Gregory, and S. Michael Halloran. Introduction. *Oratorical Culture in Nineteenth-Century America: Transformations in the Theory and Practice of Rhetoric.* Ed. Gregory Clark and S. Michael Halloran. Carbondale: Southern Illinois UP, 1993. 1–26.

Clark, Suzanne. "Argument and Composition." Jarratt and Worsham 94–99.

———. "Uncanny Millay." *Millay at 100: A Critical Reappraisal.* Ed. Diane P. Freedman. Carbondale: Southern Illinois UP, 1995. 3–26.

———. "The Unwarranted Discourse: Sentimental Community, Modernist Women, and the Case of Millay." *Critical Essays on Edna St. Vincent Millay.* Ed. William B. Thesing. New York: Hall, 1993. 248–65.

Cohen, Herman. *The History of Speech Communication: The Emergence of a Discipline, 1914–1945.* Annandale, VA: Speech Communication Association, 1994.

Connors, Robert J. *Composition-Rhetoric: Backgrounds, Theory, and Pedagogy.* Pittsburgh: U of Pittsburgh P, 1997.

———. "Mechanical Correctness as a Focus in Composition Instruction." *College Composition and Communication* 36 (1985): 61–72.

———. "Overwork/Underpay: Labor and Status of Composition Teachers since 1880." *Rhetoric Review* 9 (1990): 108–26.

———. "The Rhetoric of Explanation: Explanatory Rhetoric from 1850 to the Present." *Written Communication* 2 (1985): 49–72.

———. "Teaching and Learning as a Man." *College English* 58 (1996): 137–57.

Connors, Robert J., Lisa S. Ede, and Andrea A. Lunsford, eds. *Essays on Classical Rhetoric and Modern Discourse.* Carbondale, IL: Southern Illinois UP, 1984.

Conway, Kathryn M. "Woman Suffrage and the History of Rhetoric at the Seven Sisters Colleges, 1865–1919." Lunsford 203–26.

Cremin, Lawrence A. *The Transformation of the School: Progressivism in American Education, 1876–1957.* New York: Knopf, 1961.

Crocco, Margaret Smith. Introduction. *"Bending the Future to Their Will": Civic Women, Social Education, and Democracy.* Ed. Margaret Smith Crocco and O.L. Davis, Jr. Lanham, MD: Rowman, 1999. 1–16.

Crocco, Margaret Smith, Petra Munro, and Kathleen Weiler. "In Search of Subjectivity." *Pedagogies of Resistance: Women Educator Activists, 1880–1960.* Ed. Margaret Smith Crocco, Petra Munro, and Kathleen Weiler. New York: Teachers College P, 1999. 1–17.

Crowley, Sharon. *The Methodical Memory: Invention in Current-Traditional Rhetoric.* Carbondale: Southern Illinois UP, 1990.

———. Rev. of *Composition-Rhetoric: Backgrounds, Theory, and Pedagogy*, by Robert J. Connors. *Rhetoric Review* 16 (1998): 340–43.

Daniels, Elizabeth A. *Bridges to the World: Henry Noble MacCracken and Vassar College.* Clinton Corners, NY: College Avenue, 1994.

———. "Suffrage as a Lever for Change at Vassar College." *Vassar Quarterly* Summer 1983: 32–36.

Darlington, Beth. "Vassar's Jung Folks." *Vassar Quarterly* Winter 1998: 18–23.

Diner, Steven J. *A Very Different Age: Americans of the Progressive Era.* New York: Hill, 1998.

Donawerth, Jane, ed. *Rhetorical Theory by Women before 1900: An Anthology.* Lanham, MD: Rowman, 2002.

———. "Textbooks for New Audiences: Women's Revisions of Rhetorical Theory at the Turn of the Century." Wertheimer 337–56.

Dunkel, Harold B. *Herbart and Education.* New York: Random, 1969.

Ellis, Constance Dimock, ed., Dorothy A. Plum and George B. Dowell, comps. *The Magnificent Enterprise: A Chronicle of Vassar College.* Poughkeepsie, NY: Vassar College, 1961.

Faderman, Lillian. Foreword. *Wolf Girls of Vassar: Lesbian and Gay Experiences 1930–1990.* Ed. Anne MacKay. New York: St. Martin's, 1992. xi–xv.

Fawson, Diane. "George Pierce Baker: His Influence upon Selected Educational Theatre Systems in the U.S." Master's Thesis. U of Oregon, 1966.

Feffer, Andrew. *The Chicago Pragmatists and American Progressivism.* Ithaca: Cornell UP, 1993.

Feuer, Lewis S. "John Dewey and the Back to the People Movement in American Thought." *Journal of the History of Ideas* 20 (1959): 545–68.

Fitzgerald, Kathryn. "A Rediscovered Tradition: European Pedagogy and Composition in Nineteenth-Century Midwestern Normal Schools." *College Composition and Communication* 53 (2001): 224–50.

Flanagan, Hallie. *Dynamo.* New York: Duell, 1943.

Foss, Sonja K., and Cindy L. Griffin. "Beyond Persuasion: A Proposal for an Invitational Rhetoric." *Communication Monographs* 62 (1995): 2–18.

Fredrickson, George M. *The Black Image in the White Mind: The Debate on Afro-American Character and Destiny, 1817–1914.* 1971. Hanover, NH: Wesleyan UP, 1987.

Gage, John T. "An Adequate Epistemology for Composition: Classical and Modern Perspective." Connors, Ede, and Lunsford 152–69.

———. "Towards an Epistemology of Composition." *Journal of Advanced Composition* 1–2 (1981): 1–10.

Gaines, Billie Davis. "No Hiding Place: Civil Rights and Vassar in One Woman's Life." *Vassar Quarterly* Spring 1989: 10–18.

Garbus, Julia. "Service Learning, 1902." *College English* 64 (2002): 547–65.

Gearhart, Sally Miller. "The Womanization of Rhetoric." *Women's Studies International Quarterly* 2 (1979): 195–201.

Gilligan, Carol. *In a Different Voice: Psychological Theory and Women's Development.* Cambridge: Harvard UP, 1982.

Glenn, Cheryl. *Rhetoric Retold: Regendering the Tradition from Antiquity through the Renaissance.* Carbondale: Southern Illinois UP, 1997.

Gordon, Lynn D. *Gender and Higher Education in the Progressive Era.* New Haven: Yale UP, 1990.

Gunner, Jeanne. "Decentering the WPA." *Writing Program Administration* 18.1/2 (Fall/Winter 1994): 8–15.

Hanawalt, Leslie L. *A Place of Light: The History of Wayne State University.* Detroit: Wayne State UP, 1968.

Harmon, Sandra D. "'The Voice, Pen, and Influence of Our Women Are Abroad in the Land': Women and the Illinois State Normal University, 1857–1899." Hobbs 84–102.

Heller, Adele, and Lois Rudnick. Introduction. Heller and Rudnick 1–13.

Heller, Adele, and Lois Rudnick, eds. *1915, the Cultural Moment: The New Politics, the New Woman, the New Psychology, the New Art, and the New Theatre in America.* New Brunswick, NJ: Rutgers UP, 1991.

Heller, Rita Rubinstein. "The Women of Summer: The Bryn Mawr Summer School for Women Workers, 1921–1938." Diss. Rutgers U, The State U of New Jersey, 1986.

———. "The Women of Summer: The Bryn Mawr Summer School for Women Workers, 1921–1938." Diss. Rutgers U, The State U of New Jersey, 1986. Abstract. 16 Mar. 2006 <http://www-distance.syr.edu/heller.html>.

Henderson, Mary C. "Against Broadway: The Rise of the Art Theatre in America (1900–1920): A Photographic Essay." Heller and Rudnick 233–49.

Herman, Debra. "College and After: The Vassar Experiment in Women's Education, 1861–1924." Diss. Stanford U, 1979.

Herzberg, Bruce. "Adams Sherman Hill (1833–1910)." *Encyclopedia of Rhetoric and Composition: Communication from Ancient Times to the Information Age.* Ed. Theresa Enos. New York: Garland, 1996. 320–21.

Hobbs, Catherine, ed. *Nineteenth-Century Women Learn to Write.* Charlottesville: UP of Virginia, 1995.

Hollis, Karyn L. *Liberating Voices: Writing at the Bryn Mawr Summer School for Women Workers.* Carbondale: Southern Illinois UP, 2004.

———. "Plays of Heteroglossia: Labor Drama at the Bryn Mawr Summer School for Women Workers." *Popular Literacy: Studies in Cultural Practices and Poetics.* Ed. John Trimbur. Pittsburgh: U of Pittsburgh P, 2001. 151–74.

hooks, bell. *Teaching to Transgress: Education as the Practice of Freedom.* New York: Routledge, 1994.

Horowitz, Helen Lefkowitz. *Alma Mater: Design and Experience in the Women's Colleges from Their Nineteenth-Century Beginnings to the 1930s.* New York: Knopf, 1984.

Howton, Elizabeth. "The 'Lasuens': Academic Women at Stanford, 1920–1946." Senior Honors Thesis, Stanford U, 1991.

Jarratt, Susan C., and Lynn Worsham. *Feminism and Composition Studies: In Other Words.* New York: MLA, 1998.

Johnson, Nan. *Gender and Rhetorical Space in American Life, 1866–1910.* Carbondale: Southern Illinois UP, 2002.

Kates, Susan. *Activist Rhetorics and American Higher Education 1885–1937.* Carbondale: Southern Illinois UP, 2001.

———. "Subversive Feminism: The Politics of Correctness in Mary Augusta Jordan's *Correct Writing and Speaking* (1904)." *College Composition and Communication* 48 (1997): 501–17.

Kendall, Elaine. *"Peculiar Institutions": An Informal History of the Seven Sisters Colleges.* New York: Putnam's, 1976.

Kinne, Wisner Payne. *George Pierce Baker and the American Theatre.* Cambridge: Harvard UP, 1954.

Kitzhaber, Albert R. *A Bibliography of Rhetoric in American Colleges, 1850–1900.* Denver: Denver Public Library, 1954.

———. *Rhetoric in American Colleges, 1850–1900.* Dallas: Southern Methodist UP, 1990.

Koch, Kevin James. "Gertrude Buck and the Emergence of a Transactional Theory of Language." Diss. U of Iowa, 1992.

Lamb, Catherine E. "Beyond Argument in Feminist Composition." *College Composition and Communication* 42 (1991): 11–24. Rpt. in *Feminism and Composition: A Critical Sourcebook.* Ed. Gesa E. Kirsch, et al. Boston: Bedford, 2003. 281–93.

Lemons, J. Stanley. *The Woman Citizen: Social Feminism in the 1920s.* Urbana: U of Illinois P, 1973.

L'Eplattenier, Barbara E. "Investigating Institutional Power: Women Administrators during the Progressive Era 1890–1920." Diss. Purdue U, 1999.

———. "Questioning Our Methodological Metaphors." *Calling Cards: Theory and Practice in Studies of Race, Gender, and Culture.* Ed. Jacqueline Jones Royster and Ann Marie Simpkins. SUNY P, 2005. 133–45.

———. "Revising the Ideological Stance: Rethinking Methodologies of Archival Research." Conf. on Coll. Composition and Communication. Palmer House, Chicago. 25 Mar. 2006.

L'Eplattenier, Barbara, and Lisa Mastrangelo, eds. *Historical Studies of Writing Program Administration: Individuals, Communities, and the Formation of a Discipline.* West Lafayette, IN: Parlor, 2004.

L'Eplattenier, Barbara, and Lisa Mastrangelo. "'Is It the Pleasure of This Conference to Have Another?': Women's Colleges Meeting and Talking about Writing in the Progressive Era." L'Eplattenier and Mastrangelo 117–43.

Lindblom, Kenneth, and Patricia A. Dunn. "Cooperative Writing 'Program' Administration at Illinois State Normal University: The Committee on English of 1904–05 and the Influence of J. Rose Colby." L'Eplattenier and Mastrangelo 37–70.

Logan, Shirley Wilson. *"We Are Coming": The Persuasive Discourse of Nineteenth-Century Black Women*. Carbondale: Southern Illinois UP, 1999.

Lunsford, Andrea A., ed. *Reclaiming Rhetorica: Women in the Rhetorical Tradition*. Pittsburgh: Pittsburgh UP, 1995.

Lunsford, Andrea A., and Lisa S. Ede. "On Distinctions between Classical and Modern Rhetoric." Connors, Ede, and Lunsford 37–49.

Lynch, William O. *A History of Indiana State Teachers College: Indiana State Normal School 1870–1929*. Terre Haute: Indiana State Teachers College, 1946.

MacKay, Anne, ed. *Wolf Girls of Vassar: Lesbian and Gay Experiences 1930–1990*. New York: St. Martin's, 1992.

Mastrangelo, Lisa S. "Building a Dinosaur from the Bones: Fred Newton Scott and Women's Progressive Era Graduate Work at the University of Michigan." *Rhetoric Review* 24 (2005): 403–20.

———. "Learning from the Past: Rhetoric, Composition, and Debate at Mount Holyoke College." *Rhetoric Review* 18 (1999): 46–64.

———. "Stories of a Progressive Past: Early Feminist and Progressive Approaches to Writing Instruction." Diss. U of Albany, State U of New York, 2000.

Mattingly, Carol. *Appropriate[ing] Dress: Women's Rhetorical Style in Nineteenth-Century America*. Carbondale: Southern Illinois UP, 2002.

———, ed. *Water Drops from Women Writers: A Temperance Reader*. Carbondale: Southern Illinois UP, 2001.

———. *Well-Tempered Women: Nineteenth-Century Temperance Rhetoric*. Carbondale: Southern Illinois UP, 1998.

McHenry, Elizabeth. *Forgotten Readers: Recovering the Lost History of African American Literary Societies*. Durham: Duke UP, 2002.

"Memorial Minute: Oct. 24, 2001." [In Memoriam: Evalyn A. Clark, 1903–2001] Dept. home page. Vassar College Department of History. 19 May 2003 <http://history.vassar.edu/evalynclark/ec.minutes.html>.

Mezzacappa, Dale. "Vassar College and the Suffrage Movement." *Vassar Quarterly* Spring 1973: 2–9.

Miller, Hildy. "Postmasculinist Directions in Writing Program Administration." *Writing Program Administration* 20.1–2 (Fall/Winter 1996): 49–61. Rpt. in *The Allyn and Bacon Sourcebook for Writing Program Administrators*. Ed. Irene Ward and William J. Carpenter. New York: Longman, 2002. 78–90.

Miller, Thomas P. *The Formation of College English: Rhetoric and Belles Lettres in the British Cultural Provinces*. Pittsburgh: U of Pittsburgh P, 1997.

Morgan, Dana Hood. "Gertrude Buck's Rhetoric: The Living Expression of Thought." Master's Thesis. California State U of Dominguez Hills, 1995.

Mountford, Roxanne. "Feminization of Rhetoric?" Rev. of *Composition-Rhetoric: Backgrounds, Theory, and Pedagogy*, by Robert J. Connors. *Journal of Advanced Composition* 19 (1999): 485–92. 28 Dec. 2004 <http://jac.gsu.edu/jac/19.3/Reviews/1htm>.

————."Roxanne Mountford's Reply to *Adversus Haereses*." [Exchange over Mountford's review of *Composition-Rhetoric*.] *Journal of Advanced Composition* 19 (1999) 28 Dec. 2004 <http://jac.gsu.edu/jac/Reviewsreviewed/mountford. htm>.

Mral, Brigitte. "The Public Woman: Women Speakers around the Turn of the Century in Sweden." Sutherland and Sutcliffe 161–72.

Mulderig, Gerald. "Gertrude Buck's Rhetorical Theory and Modern Composition Teaching." *Rhetoric Society Quarterly* 14.3/4 (1984): 95–104.

Myers, D.G. *The Elephants Teach: Creative Writing Since 1880*. Englewood Cliffs, NJ: Prentice, 1996.

Noddings, Nel. *Caring: A Feminine Approach to Ethics and Moral Education*. Berkeley: U of California P, 1984.

————. *Educating Moral People: A Caring Alternative to Character Education*. New York: Teachers College P, 2002.

Paine, Charles. *The Resistant Writer: Rhetoric as Immunity, 1850 to the Present*. Albany: State U of New York P, 1999.

Painter, Nell Irvin. *Standing at Armageddon: The United States 1877–1919*. New York: Norton, 1987.

Palmieri, Patricia Ann. *In Adamless Eden: The Community of Women Faculty at Wellesley*. New Haven: Yale UP, 1995.

Pandora, Katherine. *Rebels within the Ranks: Psychologists' Critique of Scientific Authority and Democratic Realities in New Deal America*. New York: Cambridge UP, 1997.

Pappas, Gregory Fernando. "Dewey and Feminism: The Affective and Relationships in Dewey's Ethics." *Feminism and Pragmatism*. Ed. Charlene Haddock Seigfried. Spec. issue of *Hypatia* 8.2 (1993): 78–95.

Perkins, Linda M. "The Racial Integration of the Seven Sister Colleges." *Journal of Blacks in Higher Education* 19 (1998): 104–8.

Popken, Randall. "The WPA as Publishing Scholar: Edwin Hopkins and *The Labor and Cost of the Teaching of English*." L'Eplattenier and Mastrangelo 5–22.

Ricker, Lisa Reid. "'*Ars* Stripped of Praxis': Robert J. Connors on Coeducation and the Demise of Agonistic Rhetoric." *Rhetoric Review* 23 (2004): 235–52.

Ricks (Weir), Vickie. "Revisioning Traditions through Rhetoric: Studies in Gertrude Buck's Social Theory of Discourse." Diss. Texas Christian U, 1989.

Ridener, Larry R. "Charles Horton Cooley: A Summary of Ideas; The Looking-Glass Self." *Dead Sociologists' Society at Pfeiffer University*. 7 June 2004. <http://www2.pfeiffer.edu/~lridener/DSS/Cooley/COOLWRK.HTML>.

Ritchie, Joy S. "Confronting the 'Essential' Problem: Reconnecting Feminist Theory and Pedagogy." *Journal of Advanced Composition* 10 (1990): 249–73. Rpt. in *Feminism and Composition: A Critical Sourcebook*. Ed. Gesa E. Kirsch, et al. Boston: Bedford, 2003. 79–102.

Ritchie, Joy, and Kate Ronald, eds. *Available Means: An Anthology of Women's Rhetoric(s)*. Pittsburgh: U of Pittsburgh P, 2001.

———. "Riding Long Coattails, Subverting Tradition: The Tricky Business of Feminists Teaching Rhetoric(s)." Jarratt and Worsham 217–38.

Rodgers, Daniel T. "In Search of Progressivism." *Reviews in American History* 10 (1982): 113–32.

Rogers, Agnes. *Vassar Women: An Informal Study*. Poughkeepsie, NY: Vassar College, 1940.

Rosenberg, Rosalind. *Beyond Separate Spheres: The Intellectual Roots of Modern Feminism*. New Haven: Yale UP, 1982.

Rosenblatt, Louise M. *Literature as Exploration*. 1938. 3rd ed. New York: MLA, 1983.

Rothermel, Beth Ann. "A Sphere of Noble Action: Gender, Rhetoric, and Influence at a Nineteenth-Century Massachusetts State Normal School." *Rhetoric Society Quarterly* 33.1 (2003): 35–64.

Royster, Jacqueline Jones. *Traces of a Stream: Literacy and Social Change among African American Women*. Pittsburgh: U of Pittsburgh P, 2000.

Rubin, Joan Shelley. *Constance Rourke and American Culture*. Chapel Hill: U of North Carolina P, 1980.

Rynbrandt, Linda J. "The 'Ladies of the Club' and Caroline Bartlett Crane: Affiliation and Alienation in Progressive Social Reform." *Gender and Society* 11 (1997): 200–214.

Scarboro, Cheryl L. "Feminist Pedagogy." *Women's Studies Encyclopedia: Revised and Expanded Edition*. Ed. Helen Tierney. 3 vols. Westport, CT: Greenwood, 1999.

Schell, Eileen E. "The Costs of Caring: 'Feminism' and Contingent Women Workers in Composition Studies." Jarratt and Worsham 74–93.

Schultz, Lucille M. *The Young Composers: Composition's Beginnings in Nineteenth-Century Schools*. Carbondale: Southern Illinois UP, 1999.

Scott, Joan Wallach. *Gender and the Politics of History*. New York: Columbia UP, 1988.

Seigfried, Charlene Haddock. *Pragmatism and Feminism: Reweaving the Social Fabric*. Chicago: U of Chicago P, 1996.

Sharer, Wendy B. *Vote and Voice: Women's Organizations and Political Literacy, 1915–1930*. Carbondale: Southern Illinois UP, 2004.

Shaw, David Gary. "The Return of Science." *History and Theory* 38 (1999): 1–9.

Sichel, Betty A. "Different Strains and Strands: Feminist Contributions to Ethical Theory." *Newsletter on Feminism* 90.2 (1991): 90.

Simpson, Alan. "Helen Lockwood's College Years: 1908–1912. A Convocation Address by Alan Simpson, President of Vassar College." Poughkeepsie, NY: Vassar College, 1977.

Smith-Rosenberg, Carroll. *Disorderly Conduct: Visions of Gender in Victorian America*. 1985. New York: Oxford UP, 1986.

———. "The Female World of Love and Ritual: Relationships between Women in Nineteenth-Century America." *Signs: Journal of Women in Culture and Society*. 1 (1975): 1–29.

Sosnowsky, William P. "The Harriet Maria Scott Memorial Window." *The Educator: A Publication of the College of Education and College of Education Alumni Association* Spring/Summer 2004: 1–2.

Spivak, Gayatri Chakravorty. *The Post-Colonial Critic: Interviews, Strategies, Dialogues*. Ed. Sarah Harasym. New York: Routledge, 1990.

Sprinchorn, Evert. "Stagestruck in Academe: Acceptance of Theater as a Liberal Art Was No Overnight Success." *Vassar Quarterly* Spring 1991: 19–26.

Stewart, Donald C. "Fred Newton Scott and the Reform Movement of the 1890s." *Discourse Studies in Honor of James L. Kinneavy*. Ed. Rosalind J. Gabin. Potomac, MD: Scripta Humanistica, 1995. 106–20.

Stewart, Donald C., and Patricia L. Stewart. *The Life and Legacy of Fred Newton Scott*. Pittsburgh: U of Pittsburgh P, 1997.

Stumpf, Samuel Enoch. *Socrates to Sarte: A History of Philosophy*. 1966. 5th ed. New York: McGraw, 1993.

Sutherland, Christine Mason. "Women in the History of Rhetoric: The Past and the Future." Sutherland and Sutcliffe 9–31.

Sutherland, Christine Mason, and Rebecca Sutcliffe, eds. *The Changing Tradition: Women in the History of Rhetoric*. Calgary: U of Calgary P, 1999.

Swain, Barbara. "Helen Drusilla Lockwood: Class of 1912: Department of English 1927–1956: A Memoir and Appreciation by Barbara Swain, Professor Emeritus of English." Poughkeepsie, NY: Vassar College, 1977.

Tannen, Deborah. *The Argument Culture: Moving from Debate to Dialogue*. New York: Random, 1998.

Tanner, Cheryl Carithers. "An Analysis of Gertrude Buck's Originality: Do Her Textbooks Reflect a Pedagogical and Rhetorical Theory Similar to Adams Sherman Hill's?" Master's Thesis. Tarleton State U, 1999.

Thornton, Tamara Plakins. *Handwriting in America: A Cultural History*. New Haven: Yale UP, 1996.

Tong, Rosemarie. *Feminine and Feminist Ethics*. Belmont, CA: Wadsworth, 1993.

Vivian, Barbara G. "Gertrude Buck on Metaphor: Twentieth-Century Concepts in a Late Nineteenth-Century Dissertation." *Rhetoric Society Quarterly* 24.3/4 (1994): 96–103.

Wertheimer, Molly Meijer. *Listening to Their Voices: The Rhetorical Activities of Historical Women*. Columbia: U of South Carolina P, 1997.

Woods, William F. "Nineteenth-Century Psychology and the Teaching of Writing." *College Composition and Communication* 36 (1985): 20–41.

Wozniak, John Michael. *English Composition in Eastern Colleges, 1850–1940*. Washington, DC: University P of America, 1978.

INDEX

The abbreviation *pl.* indicates a pertinent plate in the gallery of illustrations following page 92.

cation of, 154, 172–80, 206–7n23; and
feminist teaching tradition at Vassar,
177–80, 189; and Hudson Shore Labor
School, 188; influences on, 154, 176–80;
retirement of, 173; students of, 211nn10,
12; and suffrage movement, 179; teaching career of, 172–73; as Vassar faculty
member and courses by, 154, 172, 173,
175, 180–89, 190, 207nn23, 24, 211n10;
and Vassar's Center for Black Studies,
10, 173; will of, 173–74; and workers'
education movement, 10, 26
logic and argumentation, 104–6, 108–10,
154, 158, 162
Lovelace, Frank B., 139–40

MacCracken, Henry Noble: and activism
of Vassar faculty, 24, 100, 188–89; administrative style of, 208n7; and budget
of Vassar, 87; and college education for
women, 54–58; and commencement
programs, 208n8; and drama workshop at Vassar, 142; and Gertrude Buck
Drama Fund, 209n13; and Poughkeepsie Community Theatre, 138, 140–41,
209n15; on Taylor, 94; on teaching of
writing at Vassar, 89; on Vassar Board
of Trustees, 203–4n1; as Vassar English
department faculty member, 203n1; on
Wylie, 84–85
MacEwan, E. J., 108
MacKaye, Hazel, 123, 207n1
MacKaye, Percy, 126
MacLean, Mildred, 114–15
Madeira, Lucy, 130
Mann, Kristine, 18–19, 115–16, 158, 175,
206n22
Mastrangelo, Lisa S., 190, 209n3
Mathison, Edith Wynne, 136
Matthews, Brander, 99
Mayhew, Katherine Camp, 127–28
McCarthy, Mary, 89, 172
metaphor, 18, 63–65, 71
Metaphor, The (Buck), 18, 63–65
Milholland, Inez, 96–97, 101
Millay, Edna St. Vincent, 26, 89, 124,
136, 149–51

Miller, Hildy, 84, 89
Mills, Herbert E., 15–16, 76, 117, 197–98n1,
203n7
Mitchell, Broadus, 211n12
Modern Language Association (MLA),
39, 78
Moore, Elizabeth, 114–15
Morris, Elisabeth Woodbridge, 18, 24,
28–34, 74, 75, 129, 200n19, 203n4
Mother-Love (Buck), 146–48, 209n17
Mount Holyoke College, 82, 95, 118,
200n13
Myers, D. G., 47, 208n

Noddings, Nel, 20, 41, 42, 65–66, 146, 149
normal schools, 11, 17–18, 41–45, 49–54,
pl., 198n7

Organic Education (H. M. Scott and Buck),
17–18, 41, 42, 49–54, 59–63, 198n7

Parker, Francis W., 59
pedagogy. *See* education; rhetoric; *specific
colleges and universities*; Vassar College
Pelham, Laura Dainty, 126–27
Perkins, Linda M., 9–10
Perry, Frances M., 114
persuasion, 22–23, 108–10, 121, 161, 163,
165, 168, 185, 205n15. *See also* rhetoric
Pestalozzi, Johann Heinrich, 44
Plato, 22–23, 67–70, 77, 163
Poems and Plays (Buck), 18, 75
Popken, Randall, 78
Poughkeepsie Community Theatre: advisory board of, 138–39; Buck's founding
of, 13, 26–27, 127, 134, 137–38, 142–43;
Buck's request for release time for, 140–
41; executive committee of, 138; finances of, 138–39; and Flanagan, 127, 142,
207n5, 208n11; goal of, 26–27, 137–38;
and MacCracken, 138, 140–41, 209n15;
plays presented by, 138–39; praise for,
139; and Stouts, 142; and Vassar College, 10, 12, 24, 124, 134, 139–42, 152;
and Wylie, 127, 138, 140
Poughkeepsie Equal Suffrage League, 24,
75, 100, 101–2, 143, 156

Poughkeepsie Woman's Suffrage Party, 97, 100

Poughkeepsie Women's City and County Club, 24, 25, 75, 100

Progressive Era: Buck on ideal of, 191; dates of, 2; definition of, 9, 195n2; and goal of education, 23, 45, 133, 190; Mills on, 15–16; and New Woman, 99; Vassar speakers on, 158; women's participation in reforms during, 124–25. *See also* democracy; education; Little Theater movement; suffrage movement

Putnam, Emily James, 16, 198n4

Quintilian, 108

Radcliffe College, 17, 26, 95, 118, 125, 128

Raymond, John Howard, 96

Reece, B. Carroll, 172

Reed, Amy L., 86–87, 203n7

Reed, Edward Bliss, 130

rhetoric: activist rhetoric instruction, 23–27; Aristotle on, 22, 69, 108, 162, 199n11; and associationism, 21, 31, 35; Buck on teaching of composition, 66–67, 104; Buck's approach to argumentation, 11–12, 14, 35–36, 93, 102–18, 121–22, 158, 161–62; and Buck's approach to drama, 142–45; Buck's social theory of, 1, 2–3, 5, 11–16, 20–23, 39–40, 63–71, 107–8, 111; and conviction, 161, 163, 165; current-traditional rhetoric, 21–22, 34–35, 199n9; definition of, 205n15; and description process, 30–32; and faculty psychology, 20–21, 27, 31, 35, 154, 161; feminine style in, 36, 53; feminist critique of, 109–10; and functional psychology, 22, 27, 31; gendered and racialized perspectives in, 1, 3–5, 23, 48–49, 112–13; inductive approach to, 25, 28–29, 33–36, 103, 121; and invention, 34–35; invitational rhetoric, 155, 168; irenic rhetoric, 14, 154; and knowledge, 35; and literary criticism, 38–39; and metaphor, 18, 63–65, 71; pedagogical practices in, 25–40, 208n6; and perception, 30–32; and persuasion, 22–23, 108–10, 121, 161, 163, 165, 168,

185, 205n15; Platonic approaches to, 14, 22–23, 67–70, 163; scholarship on, 1, 3–8; F. N. Scott on, 1, 4, 22, 39, 69–70; and sentence-diagram, 62; and Sophists, 67, 68, 163; and universal thought processes, 30–31; Wylie on teaching of writing, 73, 76–79; Yost on, 69–70; Yost on argumentation and public speaking, 22, 155, 157–67, 209n1. *See also* debate; Vassar College, English department

Rice, Joseph Mayer, 45

Ricks, Vickie, 14, 20, 115, 116, 207n2

Ritchie, Joy S., 5, 6

Rodgers, Daniel T., 9

Ronald, Kate, 5

Rosenblatt, Louise, 132

Rothermel, Beth Ann, 44

Rourke, Constance, 15, 89, 134, 198n4, 198nn1, 2

Rowland, A. Westley, 184–85

Royce, Josiah, 207n24, 208n6

Royster, Jacqueline Jones, 3

Rubin, Joan Shelley, 15, 17, 198n2

Ruskin, John, 19, 29

Rynbrandt, Linda J., 10

Salmon, Lucy Maynard: education of, 46; influence of, on Lockwood, 177, 179, 180, 189, 206n23; influences on, 2; pedagogical style of, 178, 205n13; research interests of, 48; and suffrage movement, 48, 179; at Vassar College, 42, 48, 177–80, 189, 197n1, 204n3; and Wylie, 100

Schneiderman, Rose, 96

Schultz, Lucille M., 7, 41–42, 44

Scott, Fred Newton: on Detroit Normal Training School, 49–50; on education of H. M. Scott, 202n7; influences on, 48, 49; on *Organic Education* (H. M. Scott and Buck), 17–18, 198n7; on rhetoric, 1, 4, 22, 39, 69–70; students of, at University of Michigan, 16–17, 133, 155–56, 160, 190, 210n6; writings by, 18, 113, 199n8

Scott, Harriet M.: and culture-epoch theory of education, 50–53, 155; at Detroit

Suzanne Bordelon is an associate professor in the Department of Rhetoric and Writing Studies at San Diego State University, where she coordinates the department's Upper Division Writing Program. She has published in *College Composition and Communication*, the *Journal of Teaching Writing, Nineteenth-Century Prose,* and *Rhetoric Society Quarterly.* Her articles have been anthologized in *Historical Studies of Writing Program Administration: Individuals, Communities, and the Formation of a Discipline* (2004) and *The Changing Tradition: Women in the History of Rhetoric* (1999).

Studies in Rhetorics and Feminisms

Studies in Rhetorics and Feminisms seeks to address the interdisciplinarity that rhetorics and feminisms represent. Rhetorical and feminist scholars want to connect rhetorical inquiry with contemporary academic and social concerns, exploring rhetoric's relevance to current issues of opportunity and diversity. This interdisciplinarity has already begun to transform the rhetorical tradition as we have known it (upper-class, agonistic, public, and male) into regendered, inclusionary rhetorics (democratic, dialogic, collaborative, cultural, and private). Our intellectual advancements depend on such ongoing transformation.

Rhetoric, whether ancient, contemporary, or futuristic, always inscribes the relation of language and power at a particular moment, indicating who may speak, who may listen, and what can be said. The only way we can displace the traditional rhetoric of masculine-only, public performance is to replace it with rhetorics that are recognized as being better suited to our present needs. We must understand more fully the rhetorics of the non-Western tradition, of women, of a variety of cultural and ethnic groups. Therefore, Studies in Rhetorics and Feminisms espouses a theoretical position of openness and expansion, a place for rhetorics to grow and thrive in a symbiotic relationship with all that feminisms have to offer, particularly when these two fields intersect with philosophical, sociological, religious, psychological, pedagogical, and literary issues.

The series seeks scholarly works that both examine and extend rhetoric, works that span the sexes, disciplines, cultures, ethnicities, and sociocultural practices as they intersect with the rhetorical tradition. After all, the recent resurgence of rhetorical studies has not so much been a discovery of new rhetorics; it has been more a recognition of existing rhetorical activities and practices, of our newfound ability and willingness to listen to previously untold stories.

The series editors seek both high-quality traditional and cutting-edge scholarly work that extends the significant relationship between rhetoric and feminism within various genres, cultural contexts, historical periods, methodologies, theoretical positions, and methods of delivery (e.g., film and hypertext to elocution and preaching).

Queries and submissions:
Professor Cheryl Glenn, Editor
  E-mail: cjg6@psu.edu
Professor Shirley Wilson Logan, Editor
  E-mail: Shirley_W_Logan@umail.umd.edu

Studies in Rhetorics and Feminisms
Department of English
142 South Burrowes Bldg.
Penn State University
University Park, PA 16802-6200